Making Meaning: Making Sense

Lynne Hunt

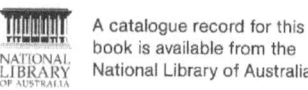

A catalogue record for this book is available from the National Library of Australia

Copyright © 2022 Lynne Hunt
All rights reserved.
ISBN-13: 978-1-922727-38-1

Linellen Press
265 Boomerang Road
Oldbury, Western Australia
www.linellenpress.com.au

Dedication

Dedicated to my grandchildren
Oliver Edwin, Thomas James, and Elsie Ruth

If we cannot tell stories about ourselves and our world, it seems we cannot really develop a sense of self, a sense that we are a unique individual in a world of many selves … We narrate our life and, in doing so, we narrate ourselves into existence. In everyday life, we understand ourselves through a kind of ongoing story. We reference our past all the time when we talk about ourselves. Without a sense of our own past and a possible future, we seem to have no continuity of self.

>   Rachel Robertson (2012) *Reaching one thousand.* Collingwood: Black Inc. p176

Contents

Dedication iii

Contents vii

Preface 1

The scaffold 11

Making meaning at school 26

Making meaning at university 44

Making sense of work 56

Making sense of place: The Cotswolds 77

Making sense of place: Devon 88

Making sense of place: Liverpool 104

Making sense of place: Australia 122

Making sense of people: Mum 146

Making sense of people: Dad 159

Making sense of people: ANZAC 171

Making sense of people: Lyall 183

Making sense of family: Marriage 203

The meaning of parenting 1990-91 236

Making sense of family: Grand-parenting 245

Making sense of family: In-laws 261

Making sense of blended families 275
Making sense of the lifecycle: Old age 304
Making sense of the lifecycle: Care-giving 324
Making sense of the lifecycle: Medical advocacy 343
Making sense of the lifecycle: Ruth's death 358
Values: Making sense of politics 372
Values: Making sense of feminism 386
Values: Making sense of courtesy 407
Values: Making sense of religion 417
Values: Making sense of secrets 429
Lifestyle and culture: The meaning of travel 440
Lifestyle and Culture: The meaning of music 453
Lifestyle and culture: The meaning of customer service ... 469
Lifestyle and culture: The meaning of one-liners 478
Conclusion: Making sense of me 490
References 512

Preface

In 2021, I went to see Jean-Paul Sartre's play, 'Huit Clos' (No Exit). It's about three people arriving in a room, and there's no way out – ever. They'd arrived in hell and would stay together for eternity. They must make sense of this situation because this wasn't at all what they expected. Imagine arriving in hell expecting torture and hell fire flames only to find yourself stuck in a bare room with three other people for eternity! From now until forever, you must make your own meaning in a seemingly meaningless situation.

Well, life can be a bit like this. We have to make sense of our own existence, and that's what this book is about – 'Making Meaning: Making Sense.' I've made a bit of a distinction between making meaning and sense. Making meaning is more about building values and ways of being. Making sense is a bit the same, but it represents areas of struggle, conflict or bewilderment: "How, on earth, do I make sense of this?'

This distinction is fluid, but I think it's important, so I've kept both words in the title of the book.

This book tells stories about how I've built meaning through school, university, work, travel and family life. The stories also talk about how I've made sense of sometimes complex and difficult situations. However, my assumption, in a book about making meaning and making sense, is that there are no straight lines between the written stories and readers' interpretations of them.

Readers will make sense of the stories in terms of their own lives; it's a bit like lecturing at university. I used to say to my students, "If I give a lecture to three hundred students, then I'm giving three hundred lectures – not just one."

Together, the stories form a memoir, of sorts, but it isn't a chronological account of my life. Rather, it's storytelling about the world in which I've made meaning with family and friends. It isn't just my memoir either. It's about the people in my world. Intergenerational family stories loom large because I'm currently the keeper of these stories, and I want to hand them on to younger generations in my British and Australian families.

However, family isn't necessarily the focus. The stories have wider import and universal meaning. So, for example, the concluding chapter not only summarises key ideas in the book. It also reflects on generational change.

Hopefully, the stories are just a good read. Who doesn't want to know a few secrets, and who isn't interested in the Papua New Guinea triplets (one of whom was killed) or the cockatoo that sang 'God Save the King' and then laughed? A good story is a good story, and that's what this book is – storytelling.

The investment of meaning intrigues me. Why are some things important and others not? Why does one story stick in my mind whilst other, possibly more significant stories, have been discounted? My UK cousin, Rosalind, recently sent me a photo of a headstone she'd found in a churchyard whilst meandering around the West Country. Using the original capitalisation, it read: 'In Memory of Sarah Jarvis who departed this life the 11th Day of December 1758 In the Hundred and Seventh Year of her age. Sometime before her Death, she had Fresh Teeth.' What, on earth, does that mean? What does it mean to have fresh teeth when you're 107 in 1758? Why would you even bother to carve this information in stone? It was obviously a very real thing to them, and what is real to people is real in its consequences.

So, this book tells stories about my reality, and that of my friends and family. I'm not very imaginative, so the only way a story gets told in this book is if it happened.

My Perth friend, Janina, is fond of saying that life's a mess, and then you die. So, I've tried to put some order to the general messiness of life by weaving my stories into themes that explore issues such as a sense of place; family; lifecycle and lifestyle matters such as travel, music, customer service, and courtesy. Each essay is stand-alone. This has resulted in some minor repetition because some stories are relevant in different contexts. However, the stand-alone stories are held together in a loose framework, which gives a nod to chronology. First, I share stories about my own development of meaning at school, university and work before moving on to make sense of important people such as Mum, Dad, my father-in-law, and my husband.

My stories are set in the Cotswolds, Liverpool,

and Devon, in the UK, and in Perth, Australia. Much of the meaning of my life engages with the strong sense of place I have with each. Finally, I've been compelled to make meaning 'of' matters such as caregiving, grand-parenting, marriage, secrecy, abandonment, old age, and sexism. The latter has particular import because I've been a feminist for most of my adult life, and I'm proud of what my generation of second-wave feminists achieved. I want our story to be told, lest future generations forget.

Some things that have happened to me are difficult to write about, such as domestic violence, secrets, gaslighting, bullying, and the death of my daughter at the age of thirty-seven. As often as I could, I've scattered these issues throughout the chapters rather than dealing with them full-on. So, for example, sexual abuse is talked about in the essay on courtesy, and bullying is covered-off under the heading of work. I feel that these stories have more poignancy and impact when treated in context rather than as dominant themes. A few friends have told me that I shouldn't tell such stories at all because it's like washing dirty linen in public – muck-raking as it's sometimes called in social research circles. Others tell me how grateful they are that I'm talking about matters, such as being a mother-in-law or step-parent because these issues resonate in their lives. In fact, sometimes, the stories come from their lives.

I believe that breaking the silence about behaviours that detract from the quality of our lives may go some way to healing the intergenerational trauma described in some of my stories. I'm not s**t-stirring; I'm simply darning the holes in the mantle of my past.

All the events happened and some beggar belief to the point that I've sometimes wondered if I've been living in the middle of a dark soap opera. This is why Perth friend, Rosemarie, thinks I shouldn't scatter the difficult issues. Rather, she thinks I should tell a composite story of 'accumulated s**t' because the real story of my life lies in the combined weight of events. I hope to hint at this in the final summary chapter: 'The meaning of me.'

I've chosen to let the stories tell themselves without too much editorialising by me. So, these are 'warts and all' chapters that contain a balance of humour, regret, real events, and the peaks and troughs of life. Even so, some stories remain untold because everybody, including me, my friends and my family, has the right to protect themselves, and there is a limit to the secrets that history needs to know.

The topics in this book were determined by the stories I've got to tell. They were not determined by a fascination with particular subject matter. For example, South African friend and colleague Wendy wrote to say I should write about mentoring, and I replied, quite simply, "I can't. I don't have any significant or funny stories about mentoring." I've tried to give a flavour of time and place because, incidentally, I'm also telling the story of my baby-boomer generation, and I want future generations in my extended family to have some understanding about what it meant to grow up as Lynne in my era. The stories about locations, music and politics probably do this the best.

I was going to write about friendship, but I ditched that idea because friends are so embedded in my life that they appear in all the stories. I am, however, very grateful to them, and to my family, for allowing me to tell their stories as well as mine.

This book has been a retirement project. It kept

me sane during the eight difficult years I cared single-handedly for my husband, Lyall, in his declining years. I like writing, and it offered me some personal space away from caregiving duties – shades of Virginia Woolf, 'A Room of One's Own.'

My challenges in the development of this book were literary. I've had to learn new writing styles. In particular, I've had to drop the academic style I used for publications during my forty-year career in universities. Now, less is more. I've kept things simple by disciplining myself to write short pieces. Most chapters are just a few pages. I've kept strictly to storytelling. It's too easy for me to slip into academic analysis, so I had to keep telling myself: "Just tell the bloody story, Lynne." My mantra has been to 'show, not tell': Just tell the stories and let readers make of it what they will. That will happen anyway because, as philosopher Hannah Arendt said, "Storytelling reveals meaning without committing the error of defining it."

"How do you write these stories so quickly?" my UK friend, Jane, asked several times. In many ways, I don't. The stories wrote themselves, and my brain charged ahead of its own accord making connections between stories and themes. I sometimes wished it wouldn't. I was at a beautiful Mozart concert recently, and I literally had to haul my brain back to focus on the music because it was busy writing the chapter about marriage. I'm not a creative writer. I attended some master classes on writing and sat there miserably with a blank page in front of me whilst the class was given 'just ten minutes' to start a sci-fi or fantasy story. Thankfully, when it came to reading out what we'd written, they allowed us to pass, which I did every time. But I am a storyteller, and I've got a lot of stories to tell.

My visual image of jig-sawing together the stories in this book is this: I have a box of stories adjacent to a box of thematic coat hangers on which to hang the stories. The stories have floated onto the coat hangers of their own accord, just like in the film 'Mary Poppins' in which objects magically tidy themselves away. I've superimposed a bit of a framework onto the stories through the themes that emerged, but these don't really matter. Each chapter can be read on its own without recourse to the framework, and you could throw all the chapters in the air and watch them come down in a different order that makes sense to you. In a book entitled 'Making meaning: Making sense,' this is entirely appropriate.

The scaffold

"I need a scaffold," Val said.

She'd read some of the stories in this book in its development stage, but it was all a bit too random for her. She wanted a chronology. She needed a scaffold to build her own meanings as she reads. So here it is – briefly.

I was born in Nuneaton in 1948, in the heart of England's Black Country. When I was five, I moved away from there and began a nomadic journey around the Cotswolds, endlessly changing primary schools until my Mother bought a house in Bishops Cleeve, near Cheltenham, when I was nine. In 1959, I started high school at Pate's Grammar School for Girls. I secured nine 'O Levels' in 1964 and three 'A Levels' in 1966. Lacking direction, I attended technical college from 1966 to 1967, gaining two more 'A Levels.' In all, I've got five 'A Levels.' These secured me a place at Liverpool University in 1967.

I specialised in languages at school, taking

exams in English language, English literature, French, Spanish and Latin. Pupils studying French 'A Level' (university entrance exams) were required to spend summer holidays with a French family. I stayed with the Labeur family in the Pyrenees. They became an important influence in my life and taught me a love of travelling that has endured. I'm now seventy-three and have visited seventy-nine countries.

At school and technical college, I focused on the social sciences. I passed exams in Tudor and Stuart history, economic history, and economics. I studied sociology at Liverpool University intending to become a medical social worker, but this never happened. Instead, I became an academic, teaching and researching in universities for forty years, finishing as a Professor and Pro Vice-chancellor at the University of Southern Queensland, but the journey to this point was circuitous.

Starting with university finals in the summer of 1970, I defied my professor's injunction to hang around in case I had to have a viva. I flogged my books to raise cash to go to the Dutch Grand Prix, returning to Liverpool in time for my graduation ceremony. I went immediately to the USA for the summer on a student ticket which, the year before, advertised itself as '$99 for 99 days.' I'd been offered a grant to do a Master's degree, so I returned to Liverpool to start my research. I also began tutoring at the University. I'd always insisted that teaching was not for me, but I found that I enjoyed tutoring. I wasn't ready to do a Master's degree, so I gave that up and got a job as a lecturer at C.F. Mott Teachers college, Huyton. I quit two years later because the whole career thing had started too soon for me. I wanted to travel. I even applied for a flight attendant's job and got through the first interview, but then I came to my senses and realised that I'm more the type to tell the business class passengers to 'sod off and get their own coffee'.

I spent the summers of 1971 and 1972 living on a Kibbutz in Israel, where I met a travelling companion with whom I planned a trip to Australia. I travelled from the UK to Brussels to meet him, and we caught trains across Europe to Moscow, where we boarded the trans-Siberian train to Vladivostok. We were arrested in Siberia for taking photos where we shouldn't, caught a boat to Japan, and stayed there a month before moving on to Okinawa, Taiwan, Philippines, Hong Kong, Thailand, Malaysia, Singapore and then Perth, Australia. My intention was to stay in Australia for two years to earn some money to travel on around the world via South America and back to the UK. However, within five weeks, I got a job as a lecturer in a college in Perth. My job became permanent, and I met and married an Australian, Lyall Hunt. He used to crow that his *suavité* had kept me in Australia. I replied that I got a job, a dog, a house, a car and a husband, in that order, so he was actually fifth on the list.

I studied for my Diploma of Education part-time at the University of Western Australia. Later, in 1978, I returned to London to study at the London School of Economics (LSE) for my Masters in Sociology. LSE is near Covent Garden, so that was the year I fell in love with opera and ballet, which, together with theatre, have provided lifelong enjoyment.

By the time I went to study in London, I'd met Lyall. He was a single father with custody of four kids. He came to London to propose marriage whilst I was studying at LSE, so our engagement was spent apart. He returned to Australia and I stayed to complete my studies. We married in Perth on 21 September 1979. It was an informal wedding under a one-hundred-year-old grapevine. That suited me because I hate the fuss and nonsense of weddings, and I never considered myself to be sufficiently 'owned' to have the need of being 'given away' by a man in a traditional wedding ceremony.

In 1982 I had our first child, Ruth, and in 1985, Samuel arrived on the scene. Lyall and I were a good intellectual match. We were both social scientists – he was an Australian historian, and I'm a sociologist – and we both wrote and published books and articles. Lyall died in 2018, and my daughter, Ruth, died in 2020.

While Lyall introduced me to instant family life, I introduced him to travel. In 1981, we availed ourselves of that wonderful Australian opportunity known as long service leave – three months of leave on full pay. We travelled around Europe for three months by train. Starting in Greece in February, where we experienced quite a severe earthquake, we moved north as spring arrived. Subsequently, we never let family life get in the way of travel. We travelled across Australia five times with various combinations of the six Hunt kids. Apart from family holidays around Asia, our children, Ruth and Sam, also accompanied us on two round-the-world trips. The first was in 1988, when they were five and three years of age. We flew across Australia, stopping in Melbourne, Sydney and Brisbane, where we saw the World Expo, then New Zealand, Fiji, Hawaii, Los Angeles and San Francisco. Subsequently, in Canada, I re-established contact with the descendants of my four British great-uncles who'd been pioneers in outback Manitoba.

I've always combined work and travel, and I've undertaken four or five international lecture and study programs. The 1988 trip with Lyall, Ruth and Sam was when I did the bulk of the research for my PhD – a study of the international women's health movement. In the early 1990s, I took two years' leave from work and completed my thesis quick time. In the mid-1990s, we took the kids around the world again, focusing on the UK and USA where we spent Christmas with our friends, Linda and Jerry, in North Carolina.

Our subsequent round-the-world ticket was without kids in 2003. It was a bizarre journey, covering five continents. We covered off on places we hadn't previously visited, including South Africa and South America. I'm glad we did travel when we could because mobility became a problem for Lyall after a knee operation in which a faulty knee implant was inserted. This gave rise to a class action and ruined the rest of his life, family relationships, and our marriage.

Lyall was fourteen years older than me, so he retired as soon as I finished my PhD thesis. He subsequently provided great support for my career, principally by editing my publications, and driving Ruth and Sam to and from school and their many sporting activities. After school, Ruth secured five university qualifications, including law. She joined the Australian Army as a lawyer and was promoted to major shortly before she died. She married secretly during the COVID lockdown of 2020, announcing the marriage four days before she died. Sam did a degree in sports science. His first job out of university was as a sports coach in Shanghai. There he met Jane, and they married in 2009. They now have three children, Oliver, Thomas and Elsie. In 2021, I built a granny house in my own back yard, and Sam and his family moved into the house in which he grew up. We are now neighbours.

My career took off quite slowly, but when it happened, it happened fast. A highlight was 2002 when I won the Prime Minister's Award for Australian University Teacher of the year. Immediately, I was promoted to the position of Associate Dean, and, in 2005, I was appointed as Professor and Director of Learning and Teaching at Charles Darwin University, which was certainly an experience – it's very much a frontier town. For the first time since I've lived in Australia, I became engaged with Indigenous issues and mentored colleagues to become the first Indigenous staff to win the Prime Minister's Award for university teachers of the year. If ever I was to cap my own success, that was the way to do it.

I became Pro-Vice-Chancellor at the University of Southern Queensland (USQ) in 2007 and retired in 2010 following one of the last highlights of my career: I won an Australian Executive Endeavour Award, which saw me working in Malaysia for five weeks at the end of 2009. My study program was helped greatly by Malaysian friends, Mazlan and Zai. I'd met Mazlan at Technical College in Cheltenham 1966-67, where we studied A-Level economics together.

I became Emeritus Professor at USQ in 2010. This is an award for lifetime achievements which include fifty-seven refereed chapters or journal articles, four books, and almost one hundred conference presentations, including occasional keynotes. I've also undertaken many consultancies and guest lectures around the world. The most special for me were in Malaysia, Macau, South Africa, and Botswana.

The cast list of significant characters in my stories includes my family of origin – Mum and Dad, Alma and Cyril Hardy, and three older sisters, Audrey, Joyce and Julie. My mother's extended Britton family hail from Devon (UK), possibly since the Norman Conquest. I know little of my Dad's family. My family of marriage includes my husband, Lyall, my daughter Ruth Ellen Kathleen (1982-2020) and Samuel Peter Lyall, who was born in 1985.

As I understood it when I married Lyall, and for the thirty-nine years of our marriage, he already had four children from his first marriage, and he had custody of them. From his death certificate, I discovered he actually had five, not four, children. This is why I write about secrets in this book. Lyall's Australian extended family have accepted me into their lives, and we rub along comfortably as friends, especially David, Peta, Meryl, Eric, Keith and Gloria. The diaspora of my own extended family stretches from the UK to Canada and Australia, and their stories feature frequently.

No woman is an island, and I haven't made meaning of my life in a vacuum. To address the importance of relatives and friends in the mosaic of my life, I considered writing some biographies, but this didn't work. Instead, I've chosen to focus on themes. So, with their permission, I refer to friends and relatives incidentally, by first name only. In this way, I can honour and value their place in the meaning of my life. In some cases, I use pseudonyms for reasons of privacy. In other cases, I have relocated stories, used pseudonyms, and changed genders because I thought a story worth telling. This is thematic storytelling, not oral history. It's a bit like the disclaimers at the start of a film, which say something like, 'The characters in this story do not refer to real people …'

The distinction between friends and family is blurred. A common cliché is that friends are the family you choose. This is particularly true for me because I'm a solo migrant in Australia, as is my Perth friend, Rosemarie, who was born in the USA and raised in Argentina. With no siblings or extended family nearby, we have become de facto sisters. So her name appears throughout the book.

It's not possible to name all significant friendships, but Jean was the first Australian friend I made in 1973, and we remain friends to this day. We have been there for each other through the birth, marriage and death lifecycle, including the arduous task of caring for our older, sick and disabled husbands. Diana, Rob, Liz, and Don are the friends who shared the parenting journey with me.

Rather than creating a list of friends, I'll simply share my mind-map of friendship, starting with school friends from my hometown, Cheltenham (UK). They are an enduring friendship group, and we have known each other for over sixty years. They now live far and wide, from Gill, in San Francisco, to Pat, in France, Julia in Germany, and me in Australia, but we have reunited frequently as a group.

After school, I attended the Technical College in Cheltenham. This was my first experience of coeducation, which meant that I made male friends for the first time in my life. I'm still in touch with Brian and Mazlan. Subsequently, I went up to Liverpool University, where I made new and enduring friendships, including with my lecturer, Professor Nikos Kokosalakis, who had a significant influence on my intellectual development.

In 1970, after graduating from university, I started my career lecturing at a college in Liverpool, and I still have friends from that era. In fact, Phil Markey, my then Head of Department, has been my anchor to Liverpool – a city I love and about which I write. I left the college in 1972 to backpack to Australia, where my first academic job was at Mt Lawley Teachers' College in Perth. I know Janina from that time. Like me, she's a sociologist, and she also migrated from the UK, and married an older Australian man. We have much in common, including publishing a book together about West Australian Women teachers:

'Claremont Cameos.'

Thereafter, the growth of my work friendships followed changes in higher education which saw teachers colleges transform into universities – in my case, Edith Cowan University (ECU).

In my journey through four campuses of ECU, I met Jodie. She's some fifteen years younger than me. We share a love of travel, connections to Liverpool, and an intent to live considered lives. At Joondalup Campus, I reconnected with Scottish Anne, who I'd met a decade before when working at another campus of ECU. In the late 1990s, Robyn became my mentor at ECU, and our friendship has grown from that. We have travelled together and even succeeded in missing a plane together.

I also met Denise at ECU. In addition, we both worked in Queensland, and her friendship and collegiality eventually led to us co-editing two editions of the textbook, 'University Teaching in Focus.'

In 2005, I was appointed to Charles Darwin University as Director of Teaching and Learning. The friendships I made there with Janet and Margaret were forged in the difficulties of getting things done. We called ourselves 'The Three Musketeers.' Subsequently, I achieved another promotional position to the University of Southern Queensland in Toowoomba, where I was the Pro-Vice-Chancellor of Learning and Teaching. My Queensland friendship groups were founded in the shared endeavour of change leadership. Pam, Ren, Liz, and Bronwyn, are still in my life. In Pam's case, we occasionally travel together because we share a love of classical music.

My academic career has afforded me opportunities to develop friendships beyond the places where I've lived and worked. My career involved international travel for conferences, consultancies and study programs. On the road, I met and have sustained friendships with: Linda (University of North Carolina), Peggy (Canberra), Pippa (London), and Marilyn. (She's American but lives in England). Marilyn and I worked together at the University of Botswana, and she facilitated our memorable trip to the Okavango. I met Jane when living on the kibbutz in Israel. She has served as my informal editor in the development of this book. These friends, and many more, have peopled my life and this book contains their stories as well as mine.

Making meaning at school

I went to eight different primary schools. It was only in the stability of two years at Broadway Primary School that my academic potential was revealed when I took out the Maths and English prizes in Year Four. My parents were poorly educated, so they never really understood or acknowledged my educational achievements. I can't remember any fuss being made when I was successful at school except when I told Dad that I'd passed my 11+ exam, which gave me entry to a selective academic high school. He raised his hands above his head in victory and emptied his pockets of pennies as a reward for me. It added up to one shilling and ninepence – in current terms, about AUS$1.75. That's my only memory of parental praise.

I had a rocky road to success. After my achievements at Broadway Primary School, I transferred to Bishops Cleeve, where I was almost demoted to class 3B – meaning the non-11+

stream. I escaped relegation and achieved a borderline pass in the important 11+ exam. Four girls from Bishops Cleeve were borderline pupils. We had to be interviewed by the headmistress for admission to the academically elite secondary school – Pate's. Two girls didn't get in, and two did. I was one of them. It's difficult to believe that it was considered OK for 11-year-olds to be interviewed and that the future career of these girls would hang by such a fine thread.

The interview was a comprehension test. I had to read a passage and then answer questions about it. I also had to say what I wanted to do when I grew up. By chance, 'Cherry Ames' came to the rescue and landed me a place at Pate's. These career education books had introduced me to the work of almoners (medical social workers), which must have been deemed an appropriately ladylike profession. But for suggesting this career, I may not have attended an elite academic school or university or become a professor.

I started at Pate's Grammar School for Girls in 1959 when it was an academically elite state school that admitted something in the order of the top 5% of girls in the region as measured by the 11+

exam. I was in my forties before I realised that girls had to pass at a higher level than boys simply because boys develop more slowly. Had the system been co-ed, the top 5% of *children* risked including a much higher percentage of girls than boys. As it was, we competed separately for single-sex schools. The 11+ was an IQ and aptitude test, much criticised for its implicit social class bias, and because it reflected the extent to which children were coached in their final year of primary school.

Coaching was facilitated by the streaming of classes in primary schools. Essentially, only the top 'A' class was expected to succeed in the 11+ examination – and only a small percentage of them. This meant that our futures might have been established as early as the age of six or seven when primary school classes were streamed. Such considerations eventually led to the demise of the academically elite state grammar school system. However, Pate's remains a grammar school to this day, and it is now one of the top state schools in the UK.

I was unwell on the first day of term when I started at Pate's in 1959. I was wound up with anxiety about the fact that I was a borderline pupil.

I must have felt as if I was beginning the race from behind the starting line. When I arrived on the second day of term, I was asked to open a classroom window together with another girl.

"Are you the Lynne Hardy who was at Broadway School?" she asked.

It was Sue, who'd been in my class at one of my eight primary schools. We were now both in class 1S with some thirty other girls destined to be together for a minimum of five years from the age of eleven. Our first-year status was declared to all by the bib and braces attached to our skirts. These could be removed when we entered third year. Our place in the hierarchy was signalled, somewhat unfortunately for those girls for whom puberty caused them to blossom behind the bib.

So, there you have it, hierarchy and order prevailed from Day One. There were four classes in each year, identified as P, Q, R, and S, to avoid any suggestion of academic streaming, such as A, B, C and D. As 11-year-old first years, we studied in our home room the whole time. Subsequently, we were streamed by some subjects but returned to our home classroom for many lessons and routine tasks, such as taking the register first thing in the morning and afternoon. That's five years of the same roll-call, twice a day. Consequently, now in our seventies, most of us can still recite the entire class register. I know this because we practiced at the 2019 Pate's Reunion. For my 1S class, it began: Baggs, Bath, Boyton, Cooke, Donnelly, Edden, Etherington, Fitzpatrick, Gibbon, Hack, Hardy (That was me, Lynne Hardy). This says a lot about the power of rote learning. It also indicates that school life was stable. There weren't many changes. A few girls left, and some arrived, but basically, this was 'US' for five years.

Each class remained together until the girls completed 'O' Levels at the age of sixteen. Then the early school-leavers departed, whilst the rest of us restructured into the Sixth Form to study for university entrance exams: 'A' Levels. That took another two years.

From a borderline pass and an apprehensive first few days, I grew in personal and academic confidence. In fact, I can date a transition point. Each class had 'form captains' – two each term per class. We were voted in by classmates, so it conferred a feeling of acceptance and belonging to be elected. I became form captain at the beginning of second year. "So, I must be OK even though I was borderline!"

Thereafter, my marks improved so that two years later, I was an 'A average' student and on track for university, even though I didn't know what it was. Without the academic push of Pate's, I would not have achieved what I did.

We were encouraged to be self-disciplined in our studies. In fact, from Year One, we had homework timetables. For example, it was Maths, Latin and History on Monday; and French, Science and Geography on Tuesday. Most homework had to be handed in the next day, so there was no getting out of study-at-home each evening.

Our memories of school are coloured by our headmistress. Some of my contemporaries remain critical of her. For my part, I never had much to do with her. I was a Bishops Cleeve girl, and we sometimes sensed that we were frowned upon. I spoke with the headmistress at my borderline interview when I was ten, and I spoke with her again when I was seventeen, just before leaving school, when I told her I wanted to study sociology at university. She determined that I go to Liverpool because her research indicated that it was one of the first universities in Britain to teach sociology. Perhaps she was impressed by the fact that the professor of sociology was also a Lord. Whatever the reason, I was agreeable because the Beatles came from there. There was also an element of revenge in this because, in Fourth Form, I'd won a prize for getting an 'A' average. We were allowed to choose our own book, and I asked for Liverpool John Lennon's newly released book, 'In his Own Write.' It was not allowed, and I was told to choose another book. I chose 'How to Avoid People without Really Trying' as a suitably offensive title. That was allowed. I still have it next to me here in my study. I've never read it – but I've kept it because it was a prize.

Our headmistress, nicknamed Flossie, set the tone of the school, and propriety loomed large with her. She was committed to the school's image and reputation, so the way her 'gels' presented themselves in public was important. She became alarmed that some of us frequented a café called Tiffany's, which she thought was a "den of vice and iniquity." We went there after school, so we were still in uniform, and this mattered.

Perhaps Flossie was right to concern herself with uniform as much as she did because after I'd been through the overlapping fashion periods of oversized sloppy-Joe jumpers and the mini-skirt, there wasn't a lot of grey skirt left showing underneath the red jumper. We were allowed to wear any kind of black or brown shoes. Most of our parents clad us in sturdy Clarkes' school shoes, but if Flossie spotted that we were getting too fashionable, she threatened us with the uniform brogue shoes of the nearby prestigious private school – The Ladies' College. That worked!

Some of us steamed our school uniform felt hats over kettles to flatten the sides and make them look like Stetsons. I think everyone in my year remembers the hat inspection story. After assembly, one day, all eight hundred of us lined up so that Flossie could inspect our hats. The one hundred good hats in the school were recycled from front to back of the line of girls so that she inspected the same one hundred good hats eight times. We always knew that something juicy was going to be discussed at assembly when our headmistress directed her gaze to the men in the room:

"Would the male members of staff mind leaving the room please?" That riveted my attention!

This happened the day after the hat inspection because Flossie's close contact with us led her to believe we smelled and needed a personal hygiene talk. On the day after her homily about taking a bath and changing our knickers regularly, it was difficult to breathe during assembly because of the overpowering smell of perfume. Girls have their own forms of silent insolence.

When I hear critiques of our headmistress, I do wonder what it must have been like for a woman to provide school leadership in the mid-twentieth century. As I see it, we needed Flossie's force with us to resist the limited social expectations for girls in the early to mid-1960s. Together with the teachers in the school, she pushed hard for us to achieve. I recently sorted my attic and found the letter my parents had to sign before my admission to Pate's. They had to agree to keep me at school until 'O' levels, when I would be sixteen – well past the minimum school-leaving age.

For parents living hand to mouth, as mine were,

this was a big commitment. However, her emphasis on propriety went too far. I was carpeted for smoking in school uniform during a school trip to Wembley. I always felt that it was the school uniform bit that mattered more than the smoking. At the time, I was bemused because we were eighteen, it was London, and it was the weekend. In any case, why were we wearing our uniform?

In 2020, the Pate's Alumni magazine, 'The Patesian', published my story of my life at Pate's, as well as another girl's story, which I read with dismay. It told of a girl a few years older than me, who I never knew. She'd transferred to Pate's because she was on track for Oxford or Cambridge University entrance. However, her photograph with Brian Jones (a local lad of Rolling Stones fame) hit the front page of the local newspaper. She was holding a beer bottle. Flossie called her into her office and told her that she was not Oxbridge material and directed her to the more appropriate red brick universities. She must have been crushed. It's a telling tale about the expected role of girls and women, and she's still miffed because she didn't even drink any beer.

Given the strong expectations about women's domestic role at that time, I was given little preparation, either at home or school, about how I might become a mother. My school friend's mum had a booklet published by a women's magazine, and I read that. That was about it apart from lessons at school. The mechanics of reproduction were taught in biology class through the study of rabbits – and I didn't make the connection to humans. In religious education classes, we were taught the morals and ethics of sexual relationships. Our teacher was a minister of the Church of England, and he explained it all in terms of cars. First, you need to know what goes on under the bonnet. That was the biological rabbit bit. Then you have to know how to drive the car. That's the morals bit. Then you need to know that cars go up and down hills. This had to do with feelings and mood swings. I'm surprised he didn't go on to discuss rabbits caught in headlights as a metaphor for teen pregnancy. As it was, my family didn't have a car, and I'm still very hazy about what goes on under the bonnet. It's a miracle that we weren't all driven to early motherhood.

We had assembly every morning, which started when the prefects paraded in ahead of the headmistress, who ascended the steps to the dais on the stage. We sang a hymn, said a prayer and then listened to school notices, including a discussion of the Tiffany café, hats, and personal hygiene.

"The endless assemblies!" one school friend wrote to me, "I loved the singing, but not the lengthy diatribe afterwards.

Quite a few of us learnt signing the alphabet to while away the time. Useful, now, as I live next door to some people with hearing and speech difficulties. Education: Never wasted!"

Traditional though it was, Pate's did a lot of things right. I look back now and marvel that a school of eight hundred girls had three orchestras and a couple of choirs. Those of us who studied languages in sixth form was expected to go and live in France or Germany to improve our language skills. I recall trips to see plays: King Lear in Nottingham, and Molière at Birmingham University. There was often a French Mademoiselle available for French conversation classes, and parents could pay for elocution lessons, in which I lasted for just one term. The teacher and I did not speak with one voice. I've never been good at accepting what I see as unreasonable authority, and the pernickety learning and exact pronunciation of vowel sounds and the enDS of wordDS put me in oppositional mode.

While the school was horizontally divided into year groups, it was vertically divided into four houses that provided opportunities for interaction across the years, particularly through junior and senior intra-school sports competitions in swimming, netball, hockey, tennis and athletics. The Houses were Normans, Saxons, Danes and Britons. I was junior and senior captain of the Norman's tennis and netball teams, and I became House Captain in my final year at school. My classmate, Jacky, recalls that she and I were the only two girls to win silver medals in athletics, as judged by national school girl standards. None of this led to my appointment as a prefect. This has come to mind, over the years, when I've advised my students to build their curricula vitae with evidence of leadership. It didn't work for me.

In the 1960s, Pate's was a monocultural society.

One of the few nods to diversity was the table for vegetarians at school lunch. I remember that these poor souls got whatever veggies the carnivores were offered, plus a lump of cheese. However, as a classmate, Pat, said, "I rather envied the vegetarians their food, because the meat was particularly horrible with gristly bits, and the fat globules floating in gravy UGH!! The only things I remember liking was cheese and potato pie, and chocolate crunch pudding."

None of the food was especially good. I stocked up on sticky buns and milk at morning recess – in pre-Thatcher days when school milk was still free.

Sue organised a lovely Pate's Reunion garden party at her house in the academic year we turned fifty. She even managed to invite some of our teachers:

"Would you like a glass of wine, Miss Jones?"

"May I offer you a piece of cake, Miss Smith?"

Accustomed to the informality of Australian society, I was quietly amused that our teachers didn't volunteer their first names at the party. I hesitate to write about our teachers because I wouldn't know who to single out or why.

I know that, in my adult years, I have looked

back at them and realised that the female teachers forged a career path for themselves through the 1950s and 60s when they would not have had the career support services that my generation of feminists fought for – no childcare services, nor maternity leave. As a consequence, many were unmarried and seemed a bit fuddy-duddy to my teenage eyes, but they were strong women who'd earned themselves a degree at university.

Strangely, after our school-leaving 'A-Level' exams had finished, we were required to stay at school until the end of term. The teachers didn't know how to keep us entertained, though I recall a bit of Wimbledon watching on the one and only school TV behind the curtains on the stage in the assembly hall. In this context, I most admired my form teacher in the Upper Sixth. She was a French teacher. To keep us occupied, she walked into our post-exam French class and plonked a piece of paper in front of us, instructing us to: "Translate that!" It was Italian, which none of us had studied. However, having studied Latin, French, and Spanish, I was able to do the translation. She was trying to give us confidence and show us that we were now linguistically competent. It was an empowering strategy.

"I think of you two or three times a week," I said to a former English teacher when I met her at the fiftieth birthday reunion. I explained that I've taught in universities all my life and ALWAYS correct students who want to centre their arguments *around* an issue.

"You can't centre around; you can only centre on. Your voice comes back to me every time."

She was horrified, "Is that all you remember about my teaching?"

Personally, I'd be pretty pleased if any of my students remembered anything at all about my teaching thirty-five years on. In any case, her wisdom has extended across continents and decades of students. I think that's a pretty good legacy. Our music teacher worked hard in running school orchestras and choirs. I still smile that he persuaded my mother that I had good finger span and offered her help if I learned the double bass. He even drove the double bass to my home so that I could practice during school holidays. He must have been desperate for double bass players in the orchestra.

Career advice was thin on the ground. It seemed

that we were expected to go to, in rough rank order: Oxbridge; any university; teacher training college; the Cheltenham based Government Communication Headquarters (GCHQ); or a bank. Interestingly, I don't remember the stereotypically female job of nursing ever being mentioned. The ambition to be an almoner (medical social worker) stayed with me. I mentioned this one day to a sixth-form friend.

"You'll need to do sociology for that," she said.

Really! What's that? So that's what I told my headmistress I wanted to do and, in that casual manner, I ended up at Liverpool University.

Like many grammar schools, Pate's had a connection with a university college. In our case, it was Corpus Christie College, Oxford. The school was established through a bequest by Richard Pate, a courtier of Queen Elizabeth I. My recollection of the Foundation Day story is that Pate's Grammar School for girls existed only because the wording in his bequest to establish a school spoke of the 'children' (not specifically boys) of Cheltenham. I've always been pleased that I went to a single-sex school. My experience is that it gave us time to become ourselves without being subject to the male gaze. A single-sex environment also provided opportunities to develop solid female friendships that have so far endured for sixty years.

We all have our opinions about the process of our education, but many of us did succeed beyond the expectations of the day. I certainly never thought that I would become a professor. We have Pate's and our own hard work to thank for that.

Making meaning at university

When I left school, I wanted to be a medical social worker, so I was advised that I should do a degree in sociology. I didn't know what it was, but my headmistress directed me to Liverpool University, which offered a three-year degree in sociology with a top-up year in social administration to qualify in social work.

I was accepted for 1967 entry and told to read a couple of prescribed books before embarking on my first year of study. One was 'Bethnal Green', a study of a working-class, East End London borough. I see now that it was designed to teach us how to research and report on social patterns of behaviour and social disadvantage in matters such as housing and education. It also showed the importance of local culture and the strong community ties in the old working-class suburbs of the UK's major cities, especially ports with strong dockland traditions. The close bonds of such communities have subsequently been captured in long-running British TV shows, like 'EastEnders,' and 'Call the Midwife.' The popularity of these television programs suggests that the sense of community they engender still resonates with viewers.

I was particularly interested in a sub-section of the study, which described the impact of social mobility through university study. In those days, not too many working-class kids gained entry to university. It would have been the same for me but for the grants that paid my tuition and accommodation fees. These weren't scholarships for the few. We all had them. We were the lucky generation of students who experienced free university education, but it came at a social cost for some. The Bethnal Green study showed the cultural disjunction experienced by working-class kids who went to university. They became educated beyond the horizons of London's East End, and this affected family dynamics.

This caught my attention because I was already experiencing this in my own life. I was the first in my entire extended family to go to university, and I didn't always know how to fit in when I returned from Liverpool to the family fold. At the same time, I was also uncertain at university because I didn't know how to behave there either. My family background lacked social capital. I hadn't been surrounded by books or engaged in the arts, like many other students, who seemed so much more sophisticated and intellectual than me. However, Pate's Grammar School and summers spent as an exchange student with my French family had given me a head start, so I dived in to enjoy undergraduate life and have fun. This wasn't difficult to do in 1960s Liverpool.

Despite my underdog view of myself, I was surprised to discover, forty years later, at our Liverpool University reunion in 2010, that I'd been seen by some as part of the 'it' crowd in our hall of residence. I'm not sure how widespread this reputation was, but it amused me to hear of it because I hadn't even known enough to understand that such things mattered.

My university education was social as well as academic, and it was middle class. The tutor in my hall of residence invited us for sherry receptions, and we were made aware of our special status as undergraduates by the requirement to wear our academic gowns to formal dinners at our hall of residence. My social life was based on formal dinner dances. We had a ball at the end of each term in our hall of residence. In addition, at the Student Guild, we attended the Guild Ball and the Medic Ball. This required formal attire – long dresses for the girls and dinner suits for the blokes. We considered ourselves rather fancy as we smoked our colourful Sobranie cigarettes. It was fun, but, as I see it now, it was also part of etiquette training for our future professional careers.

I see the early years of my undergraduate education as a parcel. I proudly plonked in front of my lecturers the parcel of my successful school education. They systematically undid the string and peeled back the brown paper that wrapped my accumulated ignorance. My first tutorial was on functionalist theory, and, apparently, I was supposed to be taking the lead. The problem was I didn't know what a tutorial was, so I wasn't prepared. Study skills weren't taught to undergraduates in 1967. I wasn't going to be caught like that again. I read a lot and grew in theoretical and philosophical understanding.

So, from this initial embarrassment, big things

grew, and I finished my career as a professor. By the time I finished my BA (Hons) Sociology at Liverpool, my Master's in Sociology at the London School of Economics, and my PhD at the University of Western Australia, I was able to offer critiques of both functionalist theory and the Bethnal Green Study – and I knew how to conduct a tutorial.

As a budding social worker in 1967, I saw the Bethnal Green study as an exciting step forward in social justice. Here we had the evidence to demonstrate the inequalities in British society. The research evidence would help us set things right. It wasn't until I started to read French philosopher Michel Foucault for my PhD that I came to see the collection of evidence about human populations as a potential form of control. Since then, social media and online purchases and interactions have exacerbated the potential privacy risks of data collection. I changed my mind again when the COVID 19 Pandemic hit. We needed detailed epidemiological data to fight this thing. Watching the ravages of the disease in India in 2021, I realised that they suffered from a lack of data. The infection and death rates were far, far higher than will ever be known, but data alone will not improve things. Political will is needed and nothing much has changed since my first reading of Bethnal Green in 1967. Social distancing for COVID prevention is no more possible in Indian slums today than it would have been in early-twentieth-century Bethnal Green. We've known the connection between poverty and poor health for centuries.

Now I see that we were 'studying down' to poverty in London's East End and not 'up' to the wealth that was bartered in the nearby City of London. The wealth data that I subsequently taught to my students shows that, in most western countries, vast portions of a country's wealth are owned by a very small percentage of the population. It doesn't matter if you live in the UK, USA or Australia, even though Australians like to see themselves as an egalitarian society. As part of my university studies, I read Karl Marx's 'Das Kapital,' which showed that the rich get richer and the poor get poorer everywhere. I'd like to say: "Come back Karl Marx, all is forgiven," but I've just watched a TV program on Russian history which indicated that Russia's President Putin is one of the richest men in the world. The praxis of communism corrupted the intent of Marxist theory. Ah, that word: Praxis! Professor Nikos Kokosalakis tried to teach me about praxis in second year Social Philosophy. I was bamboozled. I had to make an appointment to see him privately because I just didn't get it. He kindly invited me to sit down and asked what my problem was.

"I don't know," I replied, "I don't even know enough to know what I don't understand."

I subsequently told that story to generations of my own university students and they seemed to find it empowering because my message was: No question is too dumb to ask. Ironically, my PhD thesis was about the praxis of the women's health movement, so I guess I learned something along the way.

For the uninitiated, praxis just means putting theory together with practice and knowing why you are doing what you are doing. In my PhD thesis, I was able to show that the women's health movement that blossomed in the 1960s is distinguished from mainstream healthcare by its praxis. Basically, women's health workers showed how to treat women with respect and dignity. It makes a difference to be clear about process. This can be seen in Australia today, where there is a furore over the working conditions for women in the Federal Parliament. This was precipitated by the alleged rape of a young staffer just metres away from the Prime Minister's office. Her need for support following the incident appears to have taken second place to the imperative to squash the information and keep the party political machine afloat. The process was certainly not informed by a consideration of the needs of women.

I entered university having opinions, and I left as a fence-sitter, always considering both sides of the question. I wasn't particularly happy with the state of my intellectual development, until one day in 1971 when I watched a news item on TV about the Vietnam War. I found myself getting angry about what I saw. I figured that if I'm angry, I must have an opinion. I just needed to start with emotion and work backwards through theory, philosophy, sociology and politics to sort out what my opinions might be. Emotions interact with intellectual development, as one of my friends discovered in a first-year tutorial. She became distressed because our tutor informed us that cupid's arrow flies a narrow path down socio-economic channels. She'd just become engaged at the young age of eighteen, and she was in love. In her mind, mechanistic economic determinants had nothing to do with bringing her together with her fiancé. Given that she was engaged to a university graduate of the same religion and social class, the tutor probably had a point, but she didn't want to hear it.

I don't think that emotional intelligence was a part of the formal curriculum of the Sociology Department at Liverpool University, but the hidden curriculum certainly taught me compassion. The professor of my department fell ill and became confused at work, but he was not sent home to die, as would happen in corporate universities of the twenty-first century. Today, the university would want his office back quick smart if he wasn't a productive member of staff. Instead, the Sociology Department accommodated his needs and asked students if they would attend 'dummy' tutorials to keep him engaged in work and life. It was an act of pure understanding and compassion from which I learned much, much more than any lecture or tutorial could offer.

We also learned about social justice. As third-year students, we were invited to participate in research about unionism, which was published in the book 'Strike at Pilkington's.'

Later, a Liverpool University postgrad wrote a book about Liverpool car workers, which gave a new angle on their unionism and seemingly endless strikes. By working incognito on the inside, the postgraduate student was able to show how the company could provoke a strike by speeding up the assembly line beyond agreed rates. If the company was in over-supply, it helped the bottom line to have no production for a few days.

Sociology always taught me new and different ways to think about things. This started in first year when we were shown two accounts of youthful street behaviour. One concerned working-class street gangs, and the other described a bunch of undergraduates behaving in a rowdy manner during 'Rag Week,' which most British universities held once a year to raise money for charity. There really wasn't much difference in the behaviour, but the interpretation of the behaviour of street-corner gangs and a bunch of students varied significantly.

I did involve myself in Rag Week. It was called 'Panto' in Liverpool and, in a limited way, I was involved in student activism. In fact, I can claim to be a 1968er – the year of student revolutions around the world. Even my hall of residence had its little social justice moments. For starters, the Carnatic Halls of Residence were named after a slave ship, and the girl's Hall, Salisbury, was named after a governor of Rhodesia (Zimbabwe). So there were some objections to the names, but even stronger objections to the rules which allowed girls in the boys' rooms any day of the week, but the blokes could visit the girls only on weekends or Wednesday afternoon.

"Why Wednesday afternoon?" I enquired.

It transpired that it was sports afternoon. Go figure. So we had a sit-in, and the blokes came to the girls' rooms, en masse, outside of regulation hours. Rules were altered, but it was probably as much to do with emerging changes in the age of majority (twenty-one to eighteen) than our 'revolution.' Halls of Residence could no longer act in loco parentis. In fact, the Carnatic Halls of residence are no more. They were bulldozed around 2019-2020 and, along with them, many students' precious memories of their undergraduate days.

My undergraduate lecturer, Nikos, encouraged me a lot and built my confidence. When I was in third year, he was not long out of his own PhD on Ecumenism. He was open enough to hand me his thesis to critique as one of my assignments. I didn't realise, at that stage, that a PhD thesis is almost as precious as a baby and that maybe he wasn't anticipating extensive critique, but I went for it, connecting and comparing his ideas with those of other writers. I certainly honed my analytical skills. I now make connections between theoretical ideas very easily, and Nikos taught me how to do this. He was good enough to comment that I'd produced more of a critique than some of his external examiners.

I count this as an iconic moment in becoming me because Nikos was telling me that I could think. It was an enormous gift. He wrote a lovely comment telling me that my essay deserved an 'A', but he gave me an 'A-.' We are still friends. He's now in his early eighties, and I'm in my early seventies, and I often ask him why I didn't actually get an 'A.'

Making sense of work

I started work as an academic in 1970. I was helped considerably by the expansion of tertiary education, which started at that time. Student numbers surged, and colleges scrambled to employ staff. I was one of them.

My new head of Department, 'Liverpool Phil', became a lifelong friend, but he was disappointed when I left two years after he employed me. This whole career thing had started much too early for me, and I wanted to backpack around the world. Phil's farewell gift to me was 'War and Peace.' He figured I would need something hefty to read during my unemployment. The book is still on my shelves, and it has never been read. I remain actively engaged in academic writing and workshop presentations even after eleven years of retirement.

I was appointed to my first lecturing position when I was twenty-two. It was a lucky break at that age. The first feedback I received about my teaching was from a young male student.

"The social atmosphere of this class has improved enormously since you started teaching us, but you'll have to work hard to gain our respect." At least he was honest.

When I quizzed him, he said that middle-aged blokes in suits had a natural authority, mostly because they were middle-aged blokes in suits. My long hair and mini-skirt didn't quite crack it in the academic credibility stakes.

It's not uncharitable to observe that my teaching career had a head start because I followed possibly the world's worst lecturer. Bad though I was as a rookie, I could only be better than her. She described everything in terms of complex models of her own creation, leaving the students, and me, bewildered. The problem was that we not only had to understand the concept the model sought to explain, but we also had to understand her model as well. We were double-confounded. So, my first two lessons about teaching were learned: develop a positive and supportive environment in class; and keep things simple by allowing students to build their own models of understanding rather than imposing mine.

Apparently, I learned well because twenty years later, Charles, my American colleague in Perth, drawled, "Gee, Lynne, you're such a good lecturer because you're so simple-minded."

I think it was a compliment.

I started work at Mount Lawley Teachers' College in Perth in 1973, five weeks after arriving in Australia. It became Edith Cowan University (ECU) in 1991. I resigned from ECU in 2005, so it could be said that I had a stable career because I worked at the university, and its antecedent colleges, for thirty-two years. In reality, I had a complex career because the ground changed beneath my feet. I worked at four campuses in two discipline areas – the sociology of education and health – and I've lost count of the number of faculties in which I worked. Thirty-two years is a long time. But these days, longevity isn't necessarily well regarded.

"But you're not an old-timer, Lynne," a new colleague declared.

"Well, I've been here more than thirty years. How long do I have to be here to be an old-timer?"

Clearly, she had an image of old-timers that was

unrelated to longevity.

My husband, Lyall, was very involved in the academic staff union and helped to negotiate new conditions of service in all stages of change from college to university status. After one of his union meetings in the late 1980s, he came home to announce that I needed to get a PhD.

"The writing's on the wall, Lynne. You won't get any promotion without a PhD."

It didn't escape my attention that he'd been promoted to the level of associate professor without a PhD. I was still on the bottom rung to which I'd been appointed in 1973. He continued on to say that he'd support me if I took two years' leave without pay to complete a PhD. In his words, "I'll keep you in the manner to which you've become accustomed, if, the moment you go back to work, I can retire on the dot of sixty years of age."

His plan was that, when I went back to work, I could keep him in the manner to which he would like to become accustomed. So it was a deal, and I did my PhD quick time in two years. I'm not sure if the University of Western Australia had previously had a successful PhD candidate who handed back one year of a three-year postgraduate grant, but I did.

Lyall wanted to get out of the workforce because computers started to land on our desks in the early 1990s, and he didn't want a bar of them. He realised that he was old-school and that change was passing him by, so he wanted to retire. It meant we dropped a salary, but the advantage was that one parent was at home and available to our kids just before Ruth started high school. I always thought this was the most difficult stage to negotiate for working parents because primary schools have before- and after-school care, as well as holiday care, but these services drop away in high school. I didn't want latch-key kids.

The plan was good for Lyall because he carried on with research and publication in Western Australian history, which was his passion. The plan was also good for me because Lyall coped with school and sports chauffeuring, and some housework. My career took off at this point.

Through his union activities, Lyall had been instrumental in establishing a policy to facilitate the promotion of women at the university, but, in 1993, one of my feminist colleagues called by to inform me that all the promotions to senior lecturer in our faculty had gone to men. And some of them didn't have PhDs. So Lyall's prediction that I would need a PhD hadn't been entirely accurate. Apparently, I needed a PhD or a penis.

So, the women, me among them, girded their deficient loins and got their PhDs. We had a cartoon that we circulated to each other as we got the nod that we'd been successful. Visualise a small man at a cocktail party introducing himself to a tall sophisticated woman.

In the first caption of the cartoon, he's saying, "Good evening. Is that Miss?"

In the second caption, "Or Ms?"

In the third caption, she looks down at him to say, "Dr, actually."

This became an issue for me because some of the younger members of my family, my daughter, in particular, considered that I was big-noting myself because I didn't like being called 'Mrs' and wanted to be referred to as 'Dr'. But it was my choice, and I wanted to be identified in terms of my qualifications, and not my marital status.

Armed with their PhDs, the women were ready for the next round of promotions, and the following year all the promotions to senior lecturer level in my faculty went to women. It had taken me twenty years to get my first promotion.

When the news came out, a male colleague, and one of Lyall's close friends, drove to our house and interrupted our family evening meal to inform me that the only reason I'd been promoted was because I'm a woman. This man had been the so-called best man at our wedding in 1979 – and he didn't have a PhD.

Higher education is big business these days. International student fees contribute a lot to national coffers. In fact, selling university education is now Australia's fourth-largest export business, which means that teaching must be of a high standard. This focused the attention of university hierarchies on the quality of teaching. To this end, the early 1990s saw the introduction of university-based teaching awards. In my case, I could apply for an award every three years as long as each application showed growth and improvement compared to the previous one. The awards were worth AUS$3,000 each. I applied every three years and won three of them. This money enabled me to build my career. I started to research and publish about university teaching, and I gave papers at international conferences. This meant that I became better known nationally and internationally, and job offers started to arrive.

Specialist university departments opened up with the specific aim of improving university teaching. This was when I shifted my career away from teaching sociology. I made a new start in academic development to promote teaching. I became Associate Dean (Teaching and Learning) in my faculty at ECU. I became Professor and Leader of Teaching and Learning in Darwin, finishing up as Pro-Vice-Chancellor (Teaching and Learning) at a regional university in Queensland. I retired in 2010.

In 1997, Australia introduced national awards for university teaching in which candidates could win in their subject category. The winners of these categories were then judged a second time so that the 'best of the best' won the Prime Minister's Award.

My university invited me to be a candidate in 1997, but I was put in the wrong category. I taught the sociology of health, and I was entered into the health category. Unfortunately, this was reserved for doctors and nurses. My candidacy should have been in the social sciences. I was asked to apply in 1998 – this time in the correct category.

I was a finalist, but I didn't win. After that, I got sick of it because it was a lot of work to prepare the applications. Also, by this time, I'd been promoted to Associate Professor, and I wanted to get on with research and writing, which really absorbed me. Anyway, I was asked to apply again in 2002. This time I won in the social science category, and I also received the Prime Ministers Award. An academic from Queensland won the PMs Award in the same year. They simply couldn't choose between us. We didn't share the prize. We both won the full AUS$75,000.

The national awards were designed to profile university teaching. The presentation ceremonies were in Parliament House in Canberra, and the Federal Minister for Education presented the Awards. Even the Prime Minister popped in when I won in 2002. It was expected that candidates be supported in Canberra by senior members of staff from their university just to stress the importance of teaching to the powers that be. Unfortunately,

I was in Canberra alone. Things didn't improve when I got back to Perth, and the praise I received from my boss was, "Shame it was a joint award."

My preparation for the award hadn't been much better. I wrote my application whilst on stress leave. I'd been the victim of bullying. The immediate cause of the bullying was an incident involving my daughter, who was a student at the university. Her tutor wouldn't tell her when her tutorials were until a few weeks into the semester, and Ruth wanted to be able to book her hours for paid employment. I thought it was Ruth's problem to resolve, and I gave her all the strategies I could think of so that she could find out on her own. None worked, so I rang the tutor, who took umbrage, despite my low-key questions. I was a senior in the faculty so that made me intimidating in her eyes. Behind my back, she wrote letters of complaint to her Dean, my Dean and my Head of School. The matter was settled by her Dean because tutors should keep students informed in a timely manner.

However, this issue didn't go away because my immediate working environment was toxic. Almost two months later, I was summonsed to meetings with my Head of Department and the coordinator of my teaching area – both are women. They refused to tell me what the meeting was about. This had never happened to me before, and it seemed threatening, so I rang the union. They said I should not go to any such meeting without union representation. They also asked if I could think what the meetings might be about. The only thing I could think of was the incident concerning my daughter.

"But that's you in your private capacity as a mother. It's off the table for a work meeting. In any case, that was seven weeks ago," the union official exclaimed. "They're not allowed to sit on complaints until they can be weaponised."

To cut a very long story short, duty of care meant that I was told to go on stress leave, and that's when I wrote my application for the National Teaching Awards, in which I won the top prize.

As Australia's former Prime Minister, Paul Keating, once said, "This was the sweetest victory of all," but I would have preferred the circumstance of my success to be more positive and supportive.

After I extracted myself from the bullying, the union official said, "You'll leave. Victims of bullying always do." I did.

Around about 2009, I was asked to write a chapter for a book. The editor wanted to find out if feminism had helped women's careers. My answer was a decisive yes and no, partly because I found it difficult to write about my experience of woman-on-woman bullying at work. If feminism is about supporting women, then the two calling me to meetings with no known agenda were hardly helping my career. Subsequently, I went to a women's health conference in Adelaide, at which one speaker aired this controversial issue and made me understand that I was not alone. When she described her experience of woman-on-woman bullying, there was a release of tension in the room.

"My God! It's happened to her as well."

Despite overt sexism in the workplace, three male colleagues have been more helpful in my career than most female colleagues. Much of my intellectual development can be credited to my Liverpool University lecturer, Professor Nikos Kokosalakis, and my first two heads of department, both male, taught me a lot. The first was Liverpool Phil, and I married the second – Lyall. Phil could extemporise. He was an inspirational lecturer.

A member of staff was absent one day and Phil had to take over at short notice. He gave a memorable, off-the-cuff lecture on the sociology of hot pants, which were in vogue in the early 1970s. I was impressed, but it was several years before I developed the skill and confidence to extemporise in this way. Storytelling is the basis of this approach, but it's still lecturing.

When I arrived in Australia, I had the good fortune to work in a new college that was experimenting with teaching and learning styles that involved learning-by-doing and continuous assessment. As my second head of department, Lyall encouraged this move away from lectures and exams and engaged staff and students in creative, social science projects that started my career in teaching, research and publication. This set me on a path that eventually resulted in three university prizes for teaching and two national awards.

One day, when I was an Associate Dean, I

received an abrupt knock on the door. "Quick, Lynne, we've got twelve school career advisers who've come to learn about the university, and we've forgotten to prepare for them. Can you go and hold the fort?"

This was pretty important because these career advisors were from feeder schools. These are the people who guide school-leavers to universities – and universities compete for student bums on seats. So I did what I always did when I had teaching dumped on me. I took it from them and created space for them to tell their stories.

"How many of you sat in Year Twelve at school and said, 'I'm going to be a career advisor'?"

Answer – nobody.

Then we looked at what we did and didn't know when we left school, and we explored how best to guide students who were considering applying for university. They shared their stories, and I talked about my experience of being first-in-family to go to university. I knew nothing. What does BA and BSc mean? What's honours? I thought faculty was some kind of F word, and I certainly never sat at school and said, "One day, I'm going to be a professor."

When my gang of friends at Liverpool University had a reunion in 2010, I was surprised by two things. The first was how little we knew about each other's family backgrounds. We'd obviously just lived in the moment when we were undergraduates. The second was how targeted some of them had been in their career ambitions. It's probably true to say that the boys were more strategic than the girls. I wasn't ambitious when I graduated. As first-in-family to attend university, I thought I was already doing pretty well to get a degree and be appointed as a lecturer when I was fresh out of university. It was only when I saw less well-qualified colleagues, mostly men, get a promotion that I started to make comparisons. So I took action. The university initiated a mentoring program for women who wanted to get into senior management. I signed up and asked Robyn to be my mentor. I didn't really know her then, but we are now good friends.

"I don't know why you chose me," she remarked, "You're better qualified than me, and you're older."

I replied, "But you've had more promotions than me, so you must be doing something that I'm not."

There was another senior woman I could have chosen, but she took more of a counselling approach to mentoring. I didn't want hand-holding. I needed some movement in my career, and Robyn was strategic. She advised me to apply for a newly created senior position.

"You won't get it," she said, acknowledging that there was a front runner, "but you will show your wares to a new faculty hierarchy. It's not who you know but who knows you that counts."

As predicted, I didn't get the job, but the front-runner had withdrawn his application, leaving the field wide-open. I surprised everyone by coming a close second. My mentor offered to go with me to my de-briefing to find out why I didn't get it. She was prepared to defend me.

"You didn't get the job because the appointment committee said you're difficult to work with," affirmed the Chair of the selection panel.

This was probably the bullying case coming back to bite me, and maybe some reflected disdain for my husband, Lyall, who was pretty much reviled by this group for his union activities. I was gobsmacked, but Robyn launched a challenge, noting that nobody on the interview panel had ever actually worked with me.

"That was gossip and hearsay, and you should have dismissed it."

Shortly after this, the same person chaired the promotions committee, and I became an Associate Professor, which was really what I wanted. I'm guessing that Robyn's challenge had given her pause for thought. This time my achievements were looked at for what they were. All in all, 'getting there' was a bit of a struggle.

After I won the national teaching awards, I was offered promotional positions to Darwin and to Queensland. Both were leadership and management jobs. I'd never had management training, but managing is much like teaching: set ground-rules, scaffold processes so that people know what they're doing, and provide opportunities for autonomy to enable people to work effectively. Support, reward, extend horizons and sketch visions: It had worked for me in teaching so why not in management. In addition, my experiences at work had slowly inched me towards an awareness of what was needed to lead and manage in universities, though this was as much in terms of what not to do as what to do.

I was determined to be inclusive in my approach because academics are employed for their brainpower. What was the value in excluding them from the decision-making table? I developed structures for staff to participate collegially in decision-making. We experimented with communities of practice, and staff in my department were given areas of work that they could manage for themselves within frameworks that we'd all agreed.

A colleague of mine, Geoff Scott, worked with others to complete a national report on leadership and management in universities. They confirmed what we already knew: Universities are difficult and unique places to manage. The people they talked to said that academic leadership is like "Getting butterflies into formation" or "Trying to drive a nail into a wall of blanc-mange – little resistance but no result." The core issue is academic freedom, which emerged as a central tenet of universities to protect research from interference by church and state. (Remember

Galileo was put on trial for a 'strong suspicion of heresy' for his scientific research.)

I found myself tackling this issue head-on in regard to teaching: "Academic freedom never meant that you can treat students any way you like. They have a right to have their assignments marked and returned within a couple of weeks. This is not a matter of church or state censorship."

But I don't want to convey some kind of ivory tower image of lazy staff unwilling to cooperate. Most academics I know worked well over sixty hours a week just to get their teaching, research, and publication done. Universities are resource-poor, and staff must do more with less.

At one stage, I joined with a colleague to research why good university teachers quit. One respondent summarised the pressures she felt in academic life in this way:

"We've got to give students just as much education in a smaller time frame. I can be creative, but I can't be *that* creative. I can't fit a city into a house."

Another colleague observed sadly: "I no longer encourage my postgraduate students to apply for jobs in a university."

Increasing amounts of time are spent on accountability processes, and people, like me in my management positions, require a response because we must be accountable for the expenditure of public funds. Evaluating and reporting on student satisfaction with their courses takes time, not to mention reporting on your research output and community engagement activities. All this is important, but the processes do need to be at least halfway sensible. The most laughable accountability process I encountered was activity-based costing: Academics were asked to 'guesstimate' the time they spent teaching, marking, researching, and engaging with the community. The numbers had to add up to 100%. Given that most academics worked at least fifty-hour weeks, the 100% baseline of a $37^1/_2$ hour week was shot before the guessing began.

"Just tell them you do 100% teaching," went the corridor advice, "then they can't get you to do more."

We had to guesstimate online. Thoughtfully, the program provided the opportunity to indicate that things were pretty much the same this year as last year. One busy colleague thought he'd kill the job with a quick tick in this box. But these computer programs are wily. It popped back the observation that he hadn't filled it in last year either!

"Do you enjoy your work?"

This opening question of my annual performance review took me by surprise, but it was a worthy question. If everything was so difficult, why did I stay working in universities for forty years?

I remember Lyall coming home from work one day commenting that he'd had a busy but absorbing day. "Every day is different," he observed.

I agreed. I loved teaching, research and writing, and university life gave me the freedom and autonomy to organise my days so that I could do all three. Academic life is also global, and my university work enabled me to work at dozens of international universities. I was thoroughly absorbed in all aspects of my career, but time marches on, and the American-Indian expression 'Like rain without thunder' describes how retirement crept up unawares.

Making sense of place: The Cotswolds

I identify with the Cotswolds because I lived there between the ages of five and nineteen. I went to four Cotswold primary schools (Ebrington, Toddington, Broadway, and Bishops Cleeve). Then I attended high school in Cheltenham for seven years. The woman I became started in the Cotswold Hills.

The Cotswolds are rolling limestone hills. The local quarries produce the honey-coloured limestone that characterises local architecture. Many of the villages are chocolate-box pretty, and the area is now so sought after that there are controls on who can buy into the region. If you buy there, you live there. The locals want living villages, not houses used as weekend holiday homes.

My favourite Cotswold memories are associated with a farm near Snowshill, where I lived between the ages of six and eight. Mum was trying to keep a roof over our heads, and we lived there rent-free as long as she looked after the bullocks. There was no electricity, central heating or running hot water. We had a huge wood fire, lighting was by kerosene lamp, and hot water by Calor gas. It was tough for Mum raising her girls with such limited resources. We had no car, so she must have carried the groceries across the fields from the bus stop – but we had a fruit and veggie garden, and Mum had the skills of a farmer's daughter. She bottled and preserved enough food to last through the winter. She was a smart parent as well. She told my sister and me that there was a snake in the garden so that we wouldn't pinch the fruit before she got to it – and we believed her.

It was tough for Mum but good for me. I had a quiet, rural, idyllic Cotswold childhood, of the like captured by Laurie Lee in his book, 'Cider with Rosie'. I've read his book a few times just to take me home. I could roam free on the farm, pick nuts, climb trees, and play in the attics of the farmhouse. It was a tenant farmer's house that hadn't been owned by the people living in it for some time. So junk accumulated from one tenant to the next. In the attics, I found trays of birds' eggs, and abandoned clothes that I used for dressing up. Now I understand that they were knickerbockers and camisoles probably of the Victorian era. I wish I'd kept some as antique items.

In retrospect, I think two years without TV and radio was the best gift Mum could have given me, but it came at the price of isolation. As a seven-year-old, I had to walk across two fields – even in snow or dense fog – to get to the bus to take me to Broadway school. One day, the inevitable happened. I walked in circles in the fog and was found crying and yelling for Mum. Weirdly, this became a bit of a family joke. It wasn't until I had young kids of my own that I began to question why a seven-year-old was sent into the fog on her own.

In 2017, I returned to the Cotswolds for a week, and I contacted the current owners of the farm to see if it might be possible to visit. I was at pains to assure them that I wasn't a con artist and included old photos of us all at the farm in the 1950s. They took a punt and invited me to call by. We exchanged some newsy emails ahead of time in which I was warned that things had changed since I lived there. Owners in the intervening years had removed many of the original features.

"Not the mantelpiece!" I exclaimed.

I was assured that it was still in place. I was a young girl in the era when the medical fashion was in transition from removing children's tonsils willy-nilly. Mine were not removed, and so I had tonsillitis three times. In those days, sick kids stayed in bed, so I spent my sick days in Mum's bed gazing at the mantelpiece. As I recalled, the mantelpiece had 1669 carved on it. Yet something has always told me that I was wrong about the date. I was. The date is 1707.

The current owners were terrific, and they arranged for me to meet the boy who lived on the neighbouring farm when we were kids. We had played together occasionally and went to the same primary school.

"Do you remember Miss Largo?" he asked.

"Too right I do! She put me in the corner for something I didn't do."

I often tell the story as the beginning of my sense of social justice. He remained living near Snowshill, which, I'm told, features in the opening scenes of the film 'Bridget Jones' Diary' – as they all arrive for the 'Boxing Day Turkey Curry Buffet'. The village is just as I left it. It's too small for tourist buses, so it's unspoilt. Snowshill Manor, just on the outskirts, does attract a few tourists because it has car parking and an eccentric owner who amassed a collection of extraneous paraphernalia.

I love the story of the film 'The Madness of King George'. Apparently, it was destined to be called 'The Madness of George III', but it was felt that Americans wouldn't go to see it because they hadn't seen the first two films: 'The Madness of George I & II'. This is pertinent to a town at the centre of the Cotswolds – Cheltenham – because the town was kick-started as a fashionable spa when George III arrived to take the spa waters. So it blossomed as a Regency town because – well, King George was mad, so his son was Regent.

Given this history, Cheltenham gained the reputation as a town to which brigadiers retired, and it can still accord with this image. In 2003, I took Lyall to see Pate's, my old school. It's adjacent to Pittville Pump Rooms, where spa waters are dispensed. We popped in to have a look, only to find that there was a Royal Airforce function in full swing in the chandeliered ballroom. Just as we glanced in, a red-faced man, complete with a white handlebar moustache, exited, saying to his wife, "Jolly good show, what?" We thought he must have been an actor paid to do bit parts for visiting Australians.

Yet it's not all upper socioeconomic status. A friend of mine, who worked for the UK school inspection agency, told me that she was aware of children with rickets in a Cheltenham school in the 1990s. It was certainly a monocultural society in the 1950s and 60s when I was growing up there. I went to Cheltenham Technical College for a year between school and university. There, I met a Malaysian guy, Mazlan, who was to become a life-long friend. I was eighteen, and Mazlan was the first non-British person I'd befriended in England.

My cross-cultural understanding was limited. At that stage, I knew nothing about Malaysia, least of all its warm climate, relaxed culture and exquisite cuisine. Now that I do, I cringe at what Cheltenham life in the mid-1960s must have been like for him. I've challenged him about this, but he remains steadfastly Anglophile. He loved it!

"But, Lan, I ate my very first curry EVER with you. The restaurant was at the top end of Cheltenham High Street. I'm sure they would have just cooked some meat and tipped a can of curry sauce over it. How could you possibly say that was alright?"

He does concede that the food was pretty awful.

As a gang of Tech students, we went to the Mill at Withington. It's a pretty pub that served chicken in the basket, which was very trendy in the mid-1960s. It's still served at the Mill, which is reassuring because it's an eternal complaint of ex-pat British people that UK pubs have changed for the worse. Gone are the cosy little snugs and nooks. Many pubs have been taken over by hotel chains, and the connection to local communities is lost. This isn't universally true, but it has happened to one of my old favourites. In 2003, Lyall and I stayed at a Bed and Breakfast near Bishops Cleeve, where I grew up. It was in walking distance of The Apple Tree pub, which holds special memories for me of Christmas Eve lunchtime drinks in one of the little snugs. I had a sherry, whilst Brian had a beer, surrounded by rural blokes wearing tweed jackets with leather elbow patches and dogs sleeping at their feet as their owners breasted the bar. I wanted Lyall to see it. I wish I hadn't. It had been gutted and refurbished to standard hotel-chain prescription: open plan, complete with the flashing lights of game machines and mass-produced pub fare. It was pretty plastic. I'm told that it's now restored to some of its former glory.

I've always thought (still do) that Cheltenham is the best shopping venue in the UK. It's just over one hundred miles from London. It has the Government Communication Headquarters (read high level, well-dressed government officials) and the 'county set' live nearby, including several members of the royal family. Quality shops are the order of the day. However, it's a small town, so big London shops and local boutiques rub shoulders within walking distance. It's easy shopping. I'm pleased to see that when the House of Frazer chain of shops took over Cheltenham's Cavendish House, they didn't change its name. They wouldn't dare. It's a local institution.

Cheltenham is famous for horse racing – the Gold Cup in particular. It's also known for its public (meaning private) schools, especially

Cheltenham Ladies College. This is so well known that, in my forty years of working in Australia, I rarely mentioned that I hail from Cheltenham because the immediate question is:

"And did you go to Cheltenham Ladies College?"

My standard response is: "No! I went to the school for clever girls, not rich girls."

Cheltenham is also known for its music and literature festivals. In fact, Cheltenham ran the first-ever literature festival in the world more than seventy years ago.

My love of music was fostered in Cheltenham. It was all around me. It had a good pop music scene and numerous music festivals – jazz and classical. Celebrated composers, like Gustav Holst, lived in Cheltenham, which now has a Holst museum. Soprano, Dame Felicity Lott, was at my school, and Brian Jones of the Rolling Stones was born and buried in Cheltenham. The Rolling Stones performed at the Odeon in Cheltenham – a lovely art deco cinema. When I visited a few years ago, it was derelict. I thought they might at least keep the façade, but it's now gone, replaced by a row of elegantly constructed apartments. But well done, Cheltenham Town Planners, at least you stuck to Regency style.

Cheltenham architecture is elegant: Think Jane Austen's era – sweeping crescents and mews terraces. The Promenade is Cheltenham's centrepiece. There used to be a cinema on the corner behind Neptune's Fountain, but its location was of little use to me even though it was adjacent to the Royal Well Bus Station. My last bus home to Bishops Cleeve village was at 10.15 pm, and the movies didn't finish until 10.30 pm. That's if I wanted the bus that stopped right outside my house. If I really wanted to see the end of a movie, I had to catch the Green Bus, which left later but dropped me in the village. This meant walking about a mile on my own, including the road that ran between the churchyard and the primary school playing field. It was scary, so I pelted down that road. This is why, I think, I was one of only two girls at Pate's who won a silver medal in athletics. I was particularly good at sprinting. In retrospect, I had due cause and adequate reason to be scared because the notorious serial killer, Fred West, lived in a caravan in Bishops Cleeve. He killed many women, including a girl from my school.

So this is where I came from – the Cotswolds. I belong to it, and it belongs to me. I know this because when I was twenty-eight, I returned from Australia to visit Mum and Dad in Bishops Cleeve. It didn't matter that I'd got a degree and travelled the world. I returned to a village where I was identified as Mr and Mrs Hardy's daughter. If I attempted to recount my global stories, eyes glazed over and villagers waited politely until I stopped. Then they asked: "And are you courting, love?" There was only one meaningful role in life for a girl.

When I boarded the village bus to pop into Cheltenham, it was exactly the same bus that took me to high school every day for seven years, and it was the same bus driver. He gave me half-price, even though I was twenty-eight. I was so gobsmacked that I accepted it. To him, I was still a schoolgirl. This could have been my destiny, get married and stay in the village where I once belonged.

Making sense of place: Devon

It was 2005. Mum had just died, so I hastened back to the UK from my job in Darwin. I hired a car at Heathrow Airport, driving first to Gloucestershire, where Mum had lived. She wished to be buried in Peters Marland Churchyard with the rest of her Britton family, so arrangements were made to transport her back to Devon. I followed on, driving down the M5 on my own, listening to the BBC's Top 100 Classical Music contest. Just as I turned off right into North Devon, the radio played the number one piece of classical music. It was Elgar's 'Pomp and Circumstance'. The combination of Mum's death, the patriotic strains of 'Land of Hope and Glory,' and the familiar landscape of Devon proved an emotional king hit. At that moment, I felt a strong sense of belonging to the land of my extended Britton family.

As soon as we'd all arrived in Torrington, we visited the undertaker to finalise arrangements for Mum's funeral. He turned out to be twice related to me. I was the youngest girl of a batch of thirteen Britton cousins. There are a lot of us, and we all have kids and grandkids, so it was unsurprising that an undertaker might be twice related. I've often joked that if you yelled the family name down the street in Torrington, half the people about town would turn round to answer your call.

Singer, and song-writer, 'Cousin Dan.' played at a gig in Devon in 2018. The village hall was packed out, and when he asked how many people were related to him, I'd say half of those present raised their hands.

Another cousin attended one of our family reunions with the new man in her life. This caused her to show him some old family photos, including a picture of her great-great-grandparents. Coincidentally, he visited his own grandmother and mentioned the family reunion. She pulled out a photo of his great-great-grandparents. The same people! He was somewhat discomfited to find that he was in a relationship with his third cousin. He needn't have worried, though. I'd already checked that out in the back of the prayer book when I was a bored thirteen-year-old attending Anglican morning service. I discovered that it's OK to be kissing cousins, even with first cousins.

Devonshire blood runs in my veins. I know that anyway, but I did a DNA test to confirm it. Cousin Dan was among the first to pay good money for a DNA test that told him what he already knew, but he went beyond the customary commercial tests. The results showed that he is of the same haplogroup (Rb1) as most of Europe. It still seemed hardly worth paying good money for results as generalised as this. However, he also revealed a unique signature indicating that the family had stayed put for a long time. Well, we already knew that from our own lived experience in the Britton family.

I stayed with my cousin, Greta, on one of my visits to Devon. She pulled out a tin trunk from her pantry to show me the contents. Her dad had rescued it from Grandma's attic after she died. It was full of old title deeds of property that had passed through the family over centuries. The most spectacular was a large parchment dated sometime in the seventeenth century. It had a huge red wax seal ensconced in a round tin. It's a magnificent historical document.

My grandson, Thomas, loves touching historical artefacts like this. "I just love old things, NaiNai," he tells me. I really hope that he'll be able to see the parchment if he ever gets to Devon. If he doesn't, he can be assured that these documents have now been scanned for the North Devon Archives. They're available to posterity.

Cousin Dan participated in subsequent DNA analysis that links him (us) back to someone in Portugal dating back to somewhere between 800 and 1,200 years ago. We can't know exactly what the connection might be. It could be anything. We do know, for example, that slaves were taken from the Devonshire coast, and they could have been sent anywhere. It's also a possibility that 'Britton' knights may have participated in the Crusades and distributed family DNA on their way to Jerusalem.

Alternatively, the North Devon coast is treacherous, and there were many shipwrecks. So maybe this genetic connection had something to do with a shipwrecked Portuguese sailor finding his way into our family. In fact, there is a strong oral history of Portuguese blood in the family, but it didn't show up in my DNA results. Maybe, also, my ancestors helped to wreck the ship. Stories of smuggling abound along the Devonshire coast and, so I'm told, my ancestors were shipwreckers. They flashed lights to lure the ships onto the rocks so that they could collect the booty when the ship foundered. When I first made a connection with my sixth-cousin-once-removed, Nic, in Tasmania, he confirmed that he'd also heard tales of shipwreckers in the Devonshire family. True or not for the Britton family, these tales of derring-do and smuggling convey something of Devonshire history.

My cousin, Dan, has done a lot of family research, and he thinks we might be descended from younger brothers of a knightly family that came over with William the Conqueror in 1066, the last invasion of England.

"So we're Normans," I insisted during a telephone conversation with Dan.

"No, Bretons. They were allies of the Normans seeking the return of lands they'd lost when the Celts were pushed out to Brittany by invading hoards moving into the south-west of England."

Of course, none of this can be proved, but there is Domesday Book evidence showing that Alfred de Breton was given lands in North Devon after he'd participated in the Norman Conquest of England. Both the similarity in the family name and location are persuasive. So the pieces of the jigsaw do fit. Who knows?

These are the unproven, romantic, hypothetical deep-history stories about my ancestors, but I can be certain of who I belong to from the late seventeenth century forward because my cousin Jane developed a meticulously researched family tree starting with the birth of John Britton in 1690 in Devon.

I didn't realise I was bilingual until I took my Australian husband, Lyall, to meet my extended family in 1981. My cousin, Greta, organised an afternoon tea for the Brittons in the old school hall at Peter's Marland, where Mum had attended school. It was thought best to mix us all up so that we could get to know each other. It was a good idea, but I was apprehensive about Lyall. Would he understand these people? He didn't. But, no matter, because they couldn't understand his Australian accent either.

Cousin Dan has similar memories. "When I was a teenager, I took a friend called Wes down from Leicestershire to stay with Gran and Granf. Wes was from a farming background, so I thought he would have things to talk to Granf about, but I didn't count on the clash of accents. I literally had to interpret as if they were speaking different languages. Wes would say something, and Granf would look at me to interpret, then Granf would reply, and Wes would look at me to decipher! Very funny for me, but a bit embarrassing for them."

My mother was the only one of her siblings to move away, so my sister, Julie, and I were the only two of the thirteen cousins to grow up outside Devon. I grew up mostly in the Cotswolds, where the locals have the soft, rural accent of the West Country. It's similar to the Devonshire accent but not nearly as strong, so Mum always sounded a bit different. Some of my friends didn't understand her at all. My sister and I would sometimes tease her.

"Will ye put the kettle on?" Mum requested.

"Willy's not here," we'd chorus. "Do it yourself."

Mum's Devonshire accent was diluted over the

years, but she soon reverted when she visited Devon, and some aspects of her Devonshire dialect were never lost. She had a propensity for referring to 'people' as 'volk' (folk), and saying that she would do something 'dreckly' (meaning later), when she meant the exact opposite of doing anything directly, which might commonly be understood as immediately. Dan Britton picked up on the Devonshire use of 'dreckly' in the lyrics of his 'Song of the Western Brittons', which he wrote as a family anthem for our Hartland Britton website.

Grandad Daniel Britton died when I was three, but Mum remembers him commenting about me – then his toddler granddaughter, "Her be a proper little maid her be."

There's a lot of Devonshire dialect in that one small phrase. There's the use of 'her' rather than 'she' and 'be' rather than 'is'. 'Proper' is a widely used adjective meaning something like 'nice' or 'as she should be' and 'maid' means 'girl'. Later, as a young teenager, I spent several summers with Mum's sister, my Auntie Elsie. Her husband, Uncle Frank, had a broad Devonshire accent that completely bamboozled me. I tried to cover for my incomprehension by answering "I don't know" to every question asked.

"How many slices of meat do you want?" he asked as he carved the roast.

"I don't know."

"Did you ride the horses today?"

"I don't know."

These days, if I dare attempt a Devonshire accent, it's the phrases I learned at Auntie Elsie's that come to mind:

"Where be ye gwain to?" (Where are you going?);

"I be gwain abed noo." (I'm going to bed now).

In 1988, Lyall and I took our children, Ruth and Sam, to the UK to meet their kith and kin. We attended a Britton family reunion that rolled into a country dancing evening, organised by my cousin, Marina.

Lyall was not a fan of dancing. He considered it to be 'walking in agony'. So he looked askance at the prospect of this kind of event. Fortunately, various nephews and cousins whisked him away, at higher speeds than he might have liked on those narrow country roads in Devon, to a rather excellent pub at Sheepwash. I stayed and danced with my kids and spent much of the evening chatting with Auntie Elsie.

When Lyall returned, she looked him in the eye and asked, "'ave ye been to church, then?"

He agreed that he'd been to church.

"That be the one where the prayer books 'ave 'andles, be it?" she inquired.

Historically, Devon has experienced considerable poverty. If farms are passed on to first-born sons, then that leaves not only daughters, but also younger sons looking for ways to live, move and have their being. As a consequence, there was a lot of migration to the colonies, Canada in particular. I'd always vaguely known that I had Canadian cousins, but it wasn't until 1988 that I started to ask questions. I was planning a round-the-world trip to complete my PhD research about the international women's health movement, and Australia and Canada were leading countries in this field of endeavour. If I was going to Canada anyway, I thought I might as well try to meet this long-lost family. I wrote to my cousin, Marina, in Devon, and she provided me with some addresses.

To cut a long story short, I wrote to them all

and finished up at two family reunions, one on Vancouver Island and one out on the prairies in Manitoba at a town called Grandview – so-called because it doesn't have one. As my cousin, Rena, drove me to the reunion, she saw me looking at the vast, open landscape, "It's like driving on the back of a saucer, isn't it, Lynne?" I could see the horizon all around.

My cousin, Diane, took me to the small rural museum in Grandview, which houses memorabilia associated with my Grandad's four brothers, who'd been pioneers there. I was also given a history book entitled 'Pioneers of Grandview', which devotes a page or two to my great-uncles. After that first meeting in 1988, I became good friends with cousins Diane in Winnipeg, and Helah, in Calgary. There has been considerable visiting to and fro between Canada, the UK, and Australia ever since by quite a few family members. I'm particularly pleased that Mum got to Canada to meet her first cousins.

When I retired in 2010, I became aware that a lot of family research was happening around the world. Being a diligent social scientist, I thought it might be worth pulling it all together onto a website. I contacted a university colleague to ask if he could recommend a free website. I then gave those details to my nephew, Ian, in the UK, and he got it set up. After that, I worked with Ian's brother, my nephew, Michael, and with Cousin Dan and others to prepare and upload material – and so 'The Hartland Britton Website' was born. It gave rise to further contacts. For example, I thought I'd started the Australian branch of the Britton family, but I missed that honour by more than a century. I'm now in contact with my sixth cousin-once-removed, Nic, in Tasmania, and discovered that he has already written a history of the Tasmanian Brittons, some of whom own and operate what I think is the longest-running family-owned business in Tasmania – Britton Timbers.

Lyall always thought that I could rattle off relationships, such as 'third-cousin-twice-removed' because I'm a sociologist, but that's not so. It's because I'm a member of a Devonshire family where everybody knows their place. My third-cousin-once-removed, Laurie, visited me here in Perth from Calgary, Canada. Laurie brought her daughter, Erica, with her. She's a fifth cousin to my grandkids. We Brittons do actually mix and socialise with remote cousins, and it has made life interesting. There are age-old traditions in Devon that reinforce exactly where and how you belong.

In 1979, I attended my cousin's wedding in Devon with my mother and two of my sisters. I had expected to sit with them in church, but Auntie Elsie had other ideas. The groom's side of the church followed a strict protocol. Elsie, the mother of the groom, and her siblings sat, in age order, on the front pews. The next generation of cousins followed on – also in age order. As the youngest girl of my batch of first cousins, I was the last in line and next to me were the second cousins. The ushers have a very specific job to do. It made me feel that wherever I go in this world, I'll always have my place on a pew in Devon.

Years later, in 2005, I attended my mother's funeral at Peters Marland Church. It was a poignant moment as I looked at her adult grandsons standing beneath the portico, waiting to carry their grandmother on her last journey. Some cousins waited in the drizzling rain in the village square, and then, as the moment arrived to progress into the church, car doors opened and cousins emerged from all directions to line up in age order behind the coffin. Mum was going nowhere without the support of the Britton extended family that had meant so much to her. My sister, Audrey, is one of the older cousins, and she sometimes jokes that this is a disconcerting family tradition because the older you get, the closer you are to the coffin. "Us be moving up the line 'yer, my dear," an older cousin opined to Audrey at one of the family funerals.

Many of them are moving up the line to the same cemetery in Peters Marland. A few years ago, my cousin, Ros, emailed to say that she'd taken her granddaughters to Marland cemetery to lay a flower on each of the family graves. I'm guessing it was a bloody big bunch of flowers because the graves go back to our mutual great-grandparents, and there are many cousins, aunts and uncles in between, and, of course, my mother. Sadly, my daughter died, aged thirty-seven, in 2020. My sisters, Audrey and Joyce, have organised contributions from their families to plant a tree in Ruth's memory in Marland cemetery. This means that memories of generations of my family members rest in one place. This feels right for me.

I want Ruth to be remembered back where we all came from.

My niece, Elaine, has organised to plant a rowan tree, selected in memory of her own baby daughter, Rowan, who died a few hours after she was born. Elaine is a very folksy woman, so the selection also fits with her interests because, in Celtic mythology, the rowan is seen as the tree of life. When I researched this tree, I also found that, traditionally, it was planted to ward off witches. This has additional resonance with North Devon because the last witches burned at the stake in England came from Bideford, a town near Peters Marland. Dan wrote a song about this for the launch of a book about the Bideford Witches entitled 'Sins as Red as Scarlet'.

Devon is full of such stories, and people, especially my mum and her sister, Elsie, liked to tell a yarn and pass on stories. On one occasion when we were all together, my Uncle Roy turned round to me to share his opinion of Auntie Elsie: "Her be a proper old yapper, her be."

I was always raised to be proud of my links to Devon and the Britton family and, when I met my Canadian cousin, Diane, in 1988, she confirmed that she, too, had been taught that being a Britton is something special. Certainly, I saw my Devonshire aunts and uncles as giants of my childhood, and my cousin, Rosalind, said much the same about Auntie Elsie and Uncle Frank, who was the local Master of Fox Hounds. Ros had occasion to see him and Auntie Elsie dressed up for the Hunt Ball. "I thought they were like the king and queen," she said.

Making sense of place: Liverpool

"D'ya want chips with that?"

God love her! This Scouse waitress made me feel right back at home in that instant. Liverpool is, after all, one of the few places in the world where you might be offered chips with moussaka in preference to Greek salad. I have a strong sense of identity with the city, even though Scousers don't take my sentimental attachment very seriously. Liverpool Phil, for example, recorded a bit of Harry Enfield's comedy show for me because he thought I fitted the bill. Called 'The Scouse Wedding', it showed the priest saying to a young couple getting married:

"And do you promise to F**k off from Liverpool and spend the rest of your life raving about how great it is?"

Not that I was raving on the train to Liverpool when I first took my Australian family there. In fact, I quickly moved along a continuum that started with how great Liverpool is – football teams – Beatles – playwrights – poets – poverty – unemployment – violence – high crime rates ….

"Actually, it's a bit of a slum," I concluded as we pulled into Lime St Station, and my teenage kids looked in dismay at the slimy black walls in which their mother found some romance.

We were off out for a meal with friends on our first evening in Liverpool, so I decided to buy a bottle of wine for the hosts. I was driving, and Lyall hopped out of the car to get something from the bottle shop. I suddenly realised that I'd better warn him that he'd be walking into a cage.

"The bottles are displayed around the walls, and they're protected by floor-to-ceiling crim-safe mesh – so it feels like you're in a cage. Just choose a bottle and point the salesperson in the right direction."

Accustomed to acres of openly displayed bottles in Australia's wine barns, Lyall never quite got over the shock.

You don't get above yourself in Liverpool. On one return visit, I went downtown on a shopping spree for my kids before returning to Australia. I know the ropes: Bag snatching is common, so I placed my bag strap over my head, and across my chest, and held my arm firmly around the opening. It's important not to look timid, so I marched assertively down Church Street. I was the perfect traveller, wise to the ways of the world. In fact, I looked like a paragon of middle class, middle-aged virtue, and I was clocked.

"Heh, that looks like a good shoplifting bag. I need a new pair of trainers. Ger'us a pair of size tens, would ya."

The stall keeper caught my eye, and I caught his. We both collapsed laughing.

Times change, and so do cities. As well as the theatre of the street that pads out my memories of Liverpool, they now have revamped theatres, state of the art museums, and a redeveloped city shopping centre: Liverpool One. Norwegian Birger, who I knew as a student architect in Liverpool, applauds the concept of sustaining streetscapes in the shopping centre and welcomes urban renewal.

"I remember visiting Liverpool when the city centre was really run down. I felt sad that 'my city' had come to this. When we visited Liverpool again years later, it was quite a surprise. The city centre was alive again. But, it's the old buildings along Church Street, the Albert Docks, the bombed church at the top end of Bold Street, and the cathedrals that define Liverpool for me."

Despite the advantages that Liverpool One brought with it, Birger and I agree with Milan Kundera who wrote about the standardisation and globalisation of modern culture. In his view, you can go to a shopping centre in any country, and you could be anywhere. Despite this, Liverpool is a city that does have a strong sense of itself, and when I go to Liverpool, I always know that I'm somewhere.

Scouse friends think I'm doolally to return at every opportunity to the view from 'my' Number 82 bus stop in Liverpool. There I can look down the hill to where the grey skies merge with the grey Mersey that flows into the cold grey Atlantic and on out into the world.

"How can you like that when you live under blue Australian skies?" they ask.

I find the grey vista calming, and, as an undergraduate in Liverpool in the 1960s, the horizons seemed expansive in contrast to the beautiful confines of the Cotswold Hills that had encircled my childhood. Liverpool feels open to the world, and I agree with long-time campaigner for social justice in Liverpool, Margaret Simey. She said that the magic of Liverpool is that it isn't England. Liverpool is itself, an identity forged of centuries of seafaring, football fanaticism, crime, storytelling, music and humour.

The end destination of the Number 82 bus was a suburb called Speke and the bus conductor saw me coming when I boarded the bus to travel back from my first day of study at the University.

"Is this bus going to Speke?" I asked tentatively.

"Well, it hasn't said a bloody word all day, Queen, but we'll get you to where you're going."

There's a small book about Liverpool in the 'Cities on the Edge' series. It proposes that port cities of the world have more in common with each other than with their hinterlands. Ports are outward-facing and connected by seafaring trade links. For Liverpool, this has meant that it punches above its weight in its contribution to Britain's musical heritage because returning sailors bring the latest music from overseas.

The curators at the relatively new Museum of

Liverpool have a tough job trying to capture the essence of Liverpool, but it was unavoidable that they include a large section on music. How could they not when the Beatles made famous their city of origin? But there is also the Liverpool Philharmonic (Liverpool Phil), Billy Fury, Cilla Black, and Gerry and the Pacemakers, whose family joked ironically when he eventually did need to be fitted with a pacemaker.

The music section of the new museum is expansive. In contrast, the old museum had only a small room to show off the Mersey-beat sound. It contained a jukebox and a chair on which I sat as I gazed across the Mersey listening to my chosen songs: 'Ferry 'Cross the Mersey'; 'Penny Lane'; and the Beatle's 'There's a Place.' Corny and clichéd, I know, but I was so still and absorbed in the music that I gave another visitor quite a shock when I moved. She thought I was a mannequin and part of the display. A good laugh was had by all – and I haven't had a visit to Liverpool that hasn't afforded me a good laugh.

When I went to the new Museum of Liverpool, I realised just how much my identity is bound-up with the city. Indeed, aspects of my own life were on display. I spent ages in the writers' section. It's large because Liverpool has produced a lot of them. Liverpool playwright, Willy Russell, wrote 'Educating Rita' – about a mature-aged, working-class student fathoming the highbrow culture of university life. This resonates with my first response to university life in Liverpool in 1967. What did I know? I was the 'first-in-family,' as it's now classified, to enter academia. Rita barely knew what an essay was. When asked to 'Suggest how you might resolve the staging difficulties inherent in a production of Ibsen's Peer Gynt,' she submitted one sentence: 'Do it on the radio.' Good answer, but her lecturer was expecting a more academic analysis. Willy Russell's play 'Shirley Valentine' was poignantly funny, and no woman I know understands how a man can write with such insight into a woman's life.

When I first went to Liverpool, the Mersey poets dominated the scene: Roger McGough, Adrian Henri, and Brian Patten. My university friends gave me their recently-published, groundbreaking book of poems for my twenty-first birthday present. I still have it on my bookshelves, so I was somewhat confronted when I saw it on display in the museum. I'm already history!

Carla Lane wrote the gentle BBC comedies: 'Liver Birds'; 'Butterflies'; and 'Bread.' Indirectly, she has also resonated through my life because my school friend, Gill, knows her. Sometime in the 1980s, when my kids were little, Lyall arrived home from work to find me banging pots and pans around the kitchen.

"What on earth's the matter with you?" he asked.

"Well, if you'd like to know where I'd rather be – cooking chilli con carne for you lot, or dining out with Paul and Linda in the crypt of Liverpool Cathedral – I'll tell you where I'd rather be!"

I'd received a letter from Gill, who'd recently returned to Liverpool. She told me that she'd called by to see Carla, who had an invitation from Paul and Lynda McCartney to the crypt of the Catholic Cathedral. They were hosting a vegetarian supper for Liverpool family and friends whilst they were in town staging the Liverpool Oratorio.

"Come with me," Carla said to Gill. So that's how Gill is acquainted with the McCartneys and why I remained cooking chilli con carne for my

Australian family.

The writers' section of the Museum gave rise to quite a long storyline from my time living in Liverpool 1967-72, through to my life in Perth, Australia, because, in the late 1980s, Liverpool poet, Roger McGough, visited as Writer-in-Residence at Edith Cowan University, where I worked. I went to two of his poetry readings, and I asked a question at each. The first was based on a poem written in his youth:

"Do you still want to die a young man's death?"

Secondly, I wanted to know how important he thought a Liverpool accent might be when reading his poetry.

He thought accent didn't matter.

I disagree. Whenever I read his work, I always have a Liverpool accent in my head, and I can't tell a Liverpool joke without resorting to a Scouse accent.

In my first year at university, I was offended when one of my professors opined that Roger's work was, "A few drunken words dashed-off at midnight." Apart from the fact that he should have been teaching evidence-based sociology, he has been proven wrong in so many ways. For example, I recently went to see a Molière play in Perth and was intrigued by the complexities of translating rhyming couplets from French to Australian English. Subsequent investigations revealed that Roger McGough had translated several Molière plays and brought them to Merseyside in Scouse dialect. Drunk or sober that was a remarkable achievement.

Jimmy McGovern is a Liverpool playwright perhaps best known for the TV series 'Cracker.' Like most Liverpudlians, he's big on social justice. He did some great work engaging Trade Unionists in the development of a play about their life and work. Unionism was always strong in Liverpool, especially on the docks. This was particularly so when I was an undergraduate in the late 1960s because that's when containerisation started to affect the dockers' livelihoods and way of life.

Liverpool is the capital of Ireland, so the joke goes, because it has welcomed so many Irish immigrants. Its Irish heritage has breathed life into a local culture rich in storytelling and the craick. Even the word 'Scouse,' which refers to anything Liverpudlian, comes from the poverty-stricken local cuisine. It's Irish stew without the meat.

There's an old joke about an elderly Irish lady who came over to Liverpool from Dublin. She had difficulty crossing busy roads, so she asked a police officer to help her. He told her to use the traffic lights.

"When it's red, it's red for the devil, and you don't cross. When it's green, it's green for the Emerald Isles, and you can cross."

This worked, so when she saw him again, she thanked him, adding: "And I'm glad they don't give those Orange bastards much of a chance."

The religious divide in Liverpool is highlighted in the song 'In my Liverpool Home.' The lyrics tell you, 'If you want a cathedral, we've got two to spare.' The Anglican and Catholic cathedrals are within spitting distance of each other, and both dominate the Liverpool skyline. Until I went to the new museum, I'd forgotten that my advent to Liverpool life in 1967 coincided with the completion of the Catholic Cathedral, with its crown of thorns spire. This was quickly named the Mersey Funnel (to match with the Mersey Tunnel, which goes under the river). It was originally designed by Lutyens with traditional cathedral architecture in mind. These plans were started, so it's still possible to visit the Lutyens' crypt. My UK family is interested in this because my nephew lives with his family in Ashby St Ledgers, a heritage village designed by Lutyens. Just to push the story out a bit further, Ashby St Ledgers is also where the Gunpowder Plot was hatched and why the UK now has firework day: "Remember, remember, the fifth of November, the gunpowder treason and plot." In my life, the storylines from Liverpool are complex and far-reaching.

Liverpool has another religion – football. Big business that buys and sells football teams quickly discovered just how entrenched soccer fandom is in Liverpool when they tried to form a breakaway league in 2021. Fans and players objected, and the commercial plans folded. Fans of Liverpool and Everton football teams are entrenched in long family traditions. Fans don't choose their football team. It chooses them.

But the religious divide between Liverpool and Everton is easily bridged when the city is brought together in shared matters, as it was with the 1989 Hillsborough disaster in which ninety-six Liverpool football fans were killed.

At the memorial service in Anfield Stadium, the

blue scarves of Everton were intertwined with the red of the Liverpool team as Gerry (of Gerry and the Pacemakers) led them all in singing the Liverpool Club song: "You'll never walk alone." There wasn't a dry eye in Liverpool. There followed years of activism to clear the name of the football fans who were blamed for the incident. Only in 2017 were officials, rather than fans, held to account.

Liverpool waterfront is eye-catching. It has the most iconic buildings in Liverpool, and my thoughts returned to Liverpool's 'Three Graces' when I first visited the Bund in Shanghai in 1988. The similarities in architecture are remarkable. It seems port cities do have much in common. Liverpool is a red brick city, and the industrial architecture is beautiful.

If you want to know what to do in Liverpool, just walk and look up. Dale, North John, and Hope streets are particularly lovely. Stop at a pub or three on the way, including Liverpool's oldest pub: Rigby's. It was originally a staging post for horse-and-carriages on their way to Scotland – hence Scotland Road (Scottie Road to locals, like the pop star Cilla Black, who lived nearby) leads away from the pub. There's also 'Ye Crack' and 'The Phil' (Philharmonic Dining Rooms), which women should visit at 11 am if they wish to see the pink marble décor of the men's toilet.

The soul of Liverpool lies in its people. It's a hard-living multicultural city. Its China Town was established a very long time ago. That doesn't mean it's been easy for immigrants. I remember the Chinese man who owned a fish and chip shop in Penny Lane. He had an ear-to-ear scar across his neck inflicted, presumably, when he tried to resist protection rackets. My favourite Liverpool person was Lyn Owen. She was the portress in Salisbury Hall, where I lived as an undergraduate. She arrived from Wales to live in Liverpool when she was eight. At that stage, she could speak only Welsh. She contracted polio as a ten-year-old, which left her severely disabled. She and her family adopted me, and I always think of them as 'my Liverpool family.'

Lyn once said the loveliest thing that has ever been said to me: "Lynne, I never had children, but if I'd had a daughter, I'd have wanted her to be like you."

I had the utmost respect for her and her self-educated intellect, so it meant a lot to hear her say that.

Whenever I was back in Liverpool, Lyn insisted on buying me a meal at her local pub, 'The Childe of Hale.' It's named after the local 'giant,' John Middleton, who, according to legend, grew to be nine feet (2.75 metres) tall and had to sleep with his feet out of the window of his small house. Over the years, Lyn's obvious disabilities got worse. I was used to them, so I didn't notice the humpback and the callipers, but others could be taken aback. We walked into The Childe of Hale one Sunday evening. The place was buzzing with the chatter of people who'd already had a few bevvies (drinks). The sight of Lyn with her callipers and walking frame caused a sudden and embarrassing silence. Slowly, a few kind voices called out,

"Are you 'right there, Queen?"

It was all a bit awkward until one bloke, looking straight at her walking frame, yelled across: "Hey, does that thing come with an airbag?" The moment was saved with characteristic Liverpool good humour.

Self-deprecating humour is what Liverpool is all

about. It keeps you in your place, and it offers succour and comfort. Bill Bryson 'got' Liverpool in his book 'Notes from a Small Island.' He was there when neighbouring and rival city, Manchester, was bidding to host the Commonwealth Games. At least Liverpool doesn't even bother, Bryson observed. Local actor Peter Turner captured that same spirit in his account of the dying days of Hollywood actress, Gloria Graeme. He and his Liverpool family cared for her, duties which made him late for rehearsals one day. When he made his excuses, the doorman shrugged them off.

"Film stars don't die in Liverpool," he observed.

It's not possible to escape Liverpool humour. It catches you unawares. When Liverpool friend Phil and I were chatting over a drink in Rigby's one evening, he told me about the breakdown of a relationship his friend had experienced.

"Oh, what caused that?" I asked.

"He said his wife wants to be an astronaut."

I couldn't make the connection.

"Yeah, she'd told him she wanted her own space."

When I lived in Liverpool, teenage girls were called 'totties.' In the 1960s, they all looked the same with bouffant blonde hair and panda eyes framed by black eyeliner, but fashions change. These days it's about spray tan, which can look quite orange with over-enthusiastic application. With this in mind, a Liverpool comedian, Paul O'Grady, described a Saturday night out in the city, "It's like the f***ing Terracotta Army on stilettos."

Regrettably, Liverpool humour doesn't always translate across borders, as the Beatles discovered when John Lennon jested that they were more popular than Jesus. There followed USA protest burnings of Beatle's records and music.

'Fare thee well to Princes Landing Stage. River Mersey fare thee well.' These lines are from 'The Leaving of Liverpool' – a folk song of the 1960s – and the day did come, in 1972, when I left to start my backpacking journey to Australia. I walked through Sefton Park to say goodbye to a city I'd made my own. I walked further than I should and decided to catch a bus back to my flat in Aigburth Vale. I was so lost in thought that I must have appeared arrogant as I tossed my money down to buy my bus ticket:

"Aigburth Vale, please." I carried on thinking my deep thoughts about whether or not I should be leaving. Suddenly, realising I hadn't got my ticket or my change, I looked up to find the bus driver sitting with hands on hips.

"Are you just going there?" he asked, "Or would you like to buy it?" In other words, "Back in your box, girl!"

I didn't get back in my Liverpool box, but I did take it with me. As the saying goes: "You can take the girl out of Liverpool, but not Liverpool out of the girl," and so my Liverpool story ended as it started – on the buses.

Making sense of place: Australia

I arrived in Australia in 1973 after backpacking for four months. I had crossed the Soviet Union on the Trans-Siberian train and then meandered through Asian countries until I landed in Perth from Singapore. I had long black hair, and I wore jeans and a black polo neck jumper. I was quintessentially hippie. My appearance and my four months in Asia aroused the interest of border control, so, on arrival, I was detained for two hours whilst Australian officials completed a thorough search of my luggage. This made me anxious because I knew Steve was waiting for me. He's a UK bloke I'd met on the kibbutz in Israel. He'd travelled to Perth before me, and I was depending on the floor of his apartment for my first few nights of accommodation.

I knew Steve was there because in those days there was little airport security, and I'd spotted him on the observation deck on the roof of the single-storey Perth airport. It was easy to catch sight of him because he was so tall. On the kibbutz, there'd been five Steves, so they were labelled, somewhat unkindly, by their characteristics. The bloke with dropped arches was called Steve Shuffle-Foot, and tall Steve, who now waited at Perth Airport, was Steve Stretch.

When I eventually staggered out of customs and quarantine inspections, Steve said: "You put my name down as your contact in Australia, didn't you?"

Of course I had. That was the arrangement.

"Well, when I arrived," he went on to explain, "they found a small bit of cannabis in my pocket, and they'd have that on their records, so you copped the big search. Welcome to Australia."

I had to find somewhere to live and get a job, so, on my first day in Perth, I went into the city to find employment. Whilst waiting at a pedestrian crossing, I saw a man wearing a trilby hat, a long sleeve shirt with sleeve braces, tweed shorts, knee-high socks and brogue shoes. I thought, perhaps, he'd been allowed out for the day without supervision. Later, I realised that formal shorts and long socks were normal work attire for Australian men in the summer months of the 1970s. However, I'd arrived in Perth in the middle of winter, so he was one of a kind on the day I went job hunting.

I also had to tackle Australian English. This was complicated by the fact that my travelling companion was Belgian. He was a great linguist, who spoke five languages, but Australian English defeated him. He'd quickly found a job as a roustabout in the agricultural department at the local university.

Arriving home exhausted one day, he informed me that he'd had to do the work of two men because the man he normally worked with was off sick with a 'crooked leg.'

"I think you'll find that's a crook leg," I corrected, translating Australian idiomatic expression. "Crook means sick."

Subsequently, when I crossed the Nullarbor by train, I saw that the town of Cook, with a population of four, had co-opted the expression, branding itself as a mecca of medical care. 'If your crook, come to Cook,' the sign read.

I liked the Australian way of saying 'G'Day.' It's

friendly and casual, but I couldn't greet people this way when I first arrived here. It just sounded inauthentic when I said it. It was a decade before 'G'Day' fell naturally from my lips, and now I have to discipline myself not to say it when I'm back in the UK. In 1981, Lyall and I travelled around Europe for three months by train. It was an active trip with lots of walking and bike riding, and I started to get tired.

"Geez, Lyall, I'm stonkered."

He looked at me in astonishment. "Lynne, you're going to have to change your language before you reach England. Otherwise, your mother isn't going to understand you!"

I've now been in Australia for almost fifty years, and I've happily adopted the Australian diminutive. I say 'piccie,' 'rashie,' lippy (lipstick), and 'biccie' along with the best of them. Idiot people are 'drongos' and 'drop-kicks,' and I copy Lyall by deliberately dropping into Australian rhyming slang, like dead-horse for tomato sauce, so that our grandkids learn something about 'Strine' – Australian English. I also do it because it's a point of resistance to the Americanisation of Australian English.

In the UK, I'd worked as a lecturer at a teacher training college, so, as soon as I arrived, I wrote to a number of Perth colleges seeking employment. I didn't bother waiting for job advertisements. As it turned out, Mount Lawley College was desperate for a sociologist to start teaching their students as soon as possible. I was interviewed on Thursday, 13 September 1973, and I started work the following Monday. I was the only woman in my new department, and one of my new colleagues was soon to be married.

Having just arrived, I wasn't invited to the nuptials or any associated events, but my new Head of Department, Lyall Hunt, still felt comfortable asking if I had "a couple of quid for the keg for Murray's show." I had no idea what the man was talking about. I knew that a quid in the UK was one pound, but Australia used dollars. I soon discovered that Australia had decimalised on the basis of the old ten shillings – which is half a pound (quid) so, if you do the maths, 'a couple of quid' is four dollars. I also knew that beer is kept in kegs, but I didn't know that a keg can mean a party in Australia – but also still mean an actual keg. I'd never met a man called Murray. I thought it was the name of some God-forsaken river somewhere in Australia. And a show? Yes, that's performed on a stage with curtains that open and close, signalling the beginning and end of 'the show.' I didn't know it meant a party.

Making sense of Australia wasn't easy. I was a bit miffed when I figured out that I was being asked to contribute to a gift for someone I didn't know, and a party to which I wasn't invited. It seemed to me that everything in Australia, like the rent and the bond on my new flat, had to be paid up-front, but my pay-cheque was at the end of each fortnight. I was broke. Perhaps I shouldn't have been so worried because the rent on my flat at 1 Jersey Street, in Daglish, was only $19 a week. This wasn't much, but my benchmark was my last share flat in Liverpool, where my contribution to the rent had been £1 per week – AUS$2.

It was 'preference for Poms' (British) when I arrived in Australia. I could just stroll in, which is just as well because I don't remember even thinking about visas. I also didn't need to show that I could support myself. In contrast, my non-British travelling companion had to have $300, and we had only that amount between us. I gave him my money to show at the border.

Immigration rules changed shortly after my arrival. This was part of broader changes introduced by Australia's new Labor Prime Minister, Gough Whitlam. He equalised entry and citizenship rules in what seemed like a final administrative tidying up of the White Australia Policy, which had ceased to exist in 1958. It was the dawn of multicultural policies. Some leeway was given to Poms, like me, who had just walked in. If we took out Australian citizenship before the new laws came into effect, we would not be subject to the new residency period required for citizenship. So, somewhat unexpectedly, I became Australian. This was an absolute bonus for a traveller like me because I now had two passports.

I had to be interviewed before the conferral of citizenship, so Lyall appointed himself my coach. In his Australian larrikin style, he professed certainty that I would need to know about: Ned Kelly (the bushranger); Phar Lap (the famous Australian racehorse who, according to urban myth, was killed by 'the Yanks'); the boxer, Les Darcy (I think 'the Yanks' were reputed to have killed him as well); Australian Rules Football, the

Australian federal system of government; Dame Nellie Melba (the opera singer); Banjo Patterson (the poet who scribed 'Waltzing Matilda'); and, of course, the ANZACs and Gallipoli.

Back in the real world, the only question I was asked concerned the birth dates of my grandparents, which I didn't know, but they let me in any way. My private opinion was that they just wanted to check if I was white and nice, and I passed on at least one of those counts.

When I started work at Mount Lawley Teachers' College in September 1973, I realised that the Australian academic year begins in February and finishes in December, so the students were well into their course. Unfortunately, the topic for my first day of teaching was Aboriginal education. I'd been in Australia only a few weeks, and I hadn't yet met an Aboriginal person. I had only three days to prepare. I did some fast reading and decided that I had to rely on what I knew about race relations in Britain. After all, the processes of labelling, marginalisation, discrimination and poor educational and health outcomes probably had some universal application. It wasn't the best teaching I've ever done, but I managed at short notice, and I slowly grew in understanding of Indigenous issues.

Even in those early days, I knew enough to deconstruct, with my students, the titles of primary school social science books, like 'The Settlement of the Swan River Colony (Western Australia).' We considered different terminology and saw that, from an Indigenous perspective, the word 'settlement' might be replaced by 'colonisation' or 'invasion'. Later, in 2004, I was proud to have mentored a group of Indigenous teachers in the Northern Territory to success in the national university teaching awards and, in the 2012 first edition and 2021 second edition of my co-edited textbook, 'University teaching in focus', we included a chapter on Indigenous knowers and knowing. I think it may be the only university teaching textbook that provides such a clear focus on Indigenous knowledge.

The only thing I knew about Australia when I arrived was that they had a prime minister who may have been eaten by a shark. Indeed, British friends cautioned me against travelling here because they didn't like mixed bathing – sharks and people. Like many others in my country of origin, I thought of Australia as a 'Little Britain.' In fact, it's the second most multicultural society in the world after Israel. About one-quarter of the population is born overseas, and most can identify their ancestry. I was astonished to hear people describe themselves as 'half Italian, a quarter German, and a quarter British.' After all, I was English. I'd never said I'm a little bit Roman, with possibly some Hun and Viking.

As it turns out, my DNA tests show that I am 12% Norwegian, so that must have been the Vikings. Ethnic identity persists in Australia. I remember my daughter saying that when the World Soccer Cup was on, there wasn't a kid in her class who barracked for the same team. They followed the loyalties of their parents' or grandparents' country of origin. And take a look at the scenes outside the hotel of Serbian tennis champion, Novak Djokovic in 2022. He was detained at the border over concerns about his COVID vaccination status, yet Australian-Serbs danced their national dances in the street and generally turned the issue into one of national pride. Eventually, Djokovic was deported, and I did enjoy the jokes including: You can say what you like about Australians, but when it comes to tennis, we know how to return a Serb.

There are plenty of tensions between different ethnic groups in Australia, and some of these played out in my own family. Lyall didn't discover that he was one-eighth Chinese until he was in his fifties, but his older cousins couldn't believe he hadn't known because there was an incident years earlier when Lyall's half-Chinese grandmother lived in Kalgoorlie. Her brother (of the same ethnicity) had tried to visit her, and he was given five hours to get out of town. Chinese people were not tolerated on the Goldfields.

On the other side of Lyall's family, he was eighth-generation Australian. His ancestor was a little girl called Lucy Middleton, who arrived on the first boat into South Australia – the only Australian colony without a convict history. We visited a replica of that boat and saw her name on a copy of the passenger list. Small wonder that Lyall was an Australian historian and that I embraced all things Australian. Neither of us had much choice. It was our lived experience.

I was pulled into Australian history by Lyall

through his publications. When we first started going out together, he arrived at the pub with a list of people he would include in a Western Australian sesquicentenary (150 years since foundation) book that he'd just been invited to edit. Needless to say, there was not a woman among them, so I sent him back to write the list again. I can claim some kudos for getting five women included in the biographies. He also edited a book about the Yilgarn Shire, for which I wrote the chapter on women. Their stories pulled me further into Australia's embrace, as did the 'Claremont Cameos' book I co-edited with Perth colleague Janina. It was about the women who graduated from Claremont Teachers College – the first tertiary educational establishment in Western Australia, founded in 1902. In these ways, I made sense of the role of women in Australian society.

Janina and I both reckon that, as young Pommie (British) women, our starting salary in the 1970s was lower than that of male colleagues, and I was laughed at because I objected to the newly drafted conditions of service. These stated that a lecturer could take his wife and children on study leave. "Well, you know what we mean, Lynne." Yes, I did.

There were few services for women in Australia, but that was the same in the UK. When, as an adult, I asked my mother why she didn't leave her violent husband, she answered, quite simply, "Where would I have gone?"

I tried to do something about that. I started to teach health sociology in 1985, and I developed a women's health course, which eventually led to my PhD, which was about the international women's health movement. I sat on the advisory board of Perth's first Sexual Assault Referral Centre and joined in consultancies about the development of equal opportunity legislation. My embrace of Australia was cemented in feminist political activism. I've always thought this was easier to do in a small, isolated city. There was good access to power.

My circle of friends in Australia is so ethnically diverse that multiculturalism has ceased to be a thing for me. Diversity is the wallpaper of my life. This is why I didn't get Benny's joke. He's my Straits Chinese hairdresser. We're both migrants, we've both lived in Perth for a long time, and we both self-identify as Australian. So I wasn't surprised when he told me that he was off to Albany, in the south of Western Australia, for the ANZAC Day Dawn Service. The Gallipoli troops set sail from this town in 1914, so it was a comment of significance, and I listened respectfully. He couldn't believe that I took him seriously.

"Lynne, have you ever been to a Dawn Service?" he inquired.

Still behaving seriously, I told him that, when my kids were little, we took them to the service in Perth's Kings Park.

"Lynne, did you look around you? How many Asian faces did you see, huh?"

As it turned out, Benny *was* going to Albany, but he was going fishing. He was right, though, the Gallipoli story is Anglo-Australian.

I had an advantage over Benny. I learned about ANZAC traditions from immediate family in my early years in Australia because my father-in-law, Jack, had fought on the Kokoda Track. He regularly marched in the ANZAC day parade, and we took the kids to see him. Lyall and I also went to the Millennium Gallipoli celebrations in Turkey in the year 2000. I'm one of the few Australians who can say they 'set foot' on Gallipoli because I broke the other one getting off the bus and had to be medevacked to the UK.

Despite my early departure, I'd learned my lessons well and discovered that Gallipoli was more than a theatre of war. It came to represent the breaking of colonial ties with England, initiating the development of an independently minded Australia.

The first time I drove across the Nullarbor, in 1975, the road was still mostly unsealed. Everything went wrong. We had to be towed into Ceduna (the first significant town you can find driving from west to east) for engine repairs on the way over. That delayed us by a week. On the way back, the windscreen wipers broke. Shortly after that, a truck drove past and threw up a rock from the unsealed road, which smashed the windscreen. So, it no longer mattered that the windscreen wipers didn't work. It all seemed very adventurous to me.

There were eight people on our first holiday together in 1976: Lyall, me, his four kids, his Dad, Jack, and the kids' cousin. We drove Lyall's Holden and Jack's Toyota and crossed the

Nullarbor to visit parts of South Australia, Victoria, and New South Wales. By now, more of the road across was sealed. This made a difference to the culture of the Nullarbor crossing.

I'm told that, in the 1960s, meeting another car was an occasion to stop, boil the billy, make a cup of tea, and chat about the road ahead. On my first trip, in 1975, we slowed and rolled down the window to exchange a few words. When I crossed with Lyall and his family in 1976, we merely waved. That culture prevails. I drove Lyall, by now disabled, to South Australia in 2013 and had to guess the imaginary line where it's OK to wave. Too soon is uncool, too late, and you're a city slicker unaware of outback traditions. I bluffed my way through.

Lyall and I crossed the Nullarbor some eighteen times. About four of the journeys were on the Indian Pacific train. We've also travelled on the old and new Ghan trains. On five occasions, we drove various combinations of Hunt kids over to 'The Eastern States' (as they're known in Western Australia). I loved the long-distance driving. It was meditative, and the vistas were expansive. Putting all this together with my return trips from employment in Darwin and Toowoomba, I worked out that I've travelled over all of the main roads in Australia, except for the distance between Katherine and Tennant Creek on the Stuart Highway. I learned to love the Australian landscape, even though it risks getting monotonous. Lyall used to joke that when he pulled down the blinds on the Indian Pacific train and then opened them in the morning, he could swear to God that we hadn't moved. It was the same treeless landscape. "That's why it's called Nullarbor, Lyall."

I realised how Australian I'd become when my kids were in primary school. They were keen swimmers, so we all watched the world championships and the Olympics. I didn't even think about barracking for England. By then, my focus was Australia.

In 1973, when I arrived in Perth, it was a different story. I hung out with a gang of other migrants. We didn't necessarily intend to stay in Perth – but we all did. Kathy's doubts about living in Perth forever focused on the Australian way of death. She absolutely didn't want to be buried in Perth's Karrakatta Cemetery. Its grid system, which directs Catholic, Jewish, Orthodox, and Protestant corpses in different directions, seemed too assembly line for us all. It reminded me of that old joke about a woman who'd just died being shown around heaven.

"What's that brick wall for?" she asked.

"Oh, the Catholics are behind that. They think they're the only ones up here."

Far from being a morbid conversation stopper, the question about where we wanted to be buried engaged friends in a lively discussion that went to the heart of identity and a sense of belonging. At that stage, we didn't identify enough with Australia to want to be buried here.

As any good historian might, Lyall liked to take his students, and his family, on trips to cemeteries. It's possible to show the waves of migration in Australia's history in the names on the headstones, and the ages of death can reveal pandemics of childhood illnesses that were not yet controlled. He showed our Hunt kids where their great-grandparents were buried in Southern Cross and Kalgoorlie, and I could see why Lyall felt he belonged in the Goldfields – his family was all around him. But this isn't necessarily true for migrants.

On one occasion, my UK cousin, Jane, who researched our Britton family tree, asked if I might visit the graves of her Goldfields' relatives. They'd migrated from Devon almost a century earlier. I found them, but I was saddened. The contrast between the Goldfield's red mud and dust and that of the green hills of Devon made me think of Mum's grave, snug in a plot in Peter's Marland, surrounded by parents, grandparents, cousins, and in-laws.

"What's better?" I asked myself, "To be surrounded by loved ones but stay forever in the confines of rural society, or out here, where you can see the horizon all around you?"

It is, perhaps, an eternal question for migrants who never really sort out where they belong.

Rosemarie and I call ourselves de facto sisters because we're both solo migrants, and we've provided each other the familial support that we might get from aunts or siblings in our countries of origin. When our kids were younger, our families joined together for Christmas in the way that extended families might. We've also attended our families' weddings and funerals – as any relative would.

In the case of funerals, there's been far too much death and sadness in our solo migrant lives. Rosemarie's husband, Professor Chris Powell, was a top Australian geologist. He died on a plane on his way to yet another international meeting. Imagine farewelling your husband on a work trip, and then that was it! You would never see him again. I don't have to imagine what it was like for Rosemarie. I was with her when the police arrived to let her know of Chris's death. He was only in his late fifties, and my daughter died when she was thirty-seven. Young death is sad whenever it happens, but for Rosemarie and me, it seems particularly unfair that our small families were decimated in this way.

"I don't belong anywhere," Rosemarie said wistfully one day. We are both naturalised Australians, and we are both truly grateful for the opportunities and lifestyle that Australia affords us.

We have both made our contribution to Australia, and we take an interest in all things Australian, but do we feel we belong? Rosemarie's grandparents were German Jews who escaped to

Argentina just before Hitler took power. She's very private about her background, and her stories emerged only slowly over the years. In fact, so coy was she about her background that I had wondered if her slightly German accent didn't hail from a Nazi background because many of them escaped to Argentina. I never dared ask, but I was relieved to find out they were Jewish. Rosemarie's mother, Marianne, was one of their two daughters. She married an American and gave birth to Rosemarie, but by the time Rosemarie was twelve months old, her mother's multiple sclerosis had progressed. As a consequence, Rosemarie's American father booted out his wife and daughter and sent them back to the German Jewish grandparents in Argentina, where Rosemarie spoke German at home, Spanish at school, and sustained English both through her studies and because of her American heritage.

She was sixteen when her mother died, at which point she was sent back to the USA to live with her father and her stepmother. She met Chris in Chicago, and they married when she was nineteen. Subsequently, they relocated to Australia, where Chris had been raised. Small wonder that

Rosemarie doesn't feel she belongs anywhere, but she does have three passports, and she speaks three languages fluently.

"I've always thought that you really embraced Australia, Lynne," Val observed recently.

She's right. I did make an effort to understand my new country, even if, for my first two years here, I thought that I'd be returning to the UK. In the event, I met and married an Australian, I applied for citizenship, and I became Australian. So, precipitously, I needed to make sense of Australia.

The weather was an absolute catalyst in this process. When I first arrived in Australia, I understood temperatures only in Fahrenheit. I had to learn, existentially, when it was cool enough, in centigrade, for a jacket or when it was hot enough to go for a swim. I had to learn that, instead of opening windows to let in the warm sun, as I'd done in the UK, I did the opposite. Now I had to close the curtains to keep the house cool when it was sunny. I learned that in Perth, we don't moan about the rain, even if we discuss it as much as the Brits. Now I can speak intelligently about how much water is in the dams and how much rain fell over the Wheatbelt. Perth has recently been through a record-breaking period of over 40C, and then the temperature dropped to 31C. The weather reporter on television reckoned it was time to bring out the doonas (duvets). Well – yes, of course. I was in the UK in October 2019 and listened in astonishment to the weather reporter telling me that the temperature, tomorrow, would soar to 16C. Soar?

For my part, I hadn't realised how acculturated I'd become to all things Australian until I met a woman in the UK who persisted in telling me that she wanted to go to Uluru because it's the centre of Aboriginal spirituality.

"No it's not!" I exclaimed a little too abruptly. "There's no such thing! There were over three hundred language groups at the time of colonisation. Their spirituality is connected with their land. They belong to it, so spirituality is local. Uluru isn't the head of a national religion, like Canterbury Cathedral. It's not 'Little Britain,' you know. In fact, Australia wasn't a nation until 1901. How would Indigenous people even have a concept of Uluru being the spiritual centre of a country that didn't exist in their worldview?"

This conversation took place in 2019. In 1973, when I arrived in Australia, I wouldn't have had the knowledge, or the emotional and political engagement, to respond in this way. It was obvious to me that I'd finally made sense of Australia.

Making sense of people: Mum

Mum was the eighth of ten children in her family of origin and the third of three babies born in three consecutive months of May. This means that Grandma had three babies in two years. Mum was two-and-a-half pounds, born at home in 1910 with no incubator at hand. I've mused with my cousin, Rosalind, about how Mum might have survived.

"They were a farming family. They would have treated her like a lamb," Ros observed. "They'd have kept her in the chimney nook and drip-fed her milk."

She's probably right. Mum obviously survived this challenging start to her life, and the fight to live may have strengthened her immune system because she outlived all of her siblings. She died when she was ninety-five. Her body had been challenged by six pregnancies, including a miscarriage, and an awful three-day labour, which concluded when the doctor crushed the baby's head to extract the infant. The process of becoming and being a mother was never easy for her.

Mum had a strong sense of family, but she held an independent position regarding motherhood. At a family gathering, I teased her that she was responsible for the existence of all the people in the room – at that stage, four daughters, eleven grandchildren and eleven great-grandchildren. Without her, none of us would have been born.

"Gerraway," she said in her Devonshire accent. "You'm all responsible for your own decisions."

On another occasion, I sat chatting with Mum and my eldest sister. To keep Mum included in the conversation, I switched to the topic of childbirth and child-rearing because it was something we'd all done. Audrey and I swapped stories, and I could see my ninety-year-old mother concentrating on what she was going to say.

"Well, I didn't want any of mine," she blurted out.

"Great, Mum. You've got two out of four in the room with you, and now you tell us you didn't want us!" I replied.

"Well, you know what I mean," she said, "You love them when you've got them" – and she did.

I knew what she was saying, though. Her generation of women did not have the benefit of contraception. They got what they got by way of babies, and motherhood was conferred upon them by random conception and social expectations.

One set of social expectations – the male line of inheritance in farming families – trapped mothers into economic dependence. Mum's first husband died of pneumonia in the days before antibiotics. She was just twenty-six when she was widowed. The farm on which they'd lived reverted to her in-laws. I know she got some money, but she was, essentially, homeless with two small girls to care for in the 1930s. She returned to live with her own parents for about five years. There were tensions between Mum and Grandma. Why wouldn't there be? Having raised ten kids, I'm sure Grandma could have lived without two more little girls landing on her doorstep.

After five years of living with Grandma, Mum met my Dad, Cyril Hardy, at a dance, and she ran away with him. She parcelled up her daughters' clothes and lowered them from a bedroom window before she hid them in the barn and posted them one by one to her new home in Nuneaton, where my Dad's family lived. Mum told her two daughters, Audrey and Joyce, that they were going on a long train journey but they mustn't say anything to anybody. She gave them a doll each to play with, and they went on their long train journey. They arrived in Nuneaton and walked streets longer than my Devonshire sisters had ever imagined might exist, eventually arriving at Dad's sister's place. Grandma Britton was so worried about Mum and her two granddaughters that she hired a private detective to find out where they'd gone. I don't think Mum ever knew that. I wish she had because it showed that her mother cared for her, despite the tensions.

Mum's marriage to Cyril was violent and chaotic. She kept trying to keep a roof over our heads after Dad lost the greengrocery business in which she'd established him in his hometown, Nuneaton. He had a continuous pattern of letting Mum down. She was a good cook, so she referred to a women's magazine called 'The Lady' to find jobs as a cook that had tied cottages. When she worked as a cook for manor houses, she got Dad a job as the butler. But he either argued with the boss or got stuck into their alcohol. Each time this happened, we moved on. By the time we got to Broadway, Mum's work was dissociated from Dad's because he got a job in the fire brigade at Smith's Clocks and Watches Factory near Cheltenham.

In 1960, when I was twelve, I pleaded with Mum to leave Dad. She wouldn't because our house in Bishop's Cleeve had been bought with her small inheritance from her mother, and she didn't want Dad to get half. I can understand the economic imperatives of her argument. However, when Dad died in 1989, I looked back and thought just how little houses had been worth in 1960, and I realised that Mum continued to suffer through the years 1960-1989 for the sake of a few thousand pounds.

According to Mum, she didn't want any of her children, though she loved us all when we arrived, which, in the case of her third baby, was in a bit of a hurry. Mum's waters broke overnight and, accompanied by her eldest daughter, Audrey, she set off for hospital. She didn't make it, and the baby was born in the garden, hence her second name, Eve. Audrey was only thirteen at the time, and I've since asked her about her reaction to the garden birth. "I cried," she said.

It was a coincidence that I decluttered my attic close to Australian Mother's Day, 2020 because I've found a pile of letters that my mother sent to me in Australia. Their discovery made me realise that being a migrant preserved my memories of Mum. My sisters in England would have visited her or spoken on the phone, but my relationship with her was cemented in letters that reveal a lot about the person she was and the times through which we lived as mother and migrant adult daughter. Her writing was familial, and her letters long and detailed. Together with the letters she wrote to my children, it's evident that she put a massive effort into being a long-distance mother and grandmother.

As I read them, I get the sense that her pen ran ahead of her brain because she slipped bewilderingly between topics with scant attention to punctuation: Uncle Sid's funeral; the old friend she met there; the last time she saw the friend in 1935 at King George V's Jubilee celebrations at

Petrockstow; the weather; gardening; and the Chinese cabbage she'd grown from seeds she'd bought in Australia. It's a breathless read!!

She wrote as she spoke. Her rural upbringing gave her a weather eye that gave rise to meticulous meteorological observations. Writing in 1980, she noted, "It was a very cold, windy and dry spring, the seeds didn't germinate, and then the rain came, it was the wettest July since 1907 and the coldest July for three hundred years." The toings and froings of family always loomed large: "Anne brought the baby down for me to see yesterday. Joyce and Elaine came also, and we fetched Julie, Martyn and Jaime over, so I was quite busy. They put the sleeping baby in my arms, and I sat on the settee with her for four hours."

She was an untrained social scientist. Her letters are replete with whimsical observations: "Your Dad's brother, Jim, died about a fortnight ago, he was eighty years of age. None of his brothers or sisters were told until after the cremation. Perhaps they were trying to keep down expenses. It is just about as expensive to die as to live these days."

Born into a Devonshire farming family, her political views were naturally right-wing and protectionist. She felt she'd bred a red-under-the-bed in me. But I did learn from her that it's a normal thing to be politically engaged, even if from the other side of the fence. I don't think I fully appreciated the extent of her interest in politics until I heard from an old school friend who still lived in the village where I grew up. Apparently, she'd bumped into Mum at the shops and been held hostage to Mum's Thatcherite opinions for quite a lengthy conversation.

Despite her retiring nature, Mum knew how to stand her ground. On one of the occasions she stayed with me in Australia, we were having a bit of a political fight, and I cut across her when she was speaking: "Now, wait on, Lynne. You call yourself a feminist. I'm a woman. Give me a chance to speak!" OK, Mum.

I've read reports that traditional crafts, such as weaving complex patterns in rugs, use the same skills needed in coding and computing skills. If this is so, then Mum missed some career opportunities because she was ace at crocheting and knitting complex patterns. I still have the willow pattern jumper she knitted for me. The willow pattern is knitted-in, not embroidered on top. It was a highly complex pattern. I've framed it because I consider it to be women's art – all too often an ephemeral art form. The lorikeet jacket she knitted for my daughter, Ruth, is framed alongside. Both were difficult to do, and in her letters she provided a running commentary about her craft: "I had to do the finishing touches to the Christening robe. It's very lovely, the most complicated garment I have ever tackled. The baby has dark brown eyes and skin. She looks tanned.'

The baby was Abigail, one of Mum's great-granddaughters. Mum saw herself as creating family heirlooms. Almost everyone in the family has received something knitted or crocheted by her. Who knows how long Mum's memory will linger on through the crocheted tablecloths, baby shawls, christening gowns, jumpers, scarves, topsy-turvy dolls, and waistcoats she made. Right now, it's been gifted as far as her great-great-granddaughter, Emily Ross.

Mum was resourceful. My sisters tell me that when they lived on their Dad's farm, Mum made her own contribution to the family income. She bought turkey chicks and raised them to sell, dressed, at Christmas. When she returned to live with Grandma and Grandad after her first husband died, she did the same. She had to have some form of independent income. At that time, she sought out a job as a lady's companion in a nearby town. Her daughters, Audrey and Joyce, cried when she left them in the care of Grandma, but she soon returned. One of her brothers put a stop to it. He couldn't tolerate others seeing his sister in a servant role.

Small wonder that Mum grasped at straws when she ran away with my dad to his hometown, Nuneaton, with her two daughters. She had only a limited income from the turkeys, and living back with her mother was fraught. Audrey remembers Mum crying, but she doesn't know why.

Despite an unhappy marriage to my Dad, Mum continued to forge her own life. Once she was done with child-rearing, she took off to see the world through numerous holidays with friends and relatives. On some occasions, Dad accompanied her, for example, when they availed themselves of £10 a week hotel accommodation in Spain during the winter. It was a scheme to keep hotels functioning in the off-season and one which attracted British pensioners to warmer climes. They stayed several months at a time.

Among the many places she visited, Mum travelled to reconnect with Canadian cousins. She went to the USA, Germany, Holland, Austria, New Zealand, and Australia. She was competitive with me in regard to travel and particularly proud that she'd been to Iceland and I hadn't. By the time she died in 2005, she was well-travelled. I settled the score on Iceland after she died.

Mum bottled fruit and vegetables, so we always had plenty of nutritious food. She sustained her interest in gardening well into her retirement. Writing in 1980, when she was seventy, she noted, "I've got a good garden full of veg – runner beans are about to climb the canes. I have cabbage, onions, carrots, tomatoes, pineapple, spuds, cauliflower, strawberries, raspberries, sage, parsley, rhubarb, brussels, broad beans, everlasting cauliflowers, lettuce, and spring onions. So I won't be buying much, I hope. Cauliflowers have been over 40p each. It has been a cold and windy spring so it has been hard work to get anything to grow."

Mum lived through the Spanish flu pandemic,

the Great Depression, and two world wars. She took an interest in social change. I sensed her fear when the Cuban crisis challenged world peace and her delight when a man landed on the moon. She told the story of her eldest daughter, Audrey, who had seen a moon-shaped hair slide in a shop window when she was a child. She'd pleaded with Mum, "Mum, can you give me the moon?'

Recalling this, in 1969, Mum said, "Well now she's got it."

When she was young, Mum's nickname was 'Dolly' because she was so petite. She had striking brown eyes and dark good looks inherited, we think, from Portuguese input into the family. Mum's grandson, Michael Ford, completed a DNA test, and his results lend credence to the rumour, showing someone in the family of full Iberian descent approximately five to eight generations ago. Mum was always well-dressed, enjoying classically British clothes, including Jaeger. She was a smart lady and proud of her appearance.

With her smart clothes and travel, it might seem that she was a sophisticated person, yet she was demure and retiring at social gatherings. At

Christmas parties in Australia, she would shrink into a corner of the sofa and wait for people to come to her. She made little effort to join in but complained if people didn't engage with her. But get her going on murder, mayhem, politics or the weather, and there was no stopping her.

It was her wish to be buried in St Peter's Marland churchyard in Devon, where almost every grave contains someone who is related to us. Certainly, there are headstones as far back as Mum's grandparents. When the undertaker arrived at the morgue to collect Mum for transport from her home in Gloucestershire to Devon, he was told to go to a particular drawer to collect a ninety-five-year-old woman.

He returned to query the administrative staff: "Are you sure you gave me the correct drawer number? She doesn't look ninety-five."

I wanted to wake Mum and tell her that story. She would have been so pleased. Young looking and well-presented unto death.

Making sense of people:
Dad

My sister, Joyce, visited me in Australia in September 2016. We share a mum, but not a dad. Her own father, Cedric, died when Joyce was six. Sometime later, her (our) mother, Alma, married Cyril Hardy and had two more daughters, including me. Cyril met Alma when he was a soldier stationed in Devon. Subsequently, Mum, Audrey and Joyce relocated to Cyril's hometown, Nuneaton, in the heart of the Black Country, where we all lived together as four sisters, until Audrey married when I was three, and Joyce when I was four.

Surprisingly, 2016 was almost the first time in our lives that Joyce and I had the opportunity to talk one-on-one, and in-depth. We sat opposite each other at my kitchen table in Perth – she in her mid-eighties and me in my late sixties. We talked about the past, and I said things to her that

I thought were part of our shared history – apparently not. I'd never really thought about what it must have been like for Audrey and Joyce to have my Dad, Cyril Hardy, as a step-father.

"Why are you looking so shocked? Mum was so much closer in age to you. I thought she'd confided in you. You mean you didn't know about the violence?"

Of course, she did. She told me that when they first got to Nuneaton, they lived in two rooms in Cyril's sister's house. She remembered reading in the living room and, out of the blue, Cyril came in, snatched the book off her and threw it into the fire. She flew at him. She went on to tell more stories: "It was the same one Christmas when we heard him attacking Mum. Audrey and I raced downstairs to protect her. There was something against the door – probably him. I don't know where we got the strength, but we pushed the door off its hinges to get to her."

Earlier, my eldest sister, Audrey, had told me why she got married in such a hurry: "I walked upstairs with some laundry in my hands. I was headed for the ottoman under the window to put away the clean clothes. He must have thought I'd been listening outside their bedroom door. I wasn't! He hurtled into the room and started slapping me. Mum raced in behind him and pulled him off me. A couple of days later, I went to my boyfriend's house. He took me for a walk around the block because he could see I was upset. When we got back, George said we should get married. And we did – within ten days."

"One of my earliest memories," I said to Joyce, "is of him holding the carving knife to Mum's throat. I must have been about four. I can guess my age because we left Nuneaton when I was five."

I can still remember her body language: stiff, upright, frozen in the chair, looking forward, and passive: At all costs, don't provoke him!

Around the same time, he kicked-in Mum's china cabinet. She liked to have a nice house, so this was attacking where it hurt." Years later, when researching and writing about domestic violence, I came to see Cyril's behaviour as standard practice for perpetrators of domestic violence. First kick the furniture, then the cat or dog. The implicit threat is: 'Next it's you.' It happened. I saw Cyril throw his Sunday lunch against the wall, and

I remember him forcing Mum against the wall and hitting her in our Bishops Cleeve house. By this time, I was a teenager about to leave for university. I called the police to him on this occasion and three times in my last year at home.

Joyce was aghast. "I just don't know the stories you're telling me," she said. "Those were the years when I had a young family. You moved around a lot, and we didn't have telephones or emails in those days. All I could do was write letters."

'Moved around a lot' was a bit of an understatement. I went to eight different primary schools, and lived in almost as many houses. In my conversation with Joyce, I digressed into describing the different houses.

"In Rugby, we lived in some kind of gatehouse of a manor. It had a bath in the kitchen with a lid on it so that it doubled as a kitchen bench. To me, it was a wonder of modern technology because we hadn't had a bathroom at all in Nuneaton. We'd had a tin bath in front of the fire."

This prompted another question: What on earth had it been like for Audrey and Joyce sharing a house with stepfather Cyril when they had no bathroom? Joyce said they just took a bowl of water to their bedroom and had a wash-down. It wasn't the best start in life for them, but they survived through the close bond between them.

In many ways, I was protected from Dad's behaviour because I was the youngest. I think my older sister copped it more than I. That changed when she married, when I was seventeen. Shortly after her wedding, Mum went down to Devon for a family funeral, and I was left alone with Dad. He came home drunk at around 3pm on the Saturday. So, nothing new there. I went upstairs to get ready for a date. When I came down, I found that Dad had taken everything out of my handbag and arrayed the contents along the mantelpiece. What an invasion of privacy! What calculated insensitivity! What control!

I gathered my stuff, put it back in my handbag and went outside to wait for my boyfriend. I was shaking with anger. We went to the Wine Bar at Montpelier, near Cheltenham, whilst I worked out what to do. I certainly wasn't going home. It took me a while to remember that my sister was now married with a home of her own, so I went there, slept on her couch, and stayed until late on Sunday when I knew Mum would be back. Cyril did nothing about the fact that his teenage daughter had gone missing.

I'd like to say that I left Dad on the doorstep the day I went to university, but I didn't because he was down at the pub. He wasn't there to say goodbye. Mum was, and she cried: Perhaps not just because the last of her daughters was leaving home, but because she would now be alone with Cyril. Her future looked grim.

To get balance into this story, something needs to be said about Cyril Hardy himself. Dad was born into a large family in Nuneaton in 1906 to Cecilia and James Hardy. I never knew his family. In fact, I was in my fifties before I even saw a photo of Grandma Hardy, who died before I was born. As I understand it, Cyril went to school in Nuneaton. Then, like most local men, he went down the mines from whence he escaped to join the regular army, where he quickly earned his stripes. He was poorly educated, but he was bright. Joyce tells me he was a dispatch rider during the war. I've also been told he worked in Intelligence in the army – but I'm not sure. He had medals and cups for boxing, so if he was in intelligence, the potentially brutalizing kind of work he had to do might well have influenced his behaviour as a family man.

Cyril was always known as Sam. This started in the army because, so I'm told, part of the army uniform was called a 'Sam Hardy Belt.' Accordingly, all men with the surname Hardy acquired the nickname Sam. World War II happened, and Cyril found himself at Dunkirk. Eventually, he was invalided out of the army with bronchitis. My sister told me that, in his last moments of life, Dad was stomping out imaginary flames. Who knows what the brain is doing at the end of life, but she thought it might have been flashbacks to Dunkirk.

Cyril was a natural sportsman and a star athlete in the Oxford and Buckinghamshire Regiment. We had boxes of the cups and medals he won for athletics of all kinds, boxing, shooting, and football (he played football for Coventry City at one stage). I used to love rummaging through those boxes. Few cups and medals now remain in the family, and Dad's grandson (my nephew), Martyn, and I intend to donate the ones we have to The Soldiers of Oxfordshire Regimental Museum. My sister and I were pretty good at athletics as well. Dad took us training once or twice. Just think what we might have achieved with his regular encouragement. I can see Cyril in my own children – Cyril's grandchildren – Ruth and Sam. Both are Hardy descendants – both are good at sport, and Ruth joined the Australian Army as a lawyer.

Cyril could be the life and soul of the party and was known to do handstands on barstools to entertain the regulars. When he was fifty-nine, he walked the length of our driveway on his hands. While this didn't add much value to family life, it certainly was impressive. He played the spoons well. That's now a lost art. When he worked for Smith's fire brigade, he took us to London for the annual competition between the fire brigades of all Smith's factories. During the evening entertainment, he played drums for the band, giving a drum roll to draw attention to the fact that ten-year-old Lynne had just fallen flat on her face on the highly polished dance floor.

My counselling friend, William, once said, "The trouble with some clients is that they get stuck in 'Ain't it awful?' mode, and they can't get off the tram tracks."

I don't think that's what Joyce and I were doing when we chatted in my Perth kitchen in 2016 because life with Cyril *was* awful, and it can't be wished away. Not talking about it is probably worse than airing the issues because domestic violence is fostered by silence: 'Scream quietly so the neighbours don't hear.' Mum never really wanted the world to know what she had to put up with. She was ashamed, as many abused wives are, but I think her story shows tremendous strength and ingenuity. She fought like a tigress to raise her daughters properly.

This story starts with a conversation between Joyce and me in 2016. It concludes with a facetime conversation we had only yesterday. Joyce is now ninety, and I'm seventy-three, and we are still trying to make sense of Dad. Joyce is a compassionate woman, and she tries to make excuses for him.

"Maybe we should have looked up when he entered the room. Maybe it was our fault."

I couldn't believe my ears. "Joyce, it is never, ever, ever, children's fault when they are abused."

My daughter, Ruth, also tried to excuse Cyril's behaviour, thinking it might be explained by post-traumatic stress disorder. Whilst that may have been a reason, I don't see it as an excuse. He learned violent behaviour, which could be unlearned if he loved his wife and daughters. Maybe there are lessons to be learned and insights gained through telling an authentic story about Cyril. The most important lesson is that he was accountable for his own behaviour.

Just before Cyril died, he had death bed reconciliations with his step-daughters, Audrey and Joyce. In contrast, I didn't return from Australia for his funeral. I didn't want to. I don't think a man can behave as he did and then say, "Whoops, sorry," in his dying moments. I'm no orphan in this response.

My Perth friend, Rosemarie, was abandoned by her dad when she was one year old. Decades later, she told an acquaintance what'd happened and was taken aback when asked: "Have you forgiven him?"

She didn't know she was supposed to. She's been content with making him a 'nobody' in her life. Like me, she chose not to fly halfway around the world for her Dad's funeral.

I read in a magazine that former Premier of

Queensland, Anna Bligh, had a father much like Cyril, and she took the same stance. Quite simply, her dad was not part of her life. He continued to live near her. Even so, she didn't go to his funeral. This was not vengeful. This was not unfinished business. Quietly, purely and simply, he'd made his choices about how to behave in the family, and she'd made hers. It was the same for me.

Dad was never really part of my life. I thought it was normal to see him only on Good Friday and Christmas day – the two days in the UK when the pubs were shut. He went straight to the pub from work every night and he went for lunchtime and evening drinks on weekends. I rarely saw him. Some might call it neglect, but I had the freedom to sail under the radar because Dad was absent and Mum was frantic trying to survive.

I had the strength of an extended family around me. I enjoyed school. I got myself babysitting jobs. I signed up for the Girl Guides. I went horse riding, and I took myself off for long, solitary walks over Cleeve Hill. I was self-determined in the things I did, and I learned how to manage my own life.

Yet, Cyril did influence the course of all our

lives. I was once driving around North Devon with my eldest sister, Audrey, her husband, George, and their eldest son, David.

"Look down there, Lynne," Audrey called out. "If Mum hadn't married Cyril, she might have married a bloke who lived down that street."

We all froze because, if Audrey hadn't moved from Devon to Nuneaton, she wouldn't have met George, and her son, David, wouldn't have existed – and neither would I. Nor, in fact, would all of the descendants of Audrey, Joyce, Julie and Lynne. I'm sure we're all a bit pleased because, without Cyril, we wouldn't have been born.

Cyril died in 1989. He had a funeral with military honours, and he's buried in Cheltenham Cemetery. He's in good company: his grave is just a few rows down from Brian Jones of the Rolling Stones.

Making sense of people:
ANZAC

"You can tell he's knocked about a bit," my brother-in-law, George, said when visiting me in Australia in 1979.

"Yes," I replied, "Jack's a walking history of Western Australia."

My father-in-law, Jack, was a rolling stone with unschooled leadership qualities: sergeant-major, 2/6 Independent Company 1944-45; co-owner and manager, Scots Greys mine and public battery, Parker's Range, 1946-49; underground supervisor, Australian Blue Asbestos Mine, Wittenoom around 1954; elected Workmen's Inspector of Mines in the Pilbara Region, at the end of the 1960s; Chairman of Council, Town of Port Hedland, in the late 1960s (You can still see his name on the Honour Board in the town hall); and member of the Western Australian Legislative Council, 1971-74. He died in 1988 when he was seventy-five.

Born in Kalgoorlie, Jack described himself as "1912 vintage." His favourite childhood story was about sitting on the roof of his house to watch the first plane ever to fly over the Goldfields. He was so excited that he walked off the roof and broke his arm. Jack's father, Charles Edwin Hunt, was part of the migrant wave of Cornish people, many of them tin miners who travelled via South Africa to the Australian gold rushes, including Kalgoorlie.

When Jack was in his sixties, he visited Cornwall to find out where his dad had come from. He remembered his dad mentioning that he was born in a town called something like 'Peronamzouzen,' but he couldn't find it on the map. In desperation, he went into a pub to ask. The locals had no problems directing him to Perran Alms Houses. He'd been confounded by the Cornish accent.

Like many others, Jack's dad got dusted lungs working in the gold mines. Social policy in those days compensated by allocating land to the families of those afflicted by miners' diseases. So, aged sixteen, Jack was sent along with his older brother to clear the allocated land and develop a farm for the family.

After all their hard work, the 1930s depression overtook family ambitions, and Jack and his brother walked off the land because they couldn't meet repayments. The bank subsequently resold the farm, at low cost, to new waves of Italian immigrants who benefited from the land clearing Jack and his brother had completed, but Jack didn't bear a grudge. He had other things to do, and he signed up for the commandos during World War II.

I'd like to say it was a macho act of bravery. In reality, it was clever. He figured that in the regular army he'd be subject to the command of officers in whom he placed little confidence. In contrast, the commandos were left to their own initiative. He preferred this.

He told war stories of the small things: men in tears because their inappropriate tropical short sleeves and shorts failed to protect them from swarms of Papua New Guinea (PNG) mosquitoes; how they learned PNG behaviours and moved higher into the mountains to get above the mozzie line. They couldn't light fires on the Kokoda Track because it would give away their positions to the Japanese enemy. Yet, they'd been landed with only twelve days' supplies. What to do? Clearly, raw cassowary birds were not the answer. Despite beating his portion of the bird with his rifle butt, it was still inedible.

I remember his stories of the pragmatism of war. He'd escorted a comrade to the medical tent and became distressed that the doctors wouldn't attend to him. Jack's advocacy fell on deaf medical ears. The doctors already knew that his comrade's wounds were inoperable. He told, with disbelief, a story of PNG triplets. Local culture comprehended twins – one for each boob – but not triplets. One baby was killed.

He didn't tell significant war stories, and it was only in the 1980s that we found a book that described Jack's bravery on the Kokoda Track.

> *Confusion ensued. Several tracks veered off in the darkness. Pollitt took his platoon far to the right, where they found themselves in 'a complete cul-de-sac' hemmed in between the roaring waters of the creek on one side and a vertical rock wall on the other. The Japanese [were] dropping hand grenades amongst us,'*

Pollitt recalls. His men would have died were it not for Lance Corporal John Hunt, who climbed out of the hole, stalked the Japanese grenade-throwers, and shot them.'

(Page 362. Part Four: Counter-Offensive. Book unknown)

In April 2015, Jack's soldier granddaughter – my daughter, Major Ruth Hunt – took his dog tags with her when she walked the Kokoda Track in her Grandpa's memory.

'The house that Jack built' is a phrase that resonates with my father-in-law's story because he built two houses. The first was at 4 Gordon Street, Kalgoorlie, where Jack pleased his wife, Dorothy, by including a rosette around the ceiling light. I took my husband, Lyall, back to this house when he was in his late seventies, and he was delighted to see that the rosette was still in place. He remembered how important it had been to his mum. The second house was in Port Hedland. I was told that he ran chains right over this house, and it remains one of the few houses in the region to withstand cyclones. He was Shire President in

Port Hedland just as the iron ore port was opening up. This meant he hob-knobbed with entrepreneurs such as Lang Hancock, who developed mining in the Pilbara. Jack often commented, with a wry smile, that he'd been promised that dust from the new iron ore port would not affect the town. As anyone who visits Port Hedland knows, the town is now painted red with dust.

After serving as President of Port Hedland Shire Council for six years, Jack was elected to the Legislative Council of the Western Australian Parliament, representing the North Province. He served one term (1971-1974) before he retired. When I read his maiden speech online, it is evident that he concerned himself, appropriately, with local issues such as the delivery of fresh food to outback regions:

> *I was perturbed to see the quantity of perishable goods coming from other States ... [This] should not be permitted to continue, especially when Western Australia is keenly seeking increased sales of its products ... The other day I was surprised to hear my colleague ... speaking*

on the subject of daylight saving in Western Australia. He said that if South Australia advanced the clock by one hour anyone travelling from the Ord Dam would arrive two hours and ten minutes before he actually left his point of departure. If goods continue to be sent from the Eastern States to supply Wyndham and Kununurra, I would like to see the clocks put back sufficiently so that these goods never reach their destination at all!

Jack was a good athlete and excelled in cycling. In 1937, he won the Menzies-to-Kalgoorlie bike race, a distance of 130 kilometres on dirt roads. The associated cups, medals and photos are now with the Kalgoorlie Archives so that he can take his place in Goldfields' sporting history. His cycling successes followed in his dad's footsteps. Charles Edwin had won races on the Victorian Goldfields, and his cycling memorabilia is now with the Bendigo Historical Society. Unbeknown to them, both were probably drawing on British mining and working-class cycling traditions.

Jack was an easy-going father and grandfather. He liked to have fun with the kids. When he called by, he hid lollies (sweets/candy) about his person so that my toddlers, Ruth and Sam, leapt on him to find the loot.

"Say hello first!" was my constant cry.

One Christmas, he arrived complete with a bouffant wig and Edna Everage glasses to cut down to size the fashion pretensions of his teenage granddaughters. He could tell a yarn, and it took me a while to realise that I wasn't necessarily required to listen. As a career woman, step-ma of two live-in teenagers, mother of two toddlers, and wife of a union activist oft kept late at work to deal with the problems of others, I realised that somebody had to cook, especially when my father-in-law dropped in, which he frequently did. I'd dart in and out of his monologues in accordance with the requirements of food preparation. He didn't seem to mind, and it didn't matter anyway because I already knew the stories.

It's hard to think that I'm now ten years older than my father-in-law was when I first met him. To me, he was an old man. Jack was sixty-two when we met, fit, if not healthy, and he had been a widower for a couple of years. I don't feel old now, and he didn't feel old then.

I always called him ANZAC. Neither of us liked the familiarity of me calling him dad. Yet we needed some way of speaking familiarly to account for the obvious affection between us. On my wedding day, of his own volition, this widower brought his wife's wedding ring with him and had me wear it because I needed something old and borrowed. He added, pragmatically, "But I'll have it back afterwards, mind."

I married his son, Lyall, himself fourteen years my senior, and Jack became my father-in-law. I sometimes think that he was the strength of my marriage because he was genuinely on my side in my often difficult circumstances of step-parenting. He even flirted with me – just a little. If his son could pull a younger 'sheila', maybe he'd practice on me and find himself someone to love. His *joie de vivre* was always apparent in his interactions with those he liked. You knew if he didn't like you because he buggered off. He was a man of impeccable values when it came to social justice, and he fought quietly, on a one-to-one basis, for human rights.

He was of that old order of Labor Party

supporters that counted many Aboriginal people among their friends, on a one-to-one basis. Yet, Jack was completely at ease with slagging-off Indigenous Australians as a group. We still have the bark painting, shield and spears that Jack was given by his Yamatji confrères. They might be worth a bit, but we've never had them valued. They mean more as a testament to the work he did to fight for the causes of Indigenous people in Australia's North West.

He could also be disparaging about women in general, which risked conflict with me – his feminist daughter-in-law. Fortunately, I was included in the generous embrace of his one-to-one affection and humanitarianism.

"Look at her backside," he observed as he watched the news after enjoying a meal I'd cooked for a family of kids, step-kids and in-laws. "A couple of axe handles wide!"

He was walking on eggshells, but Lyall did a pretty good job of negotiating the differences between his dad and me: "Well she's done a lot for her community," he said, "despite the size of her backside."

Jack's health was poor. His resistance was low

from malaria which he'd contracted in PNG during World War II. Subsequently, he worked as the occupational health and safety officer in the Wittenoom Asbestos mines – representing the Unions. Eventually, Jack's life was taken by the disease from which he'd tried to protect others – mesothelioma. He was a knock-about bloke, but he'd also been knocked about by the circumstances of his life. He died in 1988.

In 2015, just a few years before Lyall died, I started to re-narrate what I thought about Jack.

Lyall and I were watching a TV program called 'Foyle's War.' Set at the end of World War II, this particular episode was about soldiers being demobbed. Essentially, it was about post-traumatic stress disorder (PTSD), but that language wasn't used in 1945. Suddenly Lyall blurted out, "I reckon Dad was disturbed when he got back from PNG," and from there fell out a sad story I'd never heard before.

Lyall was twelve years old when he went down to Fremantle docks to welcome his dad back from the war. His mum sent him down to another gangway in case Jack disembarked there. She knew full well where Jack would leave the ship, but she wanted Lyall out of the way. She was uncertain if she still had a marriage. It would have been the same for all married couples who'd been separated for the five years or more of war. These were difficult times. Jack, Dorothy, Lyall and his younger sister went from Fremantle to the bedsit his mum had rented in East Perth. It would have been quite a change from the mountains of PNG, and, it seems, Jack couldn't stand it. Lyall went to school one morning and when he arrived home his parents had shot through. Gone. It seemed Jack needed to go back up the bush, and he'd taken his wife and daughter with him. So, twelve-year-old Lyall was abandoned.

I was shocked to hear this story. "Why did you never tell me this before now?"

Lyall's reply echoed that of abused spouses: "I was ashamed," he said.

It was as if it were his fault. How very sad. I adored ANZAC, but now I don't know how to make sense of him.

Making sense of people:
Lyall

I first met Lyall in 1973. I'd been in Australia for just over a month. I'd written to all the colleges in Perth to spruik my qualifications and advertise that I'd already taught sociology in a UK college for two years. As chance would have it, the Social Science Department of Mount Lawley Teachers College was desperate for a replacement sociology lecturer starting the following Monday – 17 September.

As it transpired, it was Lyall's fortieth birthday on that Monday. This is why I have such a clear memory of dates. Lyall was Head of the Social Science Department, so he interviewed me wearing his crushed strawberry suit. That didn't hang around in the wardrobe after Lyall and I became an item.

My strongest memory of him on the day of the interview was that he seemed guarded, crushed and defeated. I later found out why. 1973 was the year his mother died and the year in which he divorced. He was the custodial father of his four children. He was writing his Master's history thesis. He was Head of a new department in a new college, and he was on the union executive – probably president, he often was. I can't remember. He managed by getting up at four in the morning to have some quiet time to write his thesis. He got his kids off to school and arrived promptly at work at nine. He left at four in the afternoon, which was a little early for college staff, and he went home to feed his kids. He went to bed when they did, at around eight o'clock in the evening. It was a disciplined existence.

Lyall was born in Kalgoorlie in 1933. He had a sister who was six years younger than him. His dad built them a house at 4 Gordon Street, and they were surrounded by extended family. Memories of these times were Lyall's happy place. He found Kalgoorlie's Golden Mile romantic. At night, the lights on the pit heads seemed like the fairground in the eyes of a little boy.

This all stopped suddenly when his father enlisted in the commandos for the duration of

World War II. His dad went off to war, and Lyall's mother shifted camp to Perth. Lyall never forgave her for this. She had a house and a family nearby in Kalgoorlie. Why dislocate herself and her kids from this comfort zone?

I never met Lyall's mother, so I will never know her motives. My guess is that she was a young woman with two kids, and she wanted to be close to where her husband might be if and when he got leave. I remember asking Lyall why she didn't go back to Kalgoorlie if her life in Perth didn't suit. He mentioned that houses rented out during the war could not easily be reclaimed. There was a fear that returning soldiers wanting their homes back might cause social dislocation and homelessness. It's what Lyall told me, but I've never fact-checked it.

Lyall's mother rented rooms in a house in East Perth. It's here that Lyall went to St Patrick's Catholic School. It's where he became a lifelong fan of the East Perth Football Club, which was, and still is, part of the Western Australian Football League (WAFL).

Lyall was implacably opposed to the advent of a national 'footie' competition when the West

Australian sides, 'The Eagles' joined in 1986 and 'The Dockers' in 1994. He felt that the state-based teams did a good job of training up the young lads. He also thought that the national league creamed off the best of the Western Australian players. He may have been right on both counts, but those who now support either of Western Australia's two national sides, the Eagles or the Dockers, wouldn't have any concept of what Lyall was going on about.

I saw Lyall cry only once. It was when he had a gut operation in his early sixties. It didn't work the first time, so he had to have a second operation the following day. Neither of us thought he would survive. I don't think he ever remembered that he cried. He didn't cry when his dad died, and I couldn't understand why not. When I asked, he gave his standard response, "I was ten the last time I cried – when my parents dumped me at boarding school in Toodyay."

He was harsh in his judgement of his mother for moving from Kalgoorlie to Perth, and he was equally harsh on both his parents for sending him to boarding school in Toodyay to keep him safe from the potential bombing of Perth by the

Japanese. This was a real cause for concern because Darwin and Broome were bombed in 1942, so it looked like the Japanese bombers were heading down the coast to Perth.

Boarding school had a profound influence on Lyall's life. It may well have been the start of his abandonment issues that I didn't fully recognise until he was in his eighties. I suspect that his experiences also made him a very protective father. He wouldn't treat his kids the way he'd been treated, and he didn't want to lose them through a divorce.

Boarding school certainly toughened him up, as he said in an autobiography he started to write: "After the childhood security of family life in Kalgoorlie, 1937-1941, the rest of my school days seemed ever-changing, ever tense. Mostly, I boarded away from home and family. I didn't like it much and coped by learning to be self-contained."

He raised emotional barriers that would never come down. He didn't handle conflict well, choosing to confront rather than discuss. If he felt threatened, he pulled up the drawbridge and poured scorn on his enemies. He refused to engage with matters of concern to me by announcing that he didn't worry about issues over which he had no control. Small wonder that Lyall felt that his life was out of control because, after his father returned from World War II, his parents abandoned him.

When Lyall was twelve, he went to school in Perth one morning and returned home to find himself alone. He told me his mum had left him a note and some money. He continued to go to school and bought sandwiches with the money. At the end of the week, the woman who owned the house, and had rented Lyall's mum the bedsit, told Lyall that he had to clean up his sandwich wrappings and leave the house. The rent had been paid only to the end of the week.

Lyall raced off to find his mum's sister, Auntie Marj. She had a new baby and lived in a one-bedroom flat, so she couldn't help in the long term. I don't know how they would have communicated because telephone services in the bush were limited, but somehow Auntie Marj managed to arrange for Lyall to board with another little boy at his school. According to Lyall, that was more or less it. From then on, he boarded.

His mum did come back to Perth five or six years later, but by then, Lyall would have been in his late teens. He was a grown man who'd left school and started working when he was fifteen.

Around the time Lyall turned fifty, the Speaker of the House in the West Australian Parliament was a man who'd been at high school with him. If we saw him on the news, Lyall would always make comments about this. So I decided to seize the day and make contact with the Speaker because I wanted to organise a 'This is your life' party for Lyall's fiftieth birthday party. He gave me the contact details for about ten of Lyall's old schoolmates, and they all rocked up to the party as a surprise for Lyall. Included in this number were men who'd been the kids of Italian migrants from war-torn Europe when they were at school together in the 1940s.

Lyall recalled that there were about sixty kids in his class and that one whole row was called 'mugs alley', which mainly comprised the Italian kids who couldn't speak English. They were given a hard time by the Christian Brothers, who taught them. They seemed to think that learning English could be incentivised by corporal punishment.

As was customary at the time, Lyall left school when he turned fifteen. He got a job on the Coles key cutting counter, where he was sometimes called upon to sharpen scissors. If he botched the job, he simply explained to customers that it was cheap war-time steel. Everybody accepted this explanation – it was to be expected in post-war Perth. He then got a job as an office boy in the Public Trustee Office, where he became part of a group of friends. Some of them intended to enrol in technical college to complete their school-leaving exams to secure a place in teacher training college. So Lyall tagged along behind them, eventually enrolling at the University of Western Australia (UWA) and Claremont Teachers College. Such was career guidance when Lyall left school.

He studied history and some units in geology at UWA. He loved both. I still have many of the rock samples around the house that he collected over the years. Our grandkids love looking at them. After he graduated as a teacher, his first appointment was at Boulder High School, so he went back to live on the much-loved Goldfields of his childhood. He married in 1956 and had four children that I knew of. He was subsequently appointed to John Curtin High school in Fremantle, which had something like twenty-six classes in one year. This was the beginning of the bulge in population numbers occasioned by the large numbers of babies born when soldiers returned home from World War II. In other words, my baby-boomer generation.

The classes were streamed starting at class 1A – after that working through the alphabet. Those at the latter end of the alphabet signified more difficult teaching and learning environments. Lyall's favourite story was about following a rather straight-laced older teacher into class 1J. He was a bit surprised to find the pupils sitting nicely whilst they waited for him. Then he saw what the previous teacher had written on the blackboard, 'Class 1J had a lovely tone today.' This was a far cry from the pupils who received regular caning in 'mugs' alley.' It's an endearing story illustrating the student-centred approach Lyall learned to adopt in his teaching.

Subsequently, Lyall secured promotion to Curriculum Branch as a Social Science Advisory teacher. This was a creative time for him when he made numerous educational programs for television. These were the pre-cursor to contemporary current affairs programs for schools now called 'Behind the News' (BTN). Lyall wrote the scripts and collaborated with the Australian Broadcasting Commission to bring regular programs to air. From there, he was appointed as a social science lecturer at Graylands Teacher Training College – one of the three teachers' colleges in Perth at that time. In 1970, he became the foundation head of the social science department at the new Mt Lawley Teachers College. From then on, Lyall's career fortunes were influenced by the expansion of higher education, including the eventual emergence of Edith Cowan University (ECU) from the ashes of teacher training colleges.

After the demise of Mount Lawley College, social science teaching became a thing of the past for Lyall. He served in various leadership roles at ECU before retiring as an associate professor in 1994, at the age of sixty.

However, Lyall's interest in social science, in particular Western Australian history, survived the vagaries of his career because he was part of a wave of historians that actually built Western Australian History. He was a founding member of the Western Australian Oral History Association and some years later, he was made a Fellow of the Royal Western Australian Historical Society in honour of his research and publications.

Lyall's confidence in research and publication began with his Master's thesis about Sir Walter James – a politician credited with the push for Western Australia (WA) to join the Australian Federation in 1901. Planning for the 1979 sesquicentenary of the foundation of the Swan River Colony (WA) included the production of a series of books. Lyall was invited to edit a volume of biographies entitled 'Westralian Portraits.' This put Lyall in an excellent position to respond to invitations to contribute to the Australian Dictionary of Biography, which meant that Western Australian history was recognised and valued at a national level.

It's difficult to believe that, less than a century ago, Australian school children were taught only British history. The mid-twentieth century push to teach national and local Australian history represented quite a revolutionary change in thinking and in school and university curricula. Lyall was part of this push.

Lyall's original contribution to the development of WA history lies in his support for oral history, which he saw as a democratisation of history that, more often than not, focused on the deeds of the rich and powerful. He also modelled the link between teaching and research when he edited the book 'Yilgarn: A good country for hardy people', a name now on the road sign at the border of the Yilgarn shire.

Planning for this book started about a decade before the 1988 centenary of the discovery of gold in the Yilgarn. The Shire Council approached Lyall to write the book. This was an attractive proposition for him because the farm his Dad and Uncle had cleared in the late 1920s and early 1930s was in the Yilgarn. Lyall had spent time living in the small Yilgarn town of Marvel Loch in his primary school years. However, he didn't have the time to write the book. Instead, he suggested to the Shire Council that the Social Science Department of Mount Lawley Teachers' College use the Shire as a social science laboratory. Lyall would edit the book and different academics would write one chapter each based on their own and their students' research. The project was fully integrated into students' normal assignments so that nothing extra was required of them, but they had the added value of engaging with the publication of a book. Their research was facilitated by the Shire, which permitted free use of the sports centre for student research camps, organised by the Social Science Department at Mt Lawley College.

The outcome of this combined teaching and research project was a book that was much more than a normal local history publications. It ranged over topics that were broad and diverse. Years later, when renowned West Australian historian, Professor Geoffrey Bolton, was revising his history of WA, he contacted Lyall to say the Yilgarn book offered one of the best histories to date of Indigenous people in WA. In teaching terms, this project was light years ahead of the game. Today, this level of student involvement is referred to as 'Students as Partners' and a whole journal is dedicated to this approach to teaching. By the time this journal emerged, Lyall was too old to do any more writing, so I wrote up the Yilgarn project in our joint names. I thought the initiative was worth sharing with future generations of academics.

For some five years after Lyall retired, he served as editor of the Royal WA Historical Society journal, 'Early Days'. He also wrote numerous articles for the journal. This level of involvement with the Society meant that he was around during discussions about how to celebrate the centenary of the Australian Federation in 2001.

On behalf of the Historical Society, he wrote a submission for funds to produce a book, which he edited, titled 'Towards Federation.' Basically, it collated the best articles analysing why Western Australia joined the Federation of Australia in 1901. The funds were also used to prepare free-standing panels summarising key points about WA and the Australian federation. These travelled to libraries and schools in the regions. It was a terrific way of bringing history to the people.

Lyall wrote a significant introduction to the federation book, which established the import of each included article. I edited these pages, which proved fascinating to my unschooled mind. (I didn't study any Australian history in my UK schools.) I was intrigued to discover there was a possibility that Australia might have been a combination of New Zealand and the Eastern States, leaving the Western Third as an independent country. Ironically, I'm writing about this now, at the time of the COVID pandemic and hard border controls for WA. Many joke that WA has finally achieved the early vision of separation and independence.

I also found out why the straight north-south line that separates WA from the rest of Australia is a straight line and why it sits where it does. It's an extension of the line drawn in the 1494 Treaty of Tordesillas to separate the colonial conquests of Spain and Portugal. Who would have thought? Don't ask me why this line was chosen.

"Have you heard the news?" she asked.

Lyall's niece was working the supermarket cash till during her student days. She'd found out that some man somewhere had died and that on his deathbed, he'd called for his brothers. The story is vague, but it seems his brothers had returned to China a lifetime ago. It transpired that the man who died was Lyall's great-uncle, and the import of the story was that Lyall is one-eighth Chinese. He was in his late fifties when he found that out. Lyall's great-grandmother married a Chinese man and had two children, one of whom was Lyall's grandmother Nana Barger. She was born Elsie Nom-Chong. When her dad died, his sons from an earlier marriage had returned to China. Her mother remarried a Mr Mitchell, and Elsie was raised as Kathleen Mitchell. Consequently, Lyall always thought that he had a touch of the Irish in him, but Mr Mitchell was, in fact, his step-great-grandfather. It may have been through him and then Nana Barger (née Elsie Nom Chong, alias Kathleen Mitchell) that Catholicism entered Lyall's life, so I was quick to draw conclusions: "So this means that you're actually Confucian or Buddhist."

Decades later, Lyall and I tracked down the Chinese family in Braidwood (NSW) and found the shop his Chinese great-grandfather had owned and run. They must have contributed to their community because we also found a Nom Chong family portrait in the National Portrait Gallery in Old Parliament House in Canberra.

Around about 2001, Lyall strolled into the

kitchen to get his breakfast and said, "I don't know what day it is, and I can't work out where I am."

It was the first of his Temporary Ischaemic Attacks (TIAs). The slightly misleading but simple way to explain them is to say they're like mini-strokes. He had a number of TIAs over the next few years. Just over a decade later, he was diagnosed with Normal Pressure Hydrocephalus (NPH) and it was thought then that the TIAs might have been early warning signs. He also had a stroke sometime after the NPH had been sorted with the insertion of a programmable shunt that served as a drain from his brain. He'd never been a healthy man. He was in and out of hospital throughout our married life.

My first experience of one of his health crises was in Florence in 1981. We were at the beginning of our three-month rail trip around Europe. He had a frighteningly high fever so, instead of visiting the Uffizi Art Gallery, we visited a doctor's surgery. He was fixed up for the moment, and we resumed and finished our travels. But it became a recurring problem that eventually required surgery. This was the surgery that failed the first time and had to be repeated the next day – the only time I saw Lyall cry.

Lyall was not only unhealthy, but he was also unlucky in the medical care he received over the years. The worst example was the faulty knee replacement which gave rise to a class action. Maybe that wasn't the worst. Maybe it was over-administering warfarin to him when he was in a nursing home. His levels were registering fifteen when the maximum safe level is three. Or perhaps it was inaccurate reports about his programmable brain shunt that risked knocking out the programming when he had to have an MRI. Maybe this is what my friend, Rosemarie, means when she says I should tell the story of the accumulated s**t of life with Lyall, because when I pull this series of health problems together in one paragraph, it does look awful. And it was – for him and for me. I felt incredibly sorry for him. I don't know how he endured the last decade of his life. He became grumpy and depressed. Basically, he just gave up.

Lyall was a straight-down-the-line, pragmatic man. He wrote in his will that he didn't want a fancy coffin. It was a waste of money in his eyes.

He wanted a cardboard coffin. Towards the end of his life, I tried to sort out with him what his funeral arrangements might actually look like with a cardboard coffin. By this stage he was capable of listening but not decision-making, so I took the lead. I contacted a funeral parlour to get some benchmarks. At that time, an unattended cremation cost AUS$2,000, and a full-on fancy funeral could go as high as $15,000. I suggested to Lyall that the cardboard box idea might fit an unattended cremation, but I suggested that I could use the difference between $2,000 and $15,000 to donate to student prizes in Lyall's name, one for Western Australian history and one for young lads in East Perth Football Club. These were his two great loves. He was very pleased with these ideas. So that's what happened. The history prize will continue for ten years which, as I pointed out to him, is a lot longer than most people are remembered through headstones in Karrakatta Cemetery.

Sad to say, it was difficult to find a way to give a university student prize in Western Australian history because so little of it is taught these days. All the passion and effort that Lyall, and his contemporaries, put into building a history of Western Australia seemed to have lost momentum.

There is still the WA Historical Society and a Centre for WA History at the University of Western Australia, so all is not lost. As for Lyall's publications, I scanned many of them and put them on an open-source website called ResearchGate. I didn't think much would come of it because Western Australian history is such a niche area, but I've just checked and, in the decade since I uploaded his publications, Lyall has had over one thousand reads. So he's still telling his stories of Western Australian history.

Making sense of family: Marriage

"Will you marry me? I'm ready for the renovations."

He needed to be. Lyall had never been houseproud. As a consequence, he lived in a dump in a good suburb. This proposal indicated an open-hearted awareness of the home improvements that would be needed if we married. It also contained a presumption that I would live at his place and fit in with the needs of his family. I already had my own much nicer house, which was close to our place of work, but he was the custodial father of his four children, so their schooling, understandably, came first. So, I said yes to the marriage proposal and moved in with them when we married.

When Lyall proposed, I was studying for my Master's degree at the London School of Economics (LSE) 1978-79. He came to visit me during the Christmas holiday. It was the first time he'd travelled internationally, so he discovered London during the day whilst I attended lectures and seminars. We caught up in the evening at LSE's rather scruffy student bar. This is where he chose to propose. We'd just spent a long weekend in Paris, and he could have asked me to marry him there, but that was Lyall – he never did concern himself much with the finer points of life.

Inauspiciously, my lecturer in 'Marxist Ideas and Marxist Movements' was sitting opposite us. Hopefully, he was out of earshot because Marxists aren't big on the capitalist implications of marriage and family. From a feminist perspective, I didn't necessarily want marriage either. I might have preferred to live with Lyall, but he felt that marriage automatically resolves many legal issues and that it offered me some protection as a solo migrant marrying into a ready-made Australian family of four children. As it transpired, he was right.

Lyall came with a lot of baggage, which meant that I'd had some decision-making to do even before I went to London. I needed to get my Master's degree, and I also wanted to go back to

England. I'd drifted into living in Australia when I hadn't necessarily intended to leave the UK. In fact, I loved my English life, and all my family lived there. So a year of study in London fitted the bill. I was clear in my own mind that, when I returned to Perth, I would be in a committed relationship with Lyall, or I would take the advantages of a single life. I didn't want the disadvantages of all options. I might even have considered returning to live in England.

Lyall's first question after he proposed was, "What about kids?"

I answered in terms of the existing four, but he was talking about us having kids. So, from Day One, our two children, Ruth and Sam, were very much wanted. At the time, we were staying at a friend's house. She was pregnant with her first child and heavily into all things 'baby'. When she heard about our engagement, she plied Lyall with questions.

"Will you have children? Will you be there at the birth?"

Somewhat bamboozled, he told her that he'd like to be there at the conception.

I didn't particularly want an engagement ring. In

any case, there was little time for shopping. I bought myself a little antique ring to mark the occasion, but I never wore it much, nor did I wear my wedding ring. Once I got my hands into nappy buckets, the filigree wedding ring proved insufficiently robust. Lyall's incessant joke was that he didn't buy me an engagement ring because he didn't wish to commercialise our relationship.

"But he could have asked," Rosemarie challenged.

Lyall did, however, shower me with a bouquet of flowers every month on the anniversary of our engagement. I was living in a postgraduate student residence, so I think the receptionists wondered if I was some kind of movie star.

We became engaged in January 1979, when I was about a third of the way through my MSc. I wouldn't be returning to Australia until September. LSE is right next to Australia House in London, so Lyall thought we might get married there, but it would have meant being apart for the first nine months of our marriage. In any case, I thought it would be fair to Lyall's kids to have them involved. I wanted to be inclusive. So, the wedding was deferred until I got back to Australia.

This meant that we were apart for our entire engagement.

We discussed if I should change my name when I married. He wanted me to keep 'Hardy'. I didn't see it as a feminist issue because the name I had was my Dad's, and I preferred to take the name of the man I chose to be with rather than the one foisted on me by the chance of conception. Even if I'd changed my name to my mother's maiden name, that was still my Grandad's name. It is possible to get outside of male lineage, I suppose. I once met a lesbian called Catherine, who changed her family name to Wheel. I rather liked that – Catherine Wheel.

I absolutely resisted being called Mrs. I was Ms before I got my doctorate, then Dr, and Professor after that. Lyall didn't do a PhD. So, when I became Dr Hunt, we had fun at airports watching the check-in clerks figuring out how there could be a ticket for Mr Hunt and then one for a Dr Hunt, and then it dawned on them, "Ah! Must have missed the 's' off Mrs."

Our friends, Val and Brian, had a gorgeous old grape vine in the back garden of their lovely Claremont home. We asked if we might get married there with just a few people – close friends and immediate family. Then we went back to our place for a catered party for about eighty people. I wanted a female marriage celebrant, and Lyall wrote the words for the ceremony. It was all as I wanted it to be. Mum, my eldest sister, Audrey, and her husband, George, travelled to Australia for our wedding. In honour of their visit, I chose a West Australian theme, so we had Pavlova to cut instead of a wedding cake. Lyall's youngest daughter handed out sprigs of Western Australian wildflowers for guests to wear, and my Irish friend, Genevieve, made a wonderful native flower arrangement.

I'd thought about the implications of marrying a man nearly fifteen years my senior, who was the custodial parent of his kids – albeit increasingly few of them as they grew up and left the nest. I married late and had been out with quite a few men. They were all lovely, but I knew that I needed someone who was a good intellectual match. Lyall was. He was also good fun, self-assured and confident – a man of principle, whose politics accorded with mine. His letters to me show that he was passionate about me and saw me as a loyal and giving person. He'd had other girlfriends after his first marriage ended, but I was the only one with whom he'd chosen to settle. I suspect that 'loyal and giving' were attractive qualities to him because of his kids as much as himself.

Lyall and I had a pre-wedding honeymoon a month before we married. We were determined to go on the Old Ghan train before it came off the tracks forever. We embarked in Alice Springs and switched trains at Port Pirie to travel west on the Indian Pacific across the Nullarbor to Perth. Immediately after the wedding, all we had time for was a weekend in Busselton on our own. This small town is just a couple of hours south of Perth, on the coast. Lyall had to get back to work on the Monday. Within a week, we were on the road again with my family and Lyall's. Eight of us in all. We went camping down south, but that hardly constituted a honeymoon.

Lyall's clear view about marriage was that each partner should have the space to blossom and grow. In many ways, we achieved that. I introduced him to international travel, and he introduced me to exploring Australia, 'going bush' and camping. We enjoyed these things and grew together in a shared love of writing, native plant gardening, art, theatre and opera. A shared love of writing was a particular strength in our marriage. We were always editing each other's work. For the first thirty years of our thirty-nine years of married life, I'd have rated our marriage as better and more exhilarating and adventurous than most. We facilitated each other's successful careers. In the family league table of travel, I'm winning, having visited seventy-nine countries. He's second at forty-nine. We surrounded ourselves with beautiful Western Australian and Indigenous art, and we're both well published. I think we escaped suburban banality and led engaged lives.

We both wanted children, but childbirth was delayed for a couple of years, partly because Lyall was seriously let down by a family deal that should have given him a cash lump sum. This was to pay for our house renovations, so I had to work for a longer period before taking maternity leave.

Secondly, I felt that I'd travelled a lot and that Lyall had had a lifetime of domesticity. I wanted him to enjoy some wanderlust before our babies tied him to the hearth once again. So I organised a three-month trip around Europe by train. Then we started our family. Although Lyall was an experienced parent, this was now a new era. For starters, when he had his first batch of kids, husbands were locked out of the labour ward. With our two, it was expected that he be there at the birth. That was OK because he wanted to witness the birth of our two kids, but, thinking about it from the perspective of individual choice, there isn't a lot of difference for men between being locked in or locked out.

We had discussed parenting in our letters whilst we were engaged. I was emphatic that I wanted my children to travel, and I wanted them to have the social capital that I didn't have until I lived with my French family. I wanted them to think that going to art galleries was normal. I wanted them to know how to behave in restaurants. I wanted them to enjoy theatre and music, and I wanted them to have a multicultural outlook on life. That's why we joined SERVAS, an international network that facilitated peace and friendship on a one-to-one basis through hosting international travellers.

A friend told me that the best thing I could do

for my kids was to get them into a sport that would take them through their teenage years. That worked. Ruth and Sam were actively engaged in swimming and basketball. I received other parenting advice from wise-woman friend, Val. She came to visit me in hospital when Ruth was a couple of days old.

"Lynne, you naturally love your own children. Your job is to raise them so that other people love them."

I think all maternity hospitals should pay Val to visit new parents with this message.

Regarding child-rearing, Lyall was big on routine because it leaves little room for disputation. "Toilet, teeth and bed," was his catch-cry at bedtime. One day, I looked at sixteen-year-old Ruth and fourteen-year-old Sam sitting in their bean bags watching TV. I wondered if I caught them in an unguarded moment like this if they might move into 'auto-child' mode and get up and do as told if I abruptly announced, "Toilet, teeth and bed." I didn't risk it, but it happened one day anyway when Sam was about sixteen. One of his friends had rung on our landline to tease him with some story about his wallet, implying that Sam had lost all his money. Sam got annoyed and threw the telephone down. I reacted without thinking: "Sam go to your room!" He actually went, but I instantly grabbed my brains and realised that it was years since I'd attempted to discipline him in this way.

Lyall flashed me a look. "I think that's the last time you'll get away with that."

It certainly was the last time I tried to.

We had other routines for child-rearing. One was about eating family meals together so we had time to chat. Togetherness was important.

Lyall loved musicals and wanted to introduce them into the kids' lives. He off-air recorded 'South Pacific' and 'Mary Poppins' for tiny-tot Ruth, so these movies became the wallpaper of Sam's life as he emerged from babyhood. Lyall routinely took an afternoon nap on Sundays, which left me cuddling Sam, whilst Ruth had some quiet time with me as she snuggled into her bean bag watching one of her Dad's musicals. Sam was nearly three when Lyall recorded another movie: 'The Sound of Music.'

This was when the problems started. Sam simply couldn't understand why Mary Poppins was rushing around the Austrian Alps dressed up as a nun. I tried to explain that they were both Julie Andrews, but Sam wasn't having a bar of it, especially when Julie Andrews left the convent to go to live with the Von Trapp family. What was she carrying when she left the convent? A carpet bag. What did Mary Poppins carry? A carpet bag. It was a 'gotcha' moment for Sam. He had the evidence.

Lyall emerged from his afternoon nap at about this point of the debate. He assessed the situation, looked at Sam, and said, "Mary Poppins is just pretending to be a nun." Sam found that a satisfactory explanation and returned to watching the movie.

Neighbours and friends with kids the same age were an important part of our child-rearing years and our married social life. New Zealand friends, Liz and Don, had two daughters, Brooke and Shannon, who were each just two months older than our two. So there was a lot of birthday party socialising and sometimes Christmas as well. Rosemarie and Chris arrived in Perth when all of our kids were in primary school. Rosemarie and I were both solo migrants, so we became de facto family for each other. It was a similar story with

Liz and Don. Diana and Rob lived next door with Nicole and Russell, who were also close in age to our kids. They moved in when Sam was just six months old. Thereafter, Diana and I forged a friendship that was non-judgemental about finding each other in our nighties at three o'clock in the afternoon because the pressures of parenting toddlers hadn't afforded time to grab a shower. We practically co-reared our kids. We even had a ladder over the back garden fence, and the four kids flowed into each other's houses to play together. This resulted in a few parenting errors when we thought the other set of parents was in charge. We only narrowly avoided leaving them home alone. So close was this relationship that these days I refer to Russell and Nicole as my 'other daughter and son.' It broke my heart to see them in tears at my daughter's funeral in 2020. Their 'other sister' had just died.

I saw Russell yesterday. He's now in his late thirties.

"Hey," he said, "do you remember when Sam and I were hassling you to watch the film 'Free Willy'? You brushed us off and said if we wanted to see free willies we could just pull our pants down."

Humour was important in our family, but, on the night before our wedding, wise-woman friend Val took me to one side and explained that it's the 3,436th time that you hear the same joke that is the real test of a marriage. This is why I call her a wise woman – she knew Lyall well. When it comes to jokes, Lyall had a limited repertoire, though he was a naturally witty man.

I often wished I had Lyall's capacity for witty responses, like on one occasion at work. It was my first day at a new campus of the university at which I worked. I bumped into a colleague I recognised. Seeking to integrate into my new work environment, I stopped to say 'G'Day.'

"Hi, I'm new to this campus, but I'm sure I know you from that review committee we were both on. But I'm sorry, I've forgotten your name."

He replied, "It's Marc, and that's with a C and not with a K."

Pretentious prick! I made nothing of it until I repeated the story to the family over dinner that night. "It's unimportant but really, what a pompous idiot," I concluded.

Quick as a flash, Lyall observed, "What you

should have said is, 'My name's Lynne Hunt, and that's with an H and not with a C'."

Clearly, my son remembered the lesson because he declined to call his own son Jack. He didn't think it would work well with the family name 'Hunt.'

Meeting and marrying Lyall coincided with the Whitlam era in Australia. After decades of conservative Menzies government, Whitlam forged a new society that fostered Indigenous rights, promoted the feminist cause, and developed new multicultural policies. This, coincidentally, led to me becoming a naturalised Australian faster than I expected. I sometimes think that I might not have stayed in Australia if Whitlam hadn't redefined what it meant to live here.

Of particular importance to Lyall and me was the blossoming of the arts in the 1970s. We went to many of the new Australian films: 'News Front'; 'Picnic at Hanging Rock'; 'The Getting of Wisdom,' and 'Wake in Fright.' It was fantastic stuff. Theatre was equally interesting. One that we remembered, in particular, was a one-hour play called 'Blondin.' It was based on one simple idea:

What on earth induced someone to sit on Blondin's shoulders whilst he walked across Niagara Falls on a tight-rope? For an hour, one actor sat on the shoulders of another, who bobbed up and down as if walking on a rope. My stomach was in knots; I just wanted them to stop talking and get to the other side safely. It was a relief when the play ended and they reached firm land.

Travel was also a strength of our marriage. We completed three round-the-world trips, two with Ruth and Sam. We took the kids on trips to Bali and Singapore. Given that both are closer to Perth than Sydney, this is quite an ordinary thing to do – a bit like British people going to the Costa Packet in Spain. We also took them on two interstate camping trips to introduce them to their own country. In the days when Lyall was retired, and I worked, he took them on school holiday camping trips around Western Australia. Travelling was our gift to them that kept on giving. As adults, they both travelled a lot of their own accord. In fact, Sam spent about a decade working in Shanghai.

Some differences showed up between Lyall and me when we left twenty-year-old Sam at the airport to embark on his Chinese adventure.

"I wouldn't be bloody going to work in China when I was twenty," Lyall grumbled.

"I would! Way to go, Sam."

Lyall and I did give each other room to grow and blossom. When my kids were little, I looked after them alone whilst Lyall took his older son to India. He also went to China alone whilst I worked and looked after our toddlers. My career progressed to international study and lecture programs as the kids got older, so I went away, sometimes for as long as five weeks, whilst Lyall looked after Ruth and Sam. However, when it came to me getting promotional positions in Darwin and Queensland, Lyall wouldn't come with me. He was too much of a home-lover. So I went alone, and we conducted a commuting marriage for about five years. He came over to see me a couple of times a year, and I had permission to work off-campus in Perth for two months each year.

I was a bit disgruntled with this arrangement because I'd moved to the other side of the world to marry him and fit in with his family needs. When I was offered a promotional position in

Darwin, our kids were in their early twenties, so they no longer needed us. Lyall could have joined me, and we would have been able to explore different parts of Australia together. As it was, I was alone and started to work long hours. This was the first time I'd been released from family duties, and I wrote and published a lot in these years. I actually enjoyed the freedom to do as I wished, but it wasn't without hassle because Lyall was not a well man.

One night, I received a midnight call from Lyall. He told me that he was by the back gate waiting for an ambulance. He was in excruciating pain. I had to come home immediately. I raced back to Perth from Queensland only to find that he was suffering from a kidney stone.

"What? You've had me race across the country for a frickin kidney stone!!"

In some ways, Lyall and I communicated more when we were apart than when we were together because we rang for about an hour each evening. Overall, however, he was becoming miserable, disengaged and unmotivated.

"Don't you remember?" Janina said. "You finally decided to work interstate because you came home from work one night and found Lyall and both kids watching re-runs of M.A.S.H. The dog hadn't been fed or walked, and nobody had bothered to start cooking the evening meal."

She's right. It was pure, unadulterated selfishness. In any case, I wanted to work in promotional positions because my superannuation, when I retired, would be calculated partly on my final income. I needed to up my salary in my last three years of work. Ultimately, this was all for the good of the family, but Lyall started to paint a picture of abandonment that he shared with the kids, and they all believed him – even my two. By the time I retired and returned to Perth, things were not good between us, and all he could say was, "What do you expect if you abandon your family."

The irony of this accusation of abandonment is that he could have come with me, especially in Queensland, where I rented a cottage in a retirement village. My colleagues thought I was a real hoot living in a retirement village when I was a Pro-Vice-Chancellor of the university, but it was a gated community, so I could leave my car safely when working off-campus in Perth. It was a ten-minute walk from the university, and it had a twenty-five metre heated indoor pool. This was ideal. Lyall could come over and live. I even made arrangements to bring our dog to Queensland, but Lyall wouldn't come. Even when he came to stay for a few weeks at a time, he sat in the house all day waiting for me to come home for a swim. He could have been socialising with others in the retirement village, but he didn't.

There's an old joke that serves as a metaphor for this stage of our marriage. It goes like this: A married couple was out playing golf and the husband died at the third hole. Later, when his wife recounted this story to friends, they exclaimed, "What on earth did you do?" To which she replied, "Well, it was a question of hit one and drag Fred."

This is how I see the last quarter of my marriage: Hit one and drag Lyall. I even took him with me to conferences when he was in a wheelchair. It wasn't easy. Looking back now, Lyall had already had a few Temporary Ischaemic Attacks (TIAs) before I worked interstate, and he was headed towards a diagnosis of Normal Pressure Hydrocephalus. He had brain issues, and he was getting older. He probably had dementia before I realised. This can carry with it depression and paranoia, and his behaviour suggested that this was happening.

I'd always admired Lyall for not badmouthing his first wife to their kids after she left her family, but the same courtesies were not extended to me. Lyall started to forensically comb through my emails; he contacted friends, warning them off me; he closed our joint bank account when I was overseas (I could have been left without resources), and he told the kids what he imagined I was doing. All of this happened without any discussion with me. I was completely blindsided. The kids accepted what he said at face value, including my two, and nobody felt the need to let me know what was going on – or discuss my point of view. I will never forget that lack of loyalty and care. I was a non-person, which was small reward for my years of building a blended family.

The incident of closing the bank account had its funny side, though, and Liverpool's renowned humour was there to lighten my load. We had an appointment with a Liverpudlian bank clerk to rectify the situation. I could see it from her point of view. Here's this manic old codger with a younger wife, and he's frozen the joint accounts to defend his honour. I caught her eye, which had a distinct twinkle in it, and we shared a smile at the absurdity of it all.

My career ended when Lyall rang to say I had to give up my job and return to Perth to look after him. He could no longer manage on his own. I was only four months off the end of my contract anyway, and I had a dreadful new boss, so I was willing to retire early.

Lyall flew over, and we drove my car back as far as Adelaide. Once there, we put the car and ourselves on the Indian Pacific train to return to Perth. Lyall kept telling me that our marriage was over, which was weird because he'd just called me back to look after him. So, at the time, it seemed to me that the Indian Pacific was bookending my marriage. We had our pre-wedding honeymoon on the train, and now, apparently, our marriage was over and we were back on the Indian Pacific.

One thing I'd really wanted to do on the return trip was stay in an underground hotel in Coober Pedy. We did, but I was in tears there, as I had been for most of the trip. This man was threatened, angry, and uncompromising. When we got back to Perth, I had to confront him. Did he want me to look after him or not! If he did, then he needed to change his behaviour because I was not prepared to be bullied and undermined to the kids. I look back now and wonder why I was arguing myself into looking after him because I put myself at the front end of eight years of stressful and soul-crushing caregiving. But somebody had to do it, and where else was I going to go, anyway.

Throughout our marriage, I'd often wondered why Lyall would never argue with me. I thought perhaps the break-up of his first marriage had been so bitter that he just wasn't going to 'do angry' with me. Not that I wanted him to be angry, but I resented his lack of engagement. In any case, I didn't want my relationship with him to be dictated by his first marriage. I have now re-narrated my understanding of Lyall's behaviour. I think he was guarding his anger, not through lack of engagement, but to protect our marriage. He knew that I would walk at the first signs of undue aggression, and he knew that he could get angry. He also had some very angry kids, and they were all probably angry because of intergenerational trauma arising from abandonment and divorce, but how was I supposed to understand this? I didn't know that Lyall's parents had abandoned him until we'd been married for about thirty-six years, and I didn't know that a baby had been given up for adoption in his first marriage until after Lyall died, so I was never really in a position to make a lot of sense of Lyall or our marriage.

Now, I'm able to retrofit some understanding about anger. When I started to work at Mt Lawley College in 1973, the place was agog with a story about Lyall losing his temper with the boss and storming out of a meeting. I also saw him snap at a colleague quite unreasonably. After he retired, a woman at the Historical Society approached me to say that she was concerned at the manner in which Lyall had got angry about a particular publication matter, and I'd seen signs of this anger when we dined out with friends of mine in Queensland. It was a political discussion, and one friend ventured the opinion that politics was no longer the be-all-and-end-all in public decision-making. Big industry now called some of the shots. Lyall responded with unreasonable anger for a social occasion. I was embarrassed. He'd been massively rude to one of my friends. I saw this as yet another example of me fitting in with his life, but he wouldn't fit in with mine.

So, a pattern of anger emerged, and there was me thinking I'd married a man who was the polar opposite of my Dad. After Lyall died, I spoke with a UK friend, William, who is a counsellor: "I know that daughters of drunken, violent men often marry the same kind of man. I deliberately avoided that, but it doesn't seem to have made much difference."

He replied that people who have complex childhoods, like mine, often seek complexity in adulthood. Well, I certainly walked into that one.

There was another reason for Lyall's increasing anger. When I worked at a university in Perth, I came across a research project which studied the effects of testosterone treatment in the prevention of Alzheimer's. I suggested to Lyall that he become one of the guinea pigs in the research. He had to stop quite quickly because it produced a reaction of female hormones. It was like living with a woman having a very bad menopause – menstrual as anything. But, testosterone treatment can have well-being effects, including increased stamina, so Lyall continued the treatment through his own doctor. He started to overdose because he liked the libidinal side effects. I could see what was happening. The testosterone was contributing to his anger. He was like the proverbial bull in a china shop. I couldn't talk with him about it – it was like taking candy off a baby. In the end, I had to email his doctor and get him to modify the treatment, and Lyall's behaviour improved.

I started to piece together anger management issues in the family, including my daughter. At one stage, Lyall and I had been away and returned to find a hole kicked in a door. Ruth said she slipped. It was clear that it was deliberate. When she broke up with her first serious boyfriend, he rang to say how concerned he was about her anger at the break-up. She was no orphan. The way her half-siblings treated me when Lyall died, and the hostile treatment of Sam and me at the time of Ruth's death, suggest that anger management issues may run through the whole family.

Lyall became manipulative and just plain grumpy. One of his domiciliary nurses commented, "He was cut 'n dried to the point of being rude, wasn't he?"

I told her that a sentence didn't leave his mouth that didn't begin with 'I'. It's all about him. "But when the kids come round he's full of bonhomie and his usual jokes: 'It only hurts when I laugh' or, 'my right little finger is particularly good today.' So they think nothing's wrong."

The nurse took an overview of the situation: "That's twice he's fallen over when you were out doing something for yourself. It seems like emotional blackmail to me."

Even conversation with Lyall became difficult, partly because he couldn't hear what I said. I took him to the theatre one day and started to chat about how I'd put us on several theatre e-news circuits so that we knew what would be coming up.

"What's an emu circuit?" he replied.

"Do you want some tea?"

"No, I don't need a pee."

I've recently decluttered my life in order to move into my granny house in my back garden. In so doing, I came across Lyall's loving letters when we were engaged, and I found a book he gave me when Ruth was born. It's called 'Stories of

Australian Motherhood', and his inscription said: "Thank you for adding one more story."

I also found a book he'd given me on our twentieth wedding anniversary in 1999. His inscription thanked me for twenty years of exhilarating marriage. It's been important to rediscover these things because I needed to salvage the good times. We had been happy for a long time.

Looking back, I can see that I was always treated as a bit of a second-hand rose. I told Rosemarie a story about an Easter holiday before Lyall and I married. I'd spent the long weekend helping Lyall to paint his kitchen. Then he announced, on Easter Sunday afternoon, that he was off out with the kids for a BBQ with his former sister-in-law and her family. I wasn't invited.

"And you still married him?" she scoffed.

I did marry him, and it didn't make much difference in how I was treated.

Without malice aforethought, many of Lyall's friends and relatives saw me as a second-hand rose. I was constantly told how good I was for Lyall, but it entered nobody's head to consider how good or bad he was for me. Some of Lyall's friends and relatives assumed that I was merely an interested observer of his first and, presumably, real marriage. They plied me with stories about his first wife and marriage. If I demurred, then they apologised because they hadn't realised I was jealous. Ye Gods! Damned if I defended myself, and damned if I didn't!

One of Lyall's cousins came to stay just after we were married. When I mentioned wedding gifts, she asked, "This marriage or the one before?"

Another relative could hardly believe it when Lyall's youngest daughter from his first marriage was turning fifty. "Oh, Lyall, what does it feel like to have your youngest child turn fifty?"

Silly me, and there I was thinking that our son, Sam, was his youngest child. If I looked to Lyall for support, he told me that I should be ready for these comments. It seems the problem was mine for not being adequately prepared. I'm now seventy-three, and people still talk to me as if I'm merely an interested bystander in his first and real marriage, which ended in 1973 before I arrived in Australia.

"Ah yes! I knew Lyall," said a comparative stranger I met at a party last year. "In fact, I knew his wife," they blundered on.

"You're talking to her," I snapped back. I was met with a bewildered expression. She just couldn't work out what I meant.

I wanted to live our marriage as 'our marriage' without constant reference to Lyall's first nuptials. But this proved to be impossible, partly because he and his first wife remained locked in enmity. Linda rang one day in the early 1990s. She'd recently remarried and for both Linda and her husband, Steve, it was a third marriage. She had to cut short the telephone conversation because she was going to Steve's first wife's funeral.

"Geez, Linda, with the number of previous spouses you two have, you'll be going to a funeral a week!"

I returned to my armchair to chat with Lyall.

"That was Linda on the phone. She couldn't stay long. She's off to Steve's first wife's funeral."

Lyall was galvanised by this piece of information. Normally comatose in his armchair, he sat bolt upright. "I'm buggered if I'd go to my first wife's funeral!"

Given what had happened over the years, I could see why he'd say that, but I told him, "When all's said and done, she is, and always will be, the mother of four of your children."

His response showed me that we would never be just the two of us in our marriage.

Wise woman, Val, always likes things to be nice, or, at the very least, she likes to look on the bright side.

"Did the first thirty years of marriage make it all worthwhile?" she enquired.

I had to say no, because different choices could have been made, and more support could have been brought to my table. So, singing 'Always look on the bright side of life,' like Eric Idle hanging off his crucifixion cross in the film 'Life of Brian,' is something I can't do. We could have lived the last ten years of our lives together more lovingly and with less stress, despite all the challenges. We had too much unused life in the last years of our marriage. Liverpool playwright, Willy Russell, wrote about unused life in his play, 'Shirley Valentine':

> *Why is it that there is all this unused life? ... it's not just men that do it to women. Because I've looked at [my husband] and I know it's the same for*

> him. He had more life in him than he could use, and so he carries all this waste around with him ... we always say we're fine because the vegetables are fresh and our kids grew up with their limbs intact. We say we're fine and we carry on till we die ... long before we are dead. And what kills us is the terrible weight of all this unused life that we carry around.

If I could write this eloquently, it would be my assessment of marriage with Lyall. At the end, there was no way out for either of us. Somebody had to look after him. I did try to live life as fully as possible even when he was quite disabled. I took him with me to Malaysia when I was awarded the Australian Executive Endeavour Award. He was already in a wheelchair, and I couldn't have managed the situation without the help of my Malaysian friends, Mazlan and Zai. They lent us their car and a driver to get around. I drove Lyall across the Nullarbor to visit South Australia. I took him on a cruise to the South Pacific Islands, and flew to Darwin with him and his wheelchair to catch the new Ghan train down to Adelaide before catching the Indian Pacific train back to Perth, where Lyall died in 2018. And so our married life ended.

The meaning of parenting 1990-91

Oct 7, 1990

Today marks the end of Joan Sutherland's career and of Sammy's front right tooth. I mislaid the book in which I was keeping a record of the milestones in the kids' lives, so I resorted to writing notes on scraps of paper. The best I can do now is collate my notes to convey a coherent impression of what it meant to me to parent Ruth and Sam.

Eight-year-old Ruth has had a year of ups and downs. Having gone to her first lot of Education Department swimming classes at Cottesloe Beach in the cold January of 1990, she moved on to Asthma Swimming classes, where she is now doing the equivalent of twenty Olympic laps every Sunday including a lap or two of butterfly. She continues with Italian and has taken-up drama. The latter took me by surprise. I didn't see it as one of her interests, but she seems to enjoy it, and she's demonstrated that she can express herself in theatre. By contrast, she is still uptight in social relationships generally, having suffered a lot at the hands of two dominant girls in her class. She plays mainly with the boys and accuses the girls of following the ringleaders like sheep.

I admire her independence but have worried about her happiness at school. Her teacher assures me that Ruth is not unpopular, and every time I offer to pull Ruth out of school and put her into a more 'alternative' school – Quintilian – she refuses. She always speaks of school in terms of we/us/our, so appears to strongly identify with Claremont Prac School.

Ruth's been to a few birthday parties this year and her own birthday comes up soon. We hope to make it a toy-train party at a friend's place in Gosnells. They have an acreage with a miniature train running around the property. Socially, she keeps busy starting the year at the Marina Mandarin in Singapore, where we were on holiday. Twelve thousand balloons floated down from the Atrium on the stroke of midnight. Sam didn't like that at all because the assembled crowds started to burst the balloons, which he considered a real waste. He became quite upset. I think the noise may have bothered him as well.

Ruth went to see 'Oklahoma,' with Lyall. Her dad likes musicals – I don't. She also went to 'Baba,' with her half-brother. Then Ruth and Sam both went to the 'Baby Proms,' with me, and the Emu Farm with us all, including Nana, who is here from England for four months. Today we bought our new camper trailer, and Lyall is taking the two of them away to the Murray River this week whilst I get back to work.

Much of what I've said about Ruth also applies to Sam, who has had a very successful pre-school year at Quintilian. His teachers consider him to be an "absolute delight." His theme for the first two terms was 'The alphabet.' Even the canteen was organised so that the week's letter invited the kids to lunch, just like in the TV program, 'Sesame Street'. Getting him into gear, I said. "The letter C invites you today, Sam: celery, carrot, cucumber?

"Oh no!" came the reply. "Cucumber starts with Q." So that didn't work.

He's at a very cute age linguistically and has certainly learned how to charm people. One day, 'not listening to his parents' became a problem. We both growled at him, but he can't bear for me to be cross with him, so he cuddled next to me on the settee and gave me a hundred kisses. Suddenly, I realised Sam was trying to make me happy, but not dealing with the issue. So I told him that kisses would not solve the problem.

Absolutely dumbfounded, he looked at me and said, "What about hugs then?"

This was followed the next morning by a similarly quick piece of repartee. "What will you have for breakfast, Sam?"

"I'll have eggs."

"Isn't there a word missing?" said I, looking for a 'please.'

Instead, after some thought, he said, "Yeah, bacon."

In September, he had his adenoids out. The nurse who welcomed him into the ward was good and told him what to expect. His was the first operation at 8am, and the nurse emphasised several times that he would have to get up early. He replied, 'Why did my friend sleep under the car?"

This was a complete non-sequitur, so we were a

bit perplexed until Sam explained that it was because he wanted to wake up oily. Not bad, aged five, to tell a joke in context. He liked his anaesthetist, who called him sausage.

They both do well at sport. Ruth did better than she expected in her athletics, coming second in her running race. Sam is starting to play tennis really well, with hand-eye coordination in advance of what I might expect for five-year-olds. Ruth tries hard with basketball and is always playing cricket in the backyard. They both ride bikes well. They are lovely, lively kids who bring us a lot of joy.

Sunday 3 November 1990

A week ago, Ruth was watching a dreadful Saturday afternoon movie called 'Gidget goes Hawaiian' – a rubbishy, sexist movie. I asked her to turn it off.

The reply? "Oh, but I have to watch it, Mummy, so that I can write a letter of complaint afterwards."

She has learned to manage her mother's feminism and is using my rhetoric back against me.

Last week, I took them both to Nedland's Kite

Festival. Arriving home, they proceeded to develop a game that involved finding a weight that would hold a balloon halfway between ceiling and floor. They were making a helluva row, to which I objected. Ruth's reply was that they were 'experimenting.' I asked if that was supposed to shut me up, and she said, "Yep." She's sussed out that almost anything educational goes.

Yesterday, I took them, with their Nana and a friend, to see the Spare Parts Puppet Theatre production 'Mother Goose.' I've also booked for them to see 'Queen of the Bees' – a production by George White – a lecturer at the college where I work. Last year we saw his 'Gobbledegooks' – a good panto with many layers of meaning about communication and multiculturalism. He has a knack for writing at two levels to keep parents and children engaged in his productions.

23 February 1991

We had a pleasant Christmas, though it became busy with all the end-of-year school functions. Ruth was a Hanukkah Candle in the graduation ceremony and a Guard Ant in her Drama Academy production. She had been cast in the lead role as the grasshopper, but she became sick with walking pneumonia and had to pull out. Sam had a Christmas concert and a visiting magician. We left Quintilian after his pre-school year with much regret.

Their Christmas treat was a trip to the Peter Coombes show. On Christmas Day, we had the usual stockings in which Ruth found a boogie board and Sam a Whoopsie Daisy Doll. Mum gave Sam a punch ball and Ruth some diving sticks. The 'Big Kids' came round for morning tea. By the time we'd had champagne, we cancelled lunch, and had our Christmas meal in the evening. We then had a couple of pleasant weeks at home, during which time we said goodbye to Mum when she returned to the UK.

The kids acquired some surf swimming skills at the Education Department classes at Cottesloe beach. Ruth passed Level Seven and Sam Level Three. The children then went to Quintilian Holiday care, which included a trip to Adventure World. As a family, we had a weekend away at Wedge Island, learning how to four-wheel drive over sand dunes. The kids were very impressed. They put on their swimming goggles and rolled down the sand dunes.

Ruth's had a busy start to the school year. She plays tennis before school on Monday and does Italian after school on Tuesday. Then it's drama Wednesday evening, and piano on Thursday evening. Both Sam and Ruth go to ASMA swimming classes on Sunday morning, and Sam has just re-enrolled in tap dancing on Saturday mornings. This is a sorting time. I'm giving them a go at everything to see what they like, and then we'll drop the things that don't interest them.

Ruth has blossomed into a confident giggle-pot as a Year Four girl. Sam had a poor start to the year. The new Year One teacher is very tense, rule-bound and lacking in fun. His first day at school was 44.5C, and he asked for a drink. She refused. Lyall phoned her about that. The second day at school was a State record of 45.6^0. At least at that stage, the Grade One kids were only attending for half days.

Ruth was thrilled this last week because Rebecca Smart, child actress from one of her favourite films, 'The Shiralee,' has been filming a children's TV series at her school. I took them to look at the set.

Sam and two other boys had birthdays right at the beginning of the school year, so the parents decided to have a shared birthday party for the whole of Grade One. We played party games at the Rose Gardens in Nedlands, and the parents came to our place afterwards for a Sundowner: A successful day that, hopefully, Sam will remember. We bought him cricket wickets for his birthday. Mum gave him a collection of dinosaur books. He had lots of books and puzzles from his school friends, including his favourite – a paper tree that grew crystals.

We are taking them north to Dongara for Easter, and we plan to watch a rodeo. In the meantime, they play with their friends. Ruth has joined the 'electrical club' with the boys, and last weekend she went swimming with a new girl in her class, who has arrived from Saudi Arabia. At this moment, they sit out the heat watching the original 'Lassie Come Home.' Sammy is a real softie, and is becoming very concerned about the dog. I'd better stop writing and start cuddling.

Making sense of family: Grand-parenting

My daughter-in-law, Jane, recently announced, "I can't wait to be a grandma. I want to know what it feels like." She said this with her eighteen-month-old baby, Elsie, sitting on her lap. Although her ambitions were lovingly premature, it was an interesting question and got me thinking. Well, what does it mean to be a grandmother?

When we started to teach a women's studies course at my university in the 1980s, one of my colleagues asked her students to write an essay entitled, 'My grandmother, my mother, myself.' I thought it an excellent topic because it made students think about social change, and it makes me think that being a grandmother means different things in different generations – and in different cultures. We're all living longer now, as well. My mother lived long enough to become a great-great-grandmother, and the five-generation family photograph with her eldest great-great-grandson, Elliot, made it into the local newspaper.

I didn't know my grandmother, Alice Britton, very well. She died when I was eight, and I didn't live in Devon like all of my cousins. So I visited Grandma only for summer holidays. I succeeded in contracting a childhood illness on two of those occasions. I can remember Grandma sitting on my bed telling me that three would be my lucky number and that next year I wouldn't get sick. She was right. I can also remember that she drank hot water on the grounds that it would be slimming. I was obviously sufficiently impressed with this information to remember it, but on adult reflection I've realised that hot water would hardly be fattening.

My eldest sisters, Audrey and Joyce, knew Grandma better because they lived with her when Mum was widowed. The main thing Joyce remembers is Grandma standing at the end of the table serving food. She had ten kids, so I guess that was pretty much Grandma's lot with so many mouths to feed. Mum told me that Grandma's account of her life concerned the constant baby-making.

"One at the breast and one in the belly," was how she described it.

Ten kids! No wonder Grandma had them christened in batches of five. I admire the economy of effort and the assembly-line approach to what must have been a mammoth task of mothering.

I always had the impression that my mother wasn't particularly engaged in grand-parenting. That's probably because she kept telling me that she'd raised her four, so now I could raise mine. However, I've just sorted my attic, where I found heaps of letters from Mum to my kids. They are loving letters that let her grandkids know how much she took an interest in them. Mum was very clever at knitting. As a consequence, she kept a good supply of hand-made jumpers winging their way to Ruth and Sam. She came to stay with us in Australia on a number of occasions. If I total it up, she probably lived with us for about a year. I have photos of her allowing herself to be dressed up by her grandchildren. Her favourite game to play with them was mud pies, which didn't work too well in the sandy soil of Western Australia. I had to explain to her that there's a reason why Western

Australians are called 'Sandgropers.'

My grandmother, my mother, and so to myself. What does grand-parenting mean to me? I've always wanted to make memories with my grandkids, Oli, Thomas, and Elsie, so I do a lot of storytelling with them. I'm off to headstart with Oli because he likes writing. He's watched me writing my memoir and recently announced that he'd like to write his. I suggested that he may need more than ten years behind him before he gets started. On second thoughts, maybe he should start now.

Oli and Thomas were born in China, so they were of doubtful nationality for a while because China doesn't offer citizenship to ex-pat babies born on their soil, and their mum is English and their dad is Australian. All the same, Jane bought one of them a romper suit with 'Made in China' written across the front – which I thought very cute. I was delighted to go to Shanghai to see baby Oli, not only because he was my first grandchild, but also because I love Shanghai. Its waterfront looks so much like Liverpool. It was my third trip there, but this time I got an insider's view because Sam and Jane had worked in Shanghai for many years. We walked a lot, with Oli in his stroller. His blond hair and blue eyes attracted a lot of positive attention, until the gathering crowd of Shanghainese realised that his parents were taking their baby outside before he was three months old. This is a cultural no-no in China, and strangers had no compunctions in telling Oli's parents what they thought of them. Fortunately, they both spoke some Mandarin, so they could hold their own in the debate.

When Thomas was born, I couldn't go to see him in Shanghai because Lyall's health was deteriorating, and I didn't think I'd get very far in China with a wheelchair-bound husband. Technically speaking, Thomas had been made in Australia when Sam, Jane and Oli were staying with us in Perth, so I felt that I'd witnessed his growth. They returned to Shanghai a couple of months before his birth. Later, Sam and Jane took both boys to Bali for Thomas's first birthday. I hired a villa for us all, including Ruth and her fiancée, and Lyall's daughter and her family. Lyall's health was poor, so I was concerned that he may never see Thomas if we didn't get to Bali. He'd also just won some money through the class action associated with his faulty knee implant, and I thought the best way of spending some of it would be for him to have time with his family. So, mission accomplished, but wheelchairs and Bali weren't a good combination. Thomas was too young to speak at that stage, but maybe there would have been little point because both boys were cared for by a Chinese nanny in Shanghai, and their Mandarin was as good as their English in their early years. I hope that set some foundations in their brains for future language learning because speaking Mandarin in the 'China Century' might be a real asset when they grow up.

One of the first things I had to consider when Oli was born was: "What should I be called?"

At that stage, Jane's own grandmother was still alive, so a lot of the granny and grandma names were already taken. My mother had been Nana. I didn't want that, but, in any case, I wanted to reserve that name for her in my memory. So I rang a friend. Professor Ren Yi was a work colleague of mine in Queensland, who has since become a longstanding friend.

"Quick, Ren, what's grandma in Mandarin."

"NaiNai," he replied, automatically ascribing

me the name for paternal grandmother. Had I been a maternal grandmother, I would have been LaoLao. NaiNai was a good fit. It sounded nice. It was somewhat similar to the English 'Nana.'

The kids were born in China, and Lyall was one-eighth Chinese. Therefore, my son, Sam, was one-sixteenth and the kids one thirty-second. So NaiNai it is. That name entered the limelight with the film 'The Farewell,' which was written and produced by a young ex-pat Chinese woman. It was the true story of her grandmother, who was supposedly close to the end of her life, but the family didn't want to speak to her about this reality. So one of the cousins undertook a fake wedding to bring the family together for a last farewell. That was all fine and dandy, but their NaiNai survived, so they were stuck with a film telling the story of their loving deception.

I don't do platitudes. In fact, their banality annoys me. When I spot them coming, as I did at the gym the other day, I dive for cover. A woman in my gym class was giving me the unedited version of stories about her grandkids.

"Any minute, now," I thought, and sure enough: "It's lovely to have them, but it's nice to be able to hand them back."

I wanted to be mischievous and say, "Well, actually, no. I'd prefer to keep them for longer," but I've learned to just smile and nod.

The reality is, I don't see being a grandmother as being startlingly different to being a mother, and I don't have thoughts about needing to hand them back. They are, quite simply, just around me, as and when. It doesn't matter. It's not a regulated thing. I love my three grandchildren, and I have a close sense of belonging with them in pretty much the same way I did with my own kids. I also feel protective of them, as I did with Ruth and Sam, but I know my job as a grandmother is different. Their mum and dad chart the course. They decide how their children will be raised. So, if my grandkids ask if they can do something, I invariably ask them to check with their parents first. If that's not possible, I ask what Mum and Dad might say. That's when I should have been told that some drinks in the fridge are reserved for baby Elsie. My systems are not infallible.

I'm not busy with the daily round of child-rearing as their parents are, so I can hang out with the boys. I enjoy our chats, though sometimes their questions lead me into territory that I think belongs to their parents. I often have to warn Sam and Jane about the topics we've covered because I know that, by the time they've passed through the whirlpool of Oli and Thomas's thought processes, they will emerge as something quite different to my memory of what was said. I was a teacher all my life, so I do love to seize teachable moments, and I get sucked into their stream of questions that lead I know not where. My kids used to spot these educational moments at one hundred paces and beat a retreat, but Oli and Thomas seem happy to hang around chatting.

This morning, before I dropped them at school, we covered the 'Twin Studies' in space, the significance of the length of telomeres, and how to make oxygen on a space station. I love their curiosity, though I've found that they're better at asking questions than listening to the answers. I might be unfair in saying that, because my abiding memory of Thomas will be his constant catch-cry: "Wait! So you mean …" He's obviously hearing what was said and thinking about it.

This morning it was, "Wait, so you mean the Queen sends you a birthday card when you turn one hundred? How does the Queen know that it's your one-hundredth birthday? Who will send the Queen a special birthday card when she has her one-hundredth birthday?"

This isn't a question that crops up very much, but I take it as evidence that he listens and takes things in. It didn't stop there. He obviously continued to think about regal matters overnight because the next morning he asked questions about the line of succession. I noted that, regarding the current Queen, the next in line would be King Charles and then King William, if that were to be their chosen names.

Just to make it clear, I said, "So if Daddy were king, it would be King Samuel, and then the next in line would be King Oliver, because he's the eldest."

Thomas didn't like this because Oli would get something and not him, so he tried to find loopholes in the line of succession. "Wait, so what would happen if the kids were twins?"

I pointed out that there is always one twin born first.

"Wait, so what if they were Siamese Twins?"

Fortunately, it was time to go to school, and it

was my job to take them.

I downsized into 'Lynne's Lodge' (my granny house) in my own back garden in 2021. My son, Sam, and his family moved into the main house that I vacated. So we are now neighbours. The process of downsizing entailed a lot of decluttering. This resulted in tailoring and collating the family history memorabilia into one small wooden chest. I donated some significant and larger items to museums. For example, my dad was a soldier in the Oxford and Buckinghamshire Regiment. He was an excellent athlete, so I sent his medals and memorabilia to his regimental museum, Soldiers of Oxfordshire (SOFO). Oli and Thomas had fun checking out the goods that I parcelled up. It was a very poignant moment when I looked around to see Thomas cradling my Dad's army book.

"I just love old things," he sighed.

I picked up on Thomas' interest and contacted my cousin, Jane, in England. She's been meticulous in developing a family tree dating back to 1690, but my grandkids weren't on the hard copy version I'd been given a few decades ago. I asked Jane for an update. When I received the hard copy of the family tree, Oli and Thomas were intrigued to find themselves connected by bloodlines across three centuries. This is what grandparents can be – a conduit to their grandkids' ancestry.

Elsie Ruth was born just a few months before my daughter died. I'm so pleased that Ruth had a chance to cuddle her namesake. It was such a wonderful gift from Sam and Jane to name their daughter after her. I know it meant a lot to Ruth.

Jane's mum, Julie, was extraordinarily compassionate during Ruth's illness and when she died. Julie donated a memorial brick to Ruth at the Liverpool Cathedral. It was such an appropriate gesture because our grandkids have strong connections with Liverpool. I went to university there, Granny Julie and their great-aunt Lydia went to school near Devonshire Road, and Jane's Dad, Grandad Jim, was born in Wavertree. We've got them surrounded with all things Liverpool. Anyway, Julie and I were in close correspondence about the memorial brick when one day, she signed off, "Give our grandchildren a hug from me."

It suddenly hit me that Julie and I love the same

grandchildren. That's a close bond, but there are no words in the English language to describe it. Perth friend Rosemarie later told me that in Argentina, where she grew up, this grandmotherly relationship is honoured with a name. Julie and I are 'comadres.'

I once read a study that suggested that good looking kids do better in school because adults want to interact with them. I suppose it's a story in which life spirals upwards for them. They are pretty babies, so adults 'bill-and-coo' with them, and the babes learn to blow bubbles and do raspberries back — and so on. Life is more of a struggle for babies who cry a lot or are on the lower end of the 'pretty scale.'

Well, Elsie was born with it all. She's pretty, and she's highly entertaining. She arrived as a joy-giver just when we needed her most. She's now eighteen months old, and she bosses her brothers mercilessly. Right now, she gets by on cute behaviour, but I suspect that Oli and Thomas will start to think differently about her in the not too distant future. I sent Elsie-photos to a lot of friends and relatives in the first months of her life, but I stopped doing that because I know that grandkids are really only fascinating to their grandparents. To my surprise, people asked me to keep sending because Elsie's brilliant smile was a joyful start to their day. I have, finally, stopped sending.

Grand-parenting is a complex thing. Two of my friends, Ailsa and Sally, have difficult relationships with their daughters-in-law, so their experience of grand-parenting differs markedly from mine.

Grandchildren can be weaponised, as in Ailsa's story. She has seen two of her grandchildren on only two occasions, and her other grandkids live overseas. So not much is happening for her on the granny front.

Sally's son divorced, but she's managed to keep in contact with her grandkids even though she's been undermined. She describes her relationship with her grandchildren as 'guarded.'

Darwin friend, Janet, told me about someone she knew. Let's call her Susan. She married and had two children. Susan's mum and dad contributed money to set her up in her married home. Unfortunately, Susan died young, and the kids' natural father booted them out to live with her parents – namely the maternal grandparents.

Then he took the money from the sale of the house and ran off to a new marriage. This is an extreme example of grandparents starting over as parents, but the cost of child care in Australia means that many grandparents now raise their grandkids whilst the mums and dads are at work.

For me, the most complex aspect of grand-parenting is knowing when to step in and when to stay out. I thought about this a lot when I heard on the BBC news the story of a UK child who was killed by his mother and step-father, despite the fact that the grandparents had seen the warning signs and sounded alarm bells. Just how possible is it for grandparents to be the buffer that protects their grandchildren from the difficulties they might face?

Then again, you don't need to be a grandparent to grand-parent. Perth friend, Denise, does an excellent job with her great-nieces and nephews. Her sister died at a young age, so Denise stepped up to the plate doing all the support work that grandparents normally do. She also does the fun bit of organising age-relevant excursions for pre-schoolers and teenagers. This is what I think grand-parenting is.

Grandparents should have fun and create memories with their grandkids. I know that my very earliest memory is of driving a tractor with Grandad when I was two-and-a-half years old. I know I was that age because he died the following year, and he wouldn't have been able to drive a tractor when he was that sick. I thought I was driving a tractor because Grandad must have kidded me along. In reality, I was standing between his legs and steering.

Grandpa Jack, Ruth and Sam's grandfather, would always arrive with a bag of lollies (sweets/candy) hidden about his person. They just loved clambering all over him to find them. So grand-parenting is in the joy of it. I was once told that if I started baking, then I'd be like a proper grandmother. Thankfully, I don't bake cakes. Instead, I concentrate on being a 'Crazy NaiNai' – as the boys call me. I've started playing pranks on them by hiding pebbles under the bottom sheet in their bed, and they've reciprocated. They love it, especially if I let them win. The ball's in their court at the moment, as it is with their future. Seize the day, Oli, Thomas and Elsie.

Making sense of family:
In-laws

Ailsa is in her early seventies, statuesque, sophisticated, good looking, well-travelled, well-read, and a qualified lawyer. What could possibly go wrong with her life? Well, she's also a mother, a mother-in-law, and a grandmother, and here she was on our girls' night out crying into her red wine. She's experienced long-running problems with her daughter-in-law's behaviour that have alienated her from her son and grandchildren, and she can do nothing about it. The problems have been evident for over a decade.

In the early days, her daughter-in-law visited, but she was point-blank rude and uncooperative. Then she chose not to visit at all. Quite simply, she didn't want to know her in-laws. Fortunately, she went to live overseas with her husband, Ailsa's son, and their kids. Trying to keep the door to communication open, Ailsa sent emails and presents. That kept her happy. They didn't thank her or communicate, and that, presumably, kept them happy. So it might be said that everybody was happy – but, of course, they weren't. Like many of my friends, Ailsa had expected a grown-up relationship with her adult children – even friendship.

Some years later, Ailsa rang me. "They're coming back, and so is all the hurt. I could handle it when they weren't on my doorstep. What do I do now?"

It was a difficult situation because she has two other adult children, and there were bound to be family gatherings. That day came, and she rehearsed with me how she would handle the situation at the forthcoming family party, which, as always, was to keep things as natural and low-key as possible.

"Ring me and tell me all about it," I said.

As it turned out, she'd chatted amicably with her son, addressing none of the real issues – but they spoke. That was good enough. She'd also met her grandsons for only the second time ever. They were, by then, eight and six years old. At the party, they made plans for Ailsa to take them horse riding. This was real progress, and she was thrilled. She didn't see her daughter-in-law at the party and so assumed she wasn't there.

The very next day, I got an email.

"It turns out I was wrong. She was there! She must have spent two hours dodging around furniture to avoid talking to us!"

I thought the notion of a thirty-seven-year-old woman dodging the in-laws at a family party had its funny side: "This is so ridiculous," I replied. "You have to laugh! It would make a good cartoon."

I couldn't get past the storyline: "You mean your daughter-in-law actively avoided you all afternoon? Why would she do that? HOW did she do that in a small house? Was she crawling around behind the sofa? This says more about her than you. Couldn't she make an effort just for the sake of the family? It's like the three-line whip in parliament," I exclaimed, referring to the parliamentary convention of ensuring unity in voting along party lines. In other words, there are times when you just do the right thing.

I was so shocked that I couldn't stop talking, "Good grief! It's only for one afternoon! What does it say about her relationship with her husband – your son? Is this a zero-sum game? Is this the only choice your son gets – to be friends with his wife or his mother? Why can't he have both? And what about her kids' relationship with you – their grandmother. Doesn't your daughter-in-law care about that? How would she feel if she found out that a family member had deliberately avoided her? It must have been humiliating for you to realise that everyone else at the party, including your own daughters, was in the know. It was collusion, and exclusion."

Incidentally, she was never able to take her grandsons horse riding. Her relationship with her grandchildren has been weaponised.

Before Ailsa's party story, I'd already chatted about in-law issues with members of my aqua aerobics group. We are, variously, mothers, grandmothers, step-mothers, and step-grandmothers. We are all mothers-in-law, and, in my case, I'm a stepmother-in-law. It can get complicated.

"Well I'm sick of it," Sally said, "I'm treated like a non-person by my son and his wife. In fact, I'm not allowed a say on anything. If I do, I can see them exchanging guarded looks. It's controlling. I feel constrained. I'm a social worker, so I know how not to intrude, but *anything* I say is perceived as interference. This leaves me nowhere to go, so I decided to air my concerns."

We listened in awe as she told us that she'd spoken separately with her son and her daughter-in-law to say, "We're all educated. A lot has been invested in your education – and mine – I'd hoped that we might all have the right to an intelligent and well-informed opinion. I'd like to enjoy your company."

Jen thought it a good move to separate them because she hadn't spoken to her son alone since he met his partner.

Her friend, Peggy, visiting from New Zealand, is the mother of four adult sons. She's gone on the front foot. As each son married, she gained a commitment from him to meet her once a month, alone, just for a catch-up.

Kathy demurred. "That wouldn't make any difference with my son because he just mouths his wife's opinions anyway. In fact, my daughter-in-law took me to one side to explain that her husband – my son – thinks that I don't respect his opinions. Funny he couldn't tell me that himself, isn't it? I wanted to say that if he ever has an opinion of his own, I'll try to respect it – but I didn't say anything. I just smile and nod these days. It keeps the peace."

"Hey! Remember what it was like when you were first married?" Sandra cut in. "You didn't want your in-laws around all the time, did you?"

Sally bridled, "But they want me around when they snap their fingers and call for help at short notice. In fact, I've got granny guilt today. My son just rang to ask if I would look after his three-year-old, who's sick. I said no. I'm speaking at a conference on Friday, and I don't want to catch whatever my granddaughter's got. In any case, I was just about to leave for the gym."

In fact, she'd already arrived at the gym, and we were in the locker room getting changed for our aqua class. I noticed that some younger women were taking an interest in our conversation. One of them interjected.

"Well I'd be upset if my mother-in-law wouldn't help out with a sick child if I had to get to work." However, Sally's daughter-in-law wasn't in paid employment. She was at home with a baby and just wanted rid of the sick toddler for the day.

By now, Sally was in full flight, "In any case, I resent that she always gets my son to ring with any requests that might be unreasonable. It puts a wedge between us."

I once read a story written by the mother of a transgender child who wanted to transition from girl to boy. It bothered the mother that now she would never be the preferred grandmother. Until I read that I didn't know that 'preferred grandmother' was a thing. Maybe I should have done because my mother always said she didn't want sons – only daughters. This was just as well because she had four girls. Her proverbial rationale was that 'Your daughter's your daughter for all of your life, but your son's your son till he takes a wife.'

Ailsa and Sally's sons are now husbands, so, understandably, their family of marriage was their first priority. Of course, Ailsa and Sally didn't expect to live in their son's pockets, in part because they still have their own marriages to nurture, but where were their sons when the behaviour of their wives was just plain and simply infantile, rude or aggressive? Must the onus always be on mothers-in-law to smile, nod, and tolerate it?

"You're on the scrap heap, Lynne. Get used to it."

This blunt advice from UK friend Brian signalled the message that parents of adult kids must learn to let go. I was once asked what I thought about my adult son. I replied that I think he's an excellent husband and father.

"Then you've done your job. You can let go now."

Actually, I let go a long time ago. In fact, I left home before my kids. They were aged twenty-two and twenty when I was offered (and took) a promotional position at an interstate university. My husband refused to come with me, so I left the whole family in Perth and began five years of a commuting marriage. So I found it particularly irksome to be told that I must let go of the apron strings. Firstly, I've found that adult kids retie the strings as often as they need to with requests for help, even though they want the help on a no-strings-attached basis. The other thing is that you don't actually stop being a mum just because your kids are in an adult relationship.

An overseas friend, Pauline, found it very hard to let go when her son became mentally ill and her daughter-in-law (now his next-of-kin) kept pushing for challenging, controversial and possibly damaging treatment. As his mother, she was opposed to the treatment, but she couldn't do anything about it. This made me stop and think: What if intervention on behalf of your adult child is necessary, as in domestic violence situations? It's just so difficult to make sense of all of this.

In Ailsa and Sally's cases, they each worry about their son's happiness and wellbeing. They can see that the young men are made miserable by the family tensions. As it transpired, in Sally's case (and possibly Ailsa's too), they may be dealing with mental health problems. Letting go doesn't seem like an ideal solution. They love their sons and want to support them, which is a difficult balancing act when support is seen as interference. Sally, the social worker, sought professional mediation – a round table family discussion.

"How was your son in that situation?" I asked.

"He just looked miserable," she replied.

Eventually, he split from his first wife. This hasn't really solved anything because Sally now has only limited access to her grandchildren.

Ailsa also tried to reconcile with her son and his family. On one occasion, she travelled overseas to see him and his family, but her son prevaricated. He wouldn't even cooperate in making arrangements to meet, and it quickly became apparent that no such arrangements would be in the city where he lived. They did eventually get together, and Ailsa took him out to dinner, where he told her that his wife, also a lawyer, was jealous of his mum.

"Stop, please," said Ailsa, "I can't do anything about that. That's about her own feelings of insecurity. It would be nice to get a hearing about my point of view. I've tried my best. I've told you that all I ever wanted was a close relationship with your wife. Please tell her that."

She assumes he never did because her overtures to invite them for Christmas and birthdays have been rebuffed at every point ever since. I'm not sure if that's better or worse than a daughter-in-law in my family who specialised in arriving two or three hours late for family Christmas functions. Maybe it would have been better not to come at all.

It's understandable that people in adult partnerships want to build their own lives, but the need for autonomy risks drawing boundaries that are difficult to negotiate. Rachel doesn't dare buy clothes for her two granddaughters.

"If I do, I find them in the charity box soon afterwards."

When she babysat her granddaughters for the day, she was reprimanded by her son for taking them to a shopping centre without permission because the parents need to know exactly where their daughters are at all times, even when in their grandmother's care. She accepted the slap on the wrist but was astonished a few days later when her son told her that when the girls go to their other grandmother's place, it's grandma's rules. He had no insight into the double standards he applied to his own mother.

I met a shop assistant a few years ago, and the protracted retail processes gave her a chance to explain her distress about a family situation. Her daughter-in-law was obliging her to have a whooping cough injection, even though the grandmother actually had whooping cough as a child. She thought she had immunity. She refused.

As a consequence, she wasn't allowed to hold the child until it was six months old, and, even then, she had to wear rubber gloves and a face mask. I wonder what the anti-vaxxers of the COVID era would make of this situation.

I encountered the same issue when my granddaughter was born. I thought I was immune because I had whooping cough when I was four. I can remember the awful feeling of not being able to get air – I wouldn't want that for Elsie. Anyway, I checked with my doctor and she advised getting a jab, which I did. It seemed the reasonable thing to do.

But mothers-in-law don't operate in a reasonable context. They don't get the chance to negotiate meanings and boundaries in the circumstances of their own lives. Their course is pre-set by negative social stereotypes. Mother-in-law jokes: You can Google them – whole pages of them. Try these:

I have a soft spot for my mother-in-law. It's out in the garden behind the garage;

I haven't spoken to my mother-in-law for two years. We haven't quarrelled. I just don't like to interrupt her;

How many mothers-in-law does it take to change a light globe? Just one: She just holds it up there and waits for the world to revolve around her.

And we all just laugh because this is what we expect mothers-in-law to be like. So I searched online for father-in-law jokes and didn't find anything – nor jokes about daughters-in-law or sons-in-law.

I once read a study about Bethnal Green, in the East End of London. It described close-knit communities living in tenement housing. Mother-daughter ties bound the community together across generations. When a young woman announced she was to be married, her mum would 'speak for' her to the rent-man to ensure nearby accommodation. This meant the son-in-law was pulled into the orbit of his wife's family – and this was a source of tension. This was the origin of many of the music hall jokes and stereotypes about mothers-in-law that persist today, but I bet you didn't hear the one about the mother-in-law who regularly looked after her grandkids, provided financial help to her adult kids, and was then left on her own on Christmas Day. Nobody laughed about that.

I repeated some of these in-law stories to a neighbour of mine. She just got annoyed. In her opinion, these women should stop complaining and just get on with their own lives. Well, that's exactly what's recommended in a book that Ailsa suggested I read when I was rejected by my stepkids (that's an in-law relationship). It's called 'Done with the Crying.' It draws on the stories of thousands of parents estranged from their adult kids. Basically, the book advises: If you can't change your adult kids or their spouses, then you can change your response to the situation. I'd go one step further: if I'm a non-person and if nobody cares if I live or die (except possibly for inheritance purposes), then this holds a lot of freedom.

The words of an old pop song ring in my ears. Now, I can 'do what I want to do and be what I want to be. Yeah!!'

Making sense of blended families

It was both unnecessary and a portent that Lyall and I wrote many letters to each other about his children before we married. It seemed unnecessary because we'd already spent a lot of time together as a de facto blended family in the two years before I went to study in London from 1978 to 1979, so I thought I knew how things might be if I married Lyall. It was a portent because we were to become a family of letter writing as both Lyall and I struggled to build a blended family.

When I first met Lyall, I was intrigued that he had custody of his four children – the 'Big Kids,' as we came to call them. I soon discovered that he'd defended his own divorce case in 1973. This was remarkable because, in those days, it would have been quite unusual for a father to get custody, especially without a lawyer. As I understand it, he won because he was the sole applicant.

By the time I started going out with Lyall in

1976, one daughter had already chosen to live with her mother. When we married in 1979, two of his children remained living with us and continued to do so until they were twenty-one and seventeen, respectively. We didn't have fortnightly or monthly breaks when they might have visited their mother. Visits were pretty much birthdays, Christmas and school holidays, except when we took the kids camping around Australia.

I appreciated that the children who remained living with Lyall were welcoming of me. However, I quickly discovered that Lyall wasn't big on the niceties of family life. He told me that he'd sunk as low as taking the kids to the shops on Christmas Eve to get a Mars bar because he hadn't bought them any presents.

The house was chaotic. Lyall kept up to date with the laundry – just. There was a permanent pile of clean laundry on the divan in the family room from which the kids extracted clothes as they needed them. One of his daughters told the story of the nuns at her primary school, who took her to one side and ironed her dress because it was so creased. But Lyall did his best in a context in which he received no child support.

After we married in 1979, things were good. I remember being astonished at how much my stepdaughters confided in me.

"I wouldn't have told my mother things like that," I commented to Lyall on one occasion.

"Well that's the point. You're not their mother. It's a big-sister role, isn't it?" he replied. And that's the role I took.

Perth friend Val recently reflected on my approach to step-parenting. She has a Goldilocks impression that I got it about right. I didn't step in too far, but I tried to get the context right for us all to interact positively. This meant significant catering for the many family get-togethers and considerable planning for family holidays and outings. Their mother lived in Perth, and I had no desire to usurp her role. I just wanted to establish a good Lynne-type relationship with them. Most of all, I made a promise to myself to keep Lyall and his father in touch with all the kids and to build a blended family with the children we planned to have.

Generally, I did the ordinary stuff of parenting, which Lyall described in a letter to his son in 2011.

After she joined our family, she worked

with me to organise family trips to the Eastern States for you all. She shopped, cooked and cleaned for us all, while you finished your education, and during your early years of work. Imagine, now that you have a family of your own, what it would mean to take on a ready-made family as she did. She facilitated your European trip with introductions, ideas and money from us both. She gave her all.

I also did a lot of what Janina calls the 'emotional s**t work' of blended family life, including when Lyall's kids started to have their own children. Lyall was a strong advocate of breastfeeding, so he became quite concerned when one of his daughters struggled with feeding her first baby. She was at the point of considering bottle-feeding. He phoned me at work and asked if I'd call past her place on my way home to discuss the matter. Of course, I would, but my own kids were still young, and I also wanted to get home to them after a long day at work.

I have one erstwhile friend who repeatedly accused me of looking after my step-kids to the point that I neglected my own. It was an unhelpful observation, but there may have been a kernel of truth in it. I can also remember driving between the hospital, where my father-in-law lay dying, and the children's hospital, just up the road where my toddler son, Sammy, had been admitted with a serious asthma attack. I concluded, ruefully, that my situation was a quintessential definition of middle age – sandwiched between two hospitals and caring for the generations on either side of me.

Something must have gone right in our blended family because, years later, one of my step-daughters came round for a drink, and chatted about how difficult things had been when her parents divorced. She concluded: "Then you came along, Lynne, and everything was alright."

Even at school, she'd worked out some answers for friends who patronised her with commiserations about being the child of divorced parents. She told them she was lucky. She had four parents: a dad, a mum, a step-mum, and a step-dad. I agreed with her. My narrative was that we had successfully blended a family that was good enough for everyone. And that's all we needed to be – good enough.

There are many stories about what went wrong – far too many. There were angry phone calls in 2016 about a divorce that happened in 1973. Wild and unsubstantiated accusations that I was into elder abuse when I cared for Lyall and dramatic moments when adult children split from their father. This is why we became a family of letters. Nobody would listen or talk, so writing seemed the only means of setting things right.

There was the letter that Lyall's daughter wrote to him after choosing to live with her mother when she was about sixteen. This was before we married.

Then came the letter he wrote to her when her wedding arrangements made it impossible for him to attend.

After that came the letter he wrote to his son, who chose to split with Lyall, blaming me in the process.

Finally, in a bid to be heard, I wrote 'The Story of Us' because I was sick of being vilified and ignored. I wanted to use storytelling to present my point of view. It didn't work; it just served to infuriate everybody. In fact, one of Lyall's kids dismissed my letter as rubbish.

How do I tell the story of the demise of blended family life? The problem is that the devil is in the detail. Yet rehearsal of that detail risks sounding churlish. So the focus shifts, as it often did for me when I lived in a blended family, from the behaviour of others to my reaction.

A few friends have told me that I shouldn't tell such stories at all because it's like washing dirty linen in public – muck-raking as it's sometimes called in social research circles. But this gets close to censorship. How can women break the silence and tell their stories of abuse, bullying or marginalisation if doing so opens them up to accusations of petulance or indiscretion?

In contrast, many have appreciated my open discussion of issues that seriously affect their lives. Given the rate of divorce these days, blended families and step-parenting are among those issues. Much depends on how the stories are told, and, as an experienced social researcher, I've concluded that it's best to focus on the issues and the behaviour – not the people. For my part, I see storytelling as cathartic (not necessarily therapeutic). I was a great admirer of Archbishop Tutu, who understood the human importance of his Truth and Reconciliation Commission. It couldn't actually fix the problems in South Africa when Apartheid ended, but Tutu understood that people needed to be heard before they could reshape their lives in the renewed South Africa. He saw it as restorative justice, and I need a bit of that.

The trick is to select stories that best illustrate the dynamics of our blended family and let them speak for themselves. With this in mind, less can mean more. Small stories can 'speak yards,' as my Irish friend, Kathleen, used to say. Take, for example, the time when Lyall was in hospital after three operations in one week. He was wired up like a Christmas tree and barely compos mentis. Two of his adult children had been to Sunday lunch nearby. So they decided to visit their dad with their families – at their convenience. Nine of them crowded into his room. After that, they didn't visit him again during the two weeks he was in hospital.

This was when my friends started the 'You would have thought' conversations. They instantly saw the implications of this relatively unimportant story:

"You would have thought they'd develop a

roster and spread out the visits to keep him company," or,

"You would have thought they'd let you know when they visited to maybe save you a visit or two."

Well, yes, you would have thought.

Some incidents were severe, and met the criteria for bullying and gaslighting, so the 'You would have thought' comments became shorthand conversations among my friends.

- "You would have thought, wouldn't you, that after giving her US$1000 of your own money to help with travel, she might arrive at your Christmas event with a present for you as well as the one she gave her Dad?"
- "You would have thought, wouldn't you, that if you and Lyall raised them, they might invite you for Christmas more than once each in the thirty-nine years you were married?"
- "You would have thought, wouldn't you, that they would offer to help with Lyall's end-of-life care?"
- "You would have thought, wouldn't you,

that Lyall and you would be invited to more than one of his daughters' weddings?"

- "You would have thought, wouldn't you that, if they chose to re-gift, they would, at the very least, not give you back the present that you just gave them?"

There were portents of difficult behaviour even before I married Lyall. I called by one evening and his fifteen-year-old daughter turned her back on me in a noticeably deliberate move. It was a small thing. My assessment was that I risked being used as a scapegoat because she wanted to leave Lyall to go to live with her mother. She loved her Dad, and it was a difficult move for her to make. Using Dad's girlfriend as an excuse offered an easy way out.

I didn't want any part of this, so I told Lyall that he would have to visit me at my place until things worked themselves out. When his daughter did make the move, she wrote a letter to Lyall in which she said, "Keep going out with Lynne. She's a nice person." It looks like my assessment of the situation was right on the money.

This same daughter was the first to get married.

I suggested to Lyall that it might smooth her way if we hosted an engagement party and invited her mother and her family. There had been only limited communication between Lyall and his former wife, so I hoped that an engagement party might encourage them to work together as parents. It didn't. It quickly became apparent that Lyall was to be excluded from the traditional role of a father, especially making a speech. He wasn't prepared to sit at the back of the church looking as if he'd had nothing to do with his daughter since conception, so this occasioned the first of Lyall's letters to his family. He was not at his daughter's wedding, and they were estranged for some time before I found her crying in the corridor of the hospital where Grandpa Jack lay dying. I went to her, tried to bridge the gap, and she and Lyall were slowly reconciled.

Their relationship never blossomed as it might have done. How could it? In many ways, things got worse over the years. There was a lot of awkwardness, considerable exclusive behaviour, and even complaints about the gifts I bought for birthdays and Christmas. One year, when Lyall was already dependent and disabled, she invited all members of the family to an Easter Sunday BBQ, including our son, Sam, and his family, who were actually living at our house at that time. That is … they invited all members of the family except Lyall and me. We were left alone, as we were on many other supposedly festive occasions. I asked Lyall to speak with her about it. She wrote an email of apology, explaining that the invitation list had snowballed and that deliberate exclusion was not intended.

If it was a sin of omission, it happened more than once.

On another occasion, I invited her and her family for a restaurant meal to celebrate her birthday. She selected the restaurant. I arrived, with Lyall in a wheelchair, to find that the restaurant had closed for good. In addition, she'd never changed my phone number, even though I'd kept her informed. So she hadn't been able to make contact with me. Sins of omission these may have been, but the end result was that I was stuck with a hungry eighty-year-old bloke in a wheelchair in the wind and horizontal rain, waiting for a taxi to go home. This was well past being a bloody nuisance. As usual, Lyall said nothing.

The second wedding in the family was in the early 1990s. Some of the same tensions re-emerged, but this daughter was clear that her father, who raised her, would be at her wedding and that he would make the customary father-of-the-bride speech. I thought the bride did well in trying to give a role to everyone, including me.

At the wedding reception, I was approached by her maternal aunt and asked to go to the ladies' loo because the bride was crying. Of course, but, looking around the room, I did wonder why her mother, her aunt, her great-aunt, her cousins or sisters were not there for her. After all, I was just the step-mum. It transpired she'd had a row with her mother, after which they didn't speak for about five years. I don't know who was to blame, nor do I think it matters. The point is, it happened, and it became another point of tension in the family.

Lyall's other daughter, from his first marriage, drove a truck through these events. We didn't know what her problems were, but I encouraged Lyall to talk with her. He rang and was subject to a lengthy tirade. He was ashen-faced when he sat down. I never found out what had been said.

Whatever the subject matter of the conversation, she was set to split from the family. This was the early 1990s, and we never saw her again. As far as I'm aware, she didn't speak to anybody much after that, including her mother and her sisters, or my children, her half-siblings.

My friends and UK family were agog at all this nonsense. Here we were in the early 1990s with two of Lyall's children estranged from him, despite our best efforts to build a blended family. I started to go on international lecture programs from the early 1990s forward because I was winning teaching awards that financed my travel expenses. These trips were essential for me, not only for career reasons but also because they gave me opportunities to catch up with my UK and Canadian family and friends. I desperately needed to keep a part of me that was my own, and that part was still in the UK. I also needed to be with people who were on my side. I felt like a non-person in the Hunt family, and I saw myself as being too caught up in the 'Huntness' of things. It was an unrewarding place to be. Life with Lyall and our own two kids was good and solid, but the price we all paid in our blended family was becoming too high.

My international lecture programs were organised some twelve months in advance. It was complex planning involving up to ten universities with several workshops and meetings at each. So, when Lyall's son let his dad know about his wedding plans, at only six months' notice, I was already scheduled to be away on the set date. It was too difficult to cancel, so I went. I may have been subject to some opprobrium, but I didn't think it was too much of a problem. My status as a step-mum had already been clearly signalled, and a step-mother-in-law was one step down from that.

Lyall and our kids went to what seemed to be a nicely inclusive wedding, in which our fourteen-year-old son, Sam, read out cards and telegrams, with a maturity that exceeded his years. So there were still attempts, all-round, to keep the family chugging along. At least Lyall went to this wedding without apparent tension.

Lyall always had a special relationship with his eldest son that I sought to encourage. When my kids were little, my thinking was that I'd done lots of travel before I married, yet Lyall had been locked into domesticity. It was time for Lyall to have some fun and some quality time with his son. So I cared for our babes alone so that they could travel together. I also assisted in his son's travels on other occasions. We gave him money for his first big trip to Europe, and I arranged free accommodation for him in London at my friend's house. I also spent time helping him to plan his trip, offering him information and encouragement to spend time on a kibbutz in Israel, which he did. I hoped that all this would be seen by him as positive input into his life. It was certainly intended to be.

Later, I gave significant help in the finalisation of his PhD thesis, for which he praised me, saying I'd given him more assistance than his university supervisor. Yet, within a short period of time, and without apparent cause, he walked through our house deliberately not speaking to me. This is when I said, emphatically, "I don't think so!"

Lyall had always let difficult behaviours pass without comment. My own pretty normal need to be treated with respect and dignity had been ignored too often. It was now 2011, so I started to force the issue.

"Lyall, I have put up with a lot of crap, but your children can't walk through our house and ignore me. It's just unacceptable."

Lyall tried to discuss things but he was told there would be no further contact because "Lynne is manic and difficult."

This was bewildering. Perhaps a clue to understanding lies in another comment. "I love you, Dad, but I have other family responsibilities now." The implication was that we were dealing with increasing complexity that now included in-laws as well as blended family issues.

And so, Lyall wrote another letter to the family.

"You say you love me but rarely visited me in hospital and, in my first week home, you were reluctant to enter my house and to speak to Lynne. Your behaviour is inexplicable to me."

Lyall was never able to speak with his son again.

None of us saw this split coming. There had certainly been no argument. In my view, my relationship with Lyall's son had always been as good as it could be. Of all Lyall's children, he was the most assiduous at keeping in touch with his Dad. He called by weekly with his kids, and relationships were amicable.

So, by 2011, all but one of the 'big kids' had distanced themselves from Lyall. In most cases, the process was the same – disengagement and increasingly unacceptable behaviour. There was never any discussion – no dealing with issues. We never knew what the problem was, nor were we provided an opportunity to resolve matters and rebuild family life. When I tried, I was told that my problem was that I needed to talk about things.

According to one of Lyall's daughters, my main problem was that I wanted to drag up forty years of grudges. I must confess, I have been tempted, but what I really wanted was to be heard. So it was my turn to write a letter, which I called 'The story of us.'

Later, when things got particularly difficult between me and one of Lyall's daughters, I even suggested mediation and counselling, but she'd been down that road before when she quarrelled with her mother-in-law. She classified mediation as a process in which things are said that can't be unsaid. Much later, she emailed me and all the family to tell me that I'd stolen from her father in the last years of his life and that this was tantamount to elder abuse. So, I can understand why she might be apprehensive about feedback on her behaviour.

"What? You mean she's quarrelled with her mother, her older sister, her mother-in-law and now you?" asked a friend, who is also a counsellor. "Not too difficult to draw conclusions there, is it?"

It was sad that things turned out as they did. I felt that I was living in a very dark soap opera. Kafka's trial might also serve as a metaphor because we never knew what was happening or where the next blow would come from. Lyall and I had given much, but, in the end, he was defeated by the accumulated s**t of his life. This included being abandoned by his parents, the unknown implications of the 'seventh child', a divorce, and the behaviour of his children. Towards the end of his life, all he could say, head in hands, was, "It's all so unfair." His observation referred to me, but it applied to both of us.

Lyall was a very sick man in the eight years I looked after him, so it was always a risk that he might die whilst I was away on a respite break. I couldn't have gone away without accepting this risk, and I explained it to his daughter (also alternate Guardian), ad nauseam. I made all the necessary funeral arrangements in consultation with him and kept his kids fully informed.

Lyall did die when I was away in 2018. The funeral parlour contacted me in alarm because one of his daughters wanted the more traditional flowers and coffin funeral that Lyall had specifically rejected. I had to insist on the implementation of his wishes, but the anger generated played forward to the celebration of his life that I'd organised. The attendance at this event was bizarre. Only four of his six children were there. The most loyal of his daughters was not. But the daughter who hadn't spoken to him since the early 1990s was. Only one of his twelve grandchildren came to farewell him. His sister flew in to be there, but she and Lyall hadn't spoken since about 1980. None of them spoke to me on the day. Thus Lyall died with his blended family in tatters.

Lyall's consistent approach to life was never to worry about things over which he had no control, and this extended to providing me with support in our blended family. He didn't attempt to deal with the behaviour directed at us both, or me in particular. He didn't comment when we were left out of family functions. He didn't even murmur when I'd organised Christmas events, and they arrived three hours late or with a present for him and not for me.

Speaking with friends, I've since discovered that this kind of inept response is quite common for natural fathers dealing with blended family issues. So much so that I thought of writing a story called 'Where was Cinderella's father?' because I thought she got a raw deal from her Dad. However, a five-year-old pointed out that Cinderella's Dad had died, so that metaphor didn't work, except to establish that Cinderella's story has done a lot of damage to step-mothers.

In any case, understanding our blended family requires a focus on the behaviours and not necessarily on the natural father's reaction. Had there been no poor behaviour, Lyall would not have had to avoid dealing with it.

When I was living through all this, my UK friend, Brian, emailed to say he'd been listening to a BBC Four program about step-monsters. He thought I might be interested. I bridled against this title, thinking that it was yet another discussion predicated on assumptions about wicked stepmothers.

"No, Lynne," he replied, "This was about the behaviour of step-children." Well, about bloody time!

My son's memories of blended family life are very different to mine. It was more of a non-event for him because Lyall's seventeen-year-old daughter left home shortly after Ruth was born in 1982, and his eldest son left home not long after Sam was born in 1985. After that, we were just the four of us, Lynne, Lyall, Ruth and Sam. This is all that Sam knew. Of course, I continued with blended family gatherings – about a dozen events a year, and, much to Lyall's amusement, I would chat on the phone with my stepdaughters for several hours at a time. He would bring me a cup of tea on the grounds that some husbands had found the skeletal remains of their wives – dead from dehydration on the end of the phone – the jaw bone still moving as if in conversation.

At that stage, my narrative about blended family life was that I had fulfilled the good big sister role with my step-kids and that they'd been affectionate older siblings to my kids. When their own children arrived on the scene, then my two, Ruth and Sam, were great with the little ones playing cricket and swimming in our pool together.

It seemed to me that goodwill had rocked down through the generations. We'd built a blended family with five out of six kids. The 'big-kids' started their own families, and our blended family shifted shape as Lyall and I found new roles as grandfather and step-grandmother. I organised Easter-egg hunts, birthday and Christmas parties, and steam train outings for us all, and Lyall arranged family BBQ's in the bush. Life was good, despite the tensions of weddings and Christmas and the now permanent absence of Lyall's eldest daughter.

The manner in which Lyall's son separated from his father, using me as an excuse without due cause or adequate reason was, quite frankly, a shock – and very painful. It was bewildering, and it undermined the sense that I'd made of blended family life and my sense of self. Was I really that awful? All this occurred when I was exhausted caring for Lyall single-handedly, and I was left feeling isolated, unsupported and angry.

Subsequently, my upset and distress became the cause celebre for the failure of the family. Even worse, my daughter, Ruth, had been willingly co-opted into the narratives of her half-siblings. One day, she found me crying in my study after I'd experienced the customary Christmas rejection – left alone with a disabled and demented octogenarian. When Ruth entered my study, I said, quite simply, "I'm sorry, Ruth. It's just that things are very difficult for me here."

She immediately started to yell at me (which had never happened before), telling me that I was coming between her and her sisters. She'd obviously been wound-up about something. Had I ever found my own mother in tears, for whatever reason, I cannot imagine that I would have shouted at her. Nor would I have chosen to blame the victim for family discord.

Ruth inherited the BRCA1 gene from Lyall. She had breast cancer and, at the beginning of 2020, her prognosis was poor. She asked the army (where she worked) if she might return to Perth to live out her days. She arrived with her partner, who repeatedly told me that "things must be done Ruth's way."

As it transpired, 'Ruth's way' was to position her half-sister in a matriarchal role, excluding me and marginalising her brother, Sam. At the party that Ruth organised, four days before she died, she asked her half-sister to give a speech. No mention was made of her brother, Sam, or me, in that speech.

By now, I was accustomed to exclusion, but I was surprised at the level of Sam's hurt and anger. He's normally a laid-back, even-tempered kind of bloke. Even so, he responded when Ruth's husband asked him to organise the wake after her funeral.

He wanted to organise the wake as his final gift to his sister. His half-siblings didn't help. Thank goodness for Sam's wife, Jane, and her brother, Mark, who stepped up to the plate. It was actually touch-and-go that the 'big-kids' would even come to the wake. Two out of four did.

Only one of their number acknowledged me at the funeral. It was one of Lyall's grandsons. He gave me a hug, and I asked if he would come to the wake.

"I don't know," he replied. "I'll have to go and see what the power-play is."

Unbelievable! I'm standing next to the conveyor belt that had just transported my daughter's coffin to the flames of the crematorium, and I'm being talked to about family power plays. I'm sure that Lyall's kids could document things they thought I'd done wrong over the years, but, in the abstract, nothing warrants this behaviour towards any mother whose daughter has just died.

Some of Ruth's paperwork came to me to sort out after her death, and I found the speech that her half-sister had made at Ruth's twenty-first birthday party in 2003. This story can tell itself through excerpts from the speech. She spoke first about Ruth's birth.

"Imagine my joy at being seventeen years older and having this young mind and body to manipulate," but, "By the time the eighties ended, Ruth was eight-years-old and, of course, wise enough and experienced enough to question my judgement and start to manipulate me."

This extended to a discussion of her own children, so Ruth now "had seven [and] eight-year-old minds to manipulate."

She also observed that Ruth had "inherited the Hunt gene that tells us we are always right, we always have the high moral ground, and everyone else is stupid."

I was horrified to read this speech, made some sixteen years earlier. It doesn't express the values with which Lyall and I had tried to build a blended family. I really hadn't realised that the gaslighting had been going on for so long.

After one of my respite breaks, I chatted with a Perth friend, Peter, telling him that I'd had time to think. I'd concluded that the behaviour I'd experienced in my blended family was simply wrong, in and of itself. It wasn't about me, or Lyall, or causes, or reasons.

"Yes," he replied, "but you've had to absorb it for decades."

Seeing my distress, friends tried to help by offering reasons. A number of friends suggested that they were all jealous of me. Although it was meant kindly, I wasn't sure what to do with this analysis. Perhaps sit in the corner sucking my thumb lest I upset Lyall's kids by my mere success.

School friend, Sue, wrote to ask, "Have you been blended with a family of varying degrees of seriousness on the autistic spectrum? Or a personality disorder? To an outsider, they truly do seem to behave in atypical ways."

Yes, Sue, I have thought that, and I think it could apply to more than one person in the family, including my own daughter. It's possible now to retrofit behaviours to the criteria, but, in those days, I didn't have the knowledge that would have led to this conclusion. I was aware of a complete lack of empathy, the attribution of all blame to me, and a consistent pattern of shooting the messenger when I tried to work things out. The extent to which this might have been bullying, gaslighting, or neurodivergent behaviour is still beyond my skills to analyse. What I do know is that it happened and that it seriously affected my well-being, my marriage and my relationship with my own kids.

Could things have been different?

Over coffee one day, I listened to a friend as she described her attempts to get her step-family together for a Christmas party. As I listened, I saw with complete clarity that all Anne had to do was stop trying. I also realised that the same applied to me. But, as one young friend put it to me in an email, "You were managing a spider's web of relationships, all tangled and intertwined by the winds of time. What else could you have done, realistically, other than what you did? The older children made their decisions, and all you could do is react to them."

I think things could have been different if Lyall had set some limits to behaviour early on, but, put quite simply, I think that our vision of blended family life just wasn't shared.

Making sense of the lifecycle: Old age

I recently found some letters my mother wrote when she was in her seventies. In one, she told of a family get-together in Devon when her brother, Reg, gazed in wonder at his many siblings.

"How did we get to be so old?" he asked.

Yet, to me, Uncle Reg always was old. It was his natural state of being. It just wasn't mine until the COVID pandemic hit and my baby-boomer generation was forced to identify as old because we were deemed vulnerable. We had to self-isolate. If we were lucky, our adult kids started to look after us, offering to do our shopping and offering, with even greater alacrity, not to visit lest they transmit the virus.

I rang Mum when she turned seventy, thinking that we all adjust to growing older, but I was wrong.

"I'm still me," she protested. "I'm still Alma."

In that brief statement, she made me see her as the accumulation of the little girl; the young mother; the gardener; the traveller; the craftsperson; and the battler who raised four girls virtually on her own.

Like Mum, I didn't feel particularly old when I turned seventy. In fact, I celebrated in the UK with a lovely pub lunch and, unbelievably, a drink at the champagne bar in Waitrose. The latter was a tease because I didn't believe a supermarket would actually have a champagne bar. It did.

I felt liberated when I turned seventy. I'd reached my three score years and ten: Fair shake of the tree and all that. I've had my innings, so I felt that everything, now, was a bonus. I threw myself into my septuagenarian years, during which I've published the second edition of my textbook, nominated deserving friends for awards, completed small consultancies for universities, built a house, and travelled widely. So when my grandson, Thomas, asked if I liked being my age, I answered yes, because if I were younger, I wouldn't have done all the things I've done, and I wouldn't have lovely grandchildren like him, Oli and Elsie.

In my retirement, I've taken to circulating jokes and little homilies, like the one about the elderly Clint Eastwood, who said, 'I just get up every morning and go out. And I don't let the old man in.'

One friend replied, bemoaning that he'd just spent time with a bunch of old friends who really had let the old man in. He'd determined that he would continue to think young. But it's becoming increasingly clear to me that it isn't just a matter of mind over body because the mind itself might retire. I'm sure you know the joke:

Doctor: "I've got good news and bad news. The bad news is you've got Alzheimer's."

Patient: "What's the good news?"

Doctor: "You'll forget you've got it."

But Alzheimer's isn't funny because relationships have memories. We make love, we quarrel, and we build meaning together. Conversations between friends, lovers and family members are based on a shared history that enables us to speak in shorthand and laugh at jokes that aren't even funny just because they're part of our shared intimacy. Legendary country and western singer, Glen Campbell, entered the charts with the final song of his career, 'I'm not gonna miss you.' How could he miss his loved ones as the ravages of Alzheimer's took over his life? He will no longer know who they are.

As Perth friend Vince said, with great poignancy, "What can you do when you have no yesterdays?" Maybe you just want no future.

A university friend of mine, Lyn, was diagnosed with early-onset Alzheimer's. The last time I saw her in the UK, she was in her late sixties, and she told me that she would now welcome death. For my part, I now have to communicate through her partner, John. Otherwise, I wouldn't even know if she's dead or alive.

Some memories do stick. When my mother was ninety-five, a number of mini-strokes had diminished her memory and most of her power of speech. So I conducted soliloquies in which I chatted with her about dogs we'd had, houses we'd lived in, and places to which she'd travelled. Somewhat courageously, I also rehearsed the names of her nine siblings – or at least I thought I had.

"Harold," she exclaimed when I reached the end of the list, inadvertently missing one of her brothers. She'd remembered, and she was listening intelligently. It was lovely to feel that we were having a conversation and that it wasn't just a soliloquy.

Recently, I sent out on my 'joke email circuit' a photo of a group of seventy-year-olds re-composing a picture of themselves as teenagers. I asked the question: Do women age better than men? University friend, Mac, was quick to respond.

"Hair today, gone tomorrow! I think it's totally unfair that many men lose their hair, and very few women do. God must be a woman."

He went on to tell me that he and his wife had their sons and grandkids over for Christmas and that they were now "Completely knackered! Much as we love them, we don't have the energy to keep up these days."

This confirmed my re-evaluation of myself. I had a knee replacement in 2020 and woke from the anaesthetic to find that I had a new knee and a fractured L1 vertebra, sustained during the operation. This knocked me back a lot. I still have to take regular rests to get through the day because my back aches if I do too much. I've done my best (almost). I'm back at the gym (sometimes). I walk around 'my' lake, and I swim in my backyard pool, but I still don't have much stamina. I've been blaming the injury, but now I realise that, like Mac, I may no longer have the energy to keep up.

Health issues start to dominate in older years. A UK friend came over to Australia for New Year 2022 to visit his son in Sydney. He's always been a keen sportsman, so I WhatsApped to ask if he planned to go to the test cricket that was on in Sydney at that time.

"No," he replied, "It's not worth it. I've got cataracts, and I wouldn't be able to see the ball."

That's sad. His hearing is going as well, but, on a positive note, he has blue tooth hearing aids, which make chatting by phone much easier than face-to-face.

At about the same time, Perth friend, Vince, rang to tell me that his eyesight – already poor – had taken a turn for the worse. He can no longer read emails unless they're in large font, and even that takes time and a magnifying glass. This means that I can't send any more jokes. It's in ways like this I've found that social circles start to dwindle as we get older.

Awareness of old age dawns slowly. I think I was fifty-five when I first experienced a young woman standing on public transport to offer me her seat on the Tube train leaving Heathrow. Having just flown from Australia to London, I was grateful but also mortified. I've always been told that I look younger than my years, but clearly, that hasn't stopped me from looking old enough to need a seat. But maybe it wasn't that. It could just be that I was no longer accustomed to British courtesy.

Five years older than me, Liverpool Phil couldn't decide if it was good or bad that he was offered a seat on the bus by a pregnant woman. Perth friend, Janina, thinks that her awareness of old age (and mine) was thrust upon us because we both married older men, and we've had to face their health and ageing issues before our time. In reality, we're all old, so it's been a question of the young-old looking after the old-old.

I want to grow old disgracefully, but it isn't just a matter of what I think. Other people's stereotypes about 'little old ladies' can become self-fulfilling prophecies. Friends complain that they're treated like the invisible older woman.

They know that they're no longer attractive enough to turn heads, but, at the same time, they don't want to be pushed to the back of the queue in shops.

I used to teach about this stuff to student nurses using 'An Old Lady's Poem.' It was written by a woman who died in a geriatric ward in Scotland. She asked nurses what they see: Am I a cantankerous old woman, who dribbles, or am I a daughter, sister, wife, and mother? The poem finishes: "So open your eyes, nurses, open and see … Not a crabby old woman; look closer … see ME!!"

This poem is all over the internet, and I see that nurses have now written a rejoinder: Take a look at us as well. We'd love to spend time with you, but we're exhausted and overworked.

I couldn't tolerate the way my husband was treated when he was in hospital. They infantilised him with all their "darlings, dear and ducks" communication. I didn't react because I knew they were trying to show care. Just a few years later, when I had a fractured back, I finished up on the same ward that Lyall had been on. I also tolerated the endearments. I was in no position to argue. I was sky high on painkillers after my back had been fractured. It was called a rehab ward, but I already knew it was a geriatric ward and was oddly pleased when two ward orderlies breezed past the door looking in at me. I overheard one say to the other, "They're getting younger in here, aren't they?"

I had to tell myself to get a grip. "Heavens above, Lynne! Do you really feel flattered that you overheard that you look too young for a geriatric ward?"

There was no adjustment to old age evident in my neighbour in my two-bed ward. She was intent on raging into the dark night. A newly graduated nurse came in to ask us about our goals. I used to teach student nurses, so I wanted to help her to do her duty. I said that I wanted independence and to be able to walk without pain.

"Well, I want a glass of red and a cigarette," Marie growled.

The rite of passage to geriatric wards is the dementia test, but I was ready for them. I'd had eight years of practice when I cared for Lyall. I particularly dislike the questions about the day and date. It's very work-centric. It was easy when I went to aqua aerobics because we had a different instructor each day. So that coped with days of the week, if not the date, but it didn't help with public holidays. I was busy looking after Lyall when our dog, Lizzie, needed some routine attention at the vets, so I bustled off to get that job done. When it came to paying, I was completely blindsided by a $50 surcharge because it was a public holiday. I'd had no idea. I could have gone on any day – but I had to pay.

Lyall had to answer dementia questions during that extraordinary period when Australia had a swinging back door for prime ministers. They changed at an extraordinary rate.

"Whose Australia's prime minister," the nurse asked.

"That's hardly fair," I interjected, "No bugger in Australia knows that."

The requirement to count backwards from one hundred – in sevens – became a bit of a party game among my set of friends. I had a neat system that worked, but others felt they needed to swot up before they had to do their own dementia tests.

Maintaining dignity is a 'thing' in older years. My husband hated being in a nursing home. In fact, he became quite wily about trying to get out. He knows I like travelling, so when I visited him one day, he said, "I think we should go to Mauritius."

I couldn't believe it: "Lyall, you can barely get to the bathroom unaided. How are you going to get to Mauritius?"

He'd been a man of great intellect and didn't give in to old age lightly. Even when it was noticed that he was wearing two pairs of glasses at once, he rationalised it. Apparently, the lens of one wasn't quite fit for purpose, so he needed to correct the matter by wearing two pairs of glasses. He couldn't just say he didn't know what he was doing. It was the same when he fell over. He denied that he had. "I didn't fall. I sort of slithered, and I couldn't get up."

It was sad to see him struggling to maintain his sense of self, but these stories can have a funny side.

"William, that really is very funny."

Cheshire friend, William, face-timed to tell me a story about 'Granny' in his family. Her dentures had slipped from her mouth and fallen to the floor at the family's Christmas lunch. People didn't know how to react, which created a moment of hesitation and a window of opportunity for the dog, who got to the dentures first. William was full of concern and compassion as he told the story, and I struggled to contain my mirth.

There's a difference between being alone and being lonely. Widowed friends tell me that they positively welcome aloneness, but they lack intimacy and companionship. Point taken, but these things aren't necessarily available within marriage either.

Rosemarie told me a story about her neighbours. The husband was much older than his wife, who had a lengthy chat with him one day only to realise that he was dead and had been the whole time she'd been talking. So much for companionship. She was so used to non-response that she couldn't tell if he was dead or alive.

I have two male friends who continue to live in marriages well past their use-by date. In one case, they have a shared business, and, in the other, his wife had a chronic illness. In both cases, there are adult children. One of the men moved out, no longer able to carry the burden of chronic illness in a loveless marriage. He subsequently fell in love with a needy woman, and they had ferocious arguments. One night she threw a plate of spaghetti at him. What did he do? He rang his former wife, and she came to sort him out. They were still bonded, though living apart. That may mean as much as love in older years.

A widow of my acquaintance gets up at 3 am just to watch re-runs of 'Foyles War' on television, so that she can ogle the lead actor, but what she really wants is to have her husband back so that she can talk intimately: "I want to be able to say that we have a daughter with a mental illness and discuss how we cope."

Even though her friends give her a hearing when she worries about her kiddults, the fact is they are not their kids. Intimacy involves being concerned about the same issues and people. That kind of intimacy dies with your partner. This is irrevocable loneliness.

I was recently told that I look too fresh to be seventy-three.

"What's a seventy-three-year-old supposed to look like?" I asked.

It made me realise that expectations of old age are mostly negative. This was certainly true for me when I was asked to write for an online journal.

"Write about the ten best things about being

over fifty," the editor suggested.

"Are there ten best things?" I asked.

The suggestion seemed silly to me because I couldn't understand how ten new best things might suddenly emerge after the age of forty-nine. In any case, nobody ever asked me to think of ten good reasons for being over twenty or thirty. It struck me that we really do make a negative thing out of being old.

When I asked friends about their ten best things, I mostly got flippant answers like, "Being over fifty is better than the alternative," but that's not necessarily true, either. My mother died at ninety-five but prayed aloud for the Lord to take her immediately. Nobody wants to be sick and in pain for endless years. Nobody wants to suffer mental deterioration. Indeed, my thirty-seven-year-old son, Sam, shocked his work colleagues by saying that he wants to get to seventy, and that's it. I was seventy-three when he told me this story.

My baby-boomer generation grew up in 1960s Britain, and we're credited with a social and sexual revolution that is now playing forward to redefining old age. Seventy is the new sixty, in case you hadn't heard. The cards that friends send show that we can laugh at old age and resist stereotypes. My fiftieth birthday card from a university friend depicted a skinhead (bovver boy, punk rocker, Bogan) standing at a bus stop next to an old lady.

"Show us your tits," he commanded. So she lifted up the hem of her skirt.

We may be redefining old age, but gravity also has a say, as wise-woman Val commented after looking at herself in the mirror: "Who needs these things anymore? I might as well just throw them over my shoulder and forget about them."

Getting old and wondering who is looking back at you in the mirror has its compensations, as Janina noted, "It's a great relief to find that the 'judgmental anonymous other' has disappeared." That's alright for her to say: She still looks fantastic.

Artist friend, Felicity, didn't want to 'just be' in her old age. She wanted to grow old outrageously. So she grabbed a mirror – lobbed out her boobs, and started a series of nude self-portraits depicting the corporeal reality of her late fifties.

Friends have surprised me by becoming more outrageous as they grow older. Rosemarie now has her favourite birthday card pinned to the fridge, declaring that: 'the older I get, the more everyone can kiss my a**e.' Who would have thought that mild-mannered Rosemarie would arrive at this point in her early seventies?

"You're saving in your retirement,' an old friend observed. 'Shrouds don't have pockets! You should be spending the kids' inheritance!"

I was spending mine on travel until the COVID-19 pandemic hit in 2020. So, for the last two years. I've spent my money planning and building an ancillary dwelling (granny house) in my back garden. I designed it to disability standards, but I did get fed up with the constant talk about wide doors to allow for Lynne's wheelchair, which I don't yet possess. I had to accept it, though. It was a question of planning for the worst whilst building for the best that old age might bring.

I once wrote a piece about sex in the sixties, which was a spoof on the TV program called 'Sex in the City.' It was also a critique of attitudes about love and sex in older years. For the young, this is the stuff of smutty jokes: "I should warn you," the old woman said as she undressed, "I've got acute angina." "Just as well," he replied, "because your tits are bloody awful."

In reality, the feelings are all still there: "Of course, I've had yearnings over the years," said a single friend who'd found love in her sixties. "I just didn't think I'd find it with a woman." She's gloriously happy.

It seems that sexual urges may continue well past the mind's capacity to filter out inappropriate behaviour. My Perth friend, Vince, is a very proper gentleman who knows how to tell a good story. He recently had me crying with laughter as he told of visiting a bed-ridden friend in a twin-bed room in a nursing home. He was busy feeding her when he turned around to find an elderly male resident trying to get into bed with the other woman in the room.

"I'm sure that's not right," Vince pondered to himself.

Genuine love in old age can be a poignant affair. I was saddened by a news item I heard today. An elderly couple lived together for fifteen years in Queensland, but the woman became increasingly incapacitated, so her Westralian family took charge and relocated her to a nursing home on the other side of the country. He followed and took her from her nursing home, without permission, so that they could be together. Legally this is probably kidnapping, so he was arrested and charged. I hope the courts deal with him compassionately because it was an act of pure love. Yet love and caregiving is a volatile mix. For me, and at least two of my friends, caring for an increasingly depressed, angry and grumpy old man destroyed love. I did my best. I tried to keep him happy with holidays and outings, but there was little response. It was an emotionally unrewarding eight years.

For Lyn's partner, John, coping with her early-onset Alzheimer's challenged the lifetime of affection they'd shared. In his own words, "The mix of constant surprise and denial, with occasional apparent clarity and comprehension, is very wearing. But we are coping – somehow – together."

A Perth friend has just been given a poor prognosis, which we discussed over dinner one night. "I've never had the grand passion," she blurted out. "In the 1950s, we just got married to the nearest nice bloke."

Her first husband committed suicide. In her

forties, she teamed up with another man, who she threw out some twenty years later because he was grumpy and gave her no companionship. What was the point? She's eighty, has a poor prognosis, and passion is at the top of her mind. She has regrets as passionately as Edith Piaf had 'No regrets.'

Another friend, recently widowed, opened-up about how her seemingly good marriage had been marred by domestic violence and coercive control. Looking back, she now wishes that she'd left him and had relationships with other men.

"He was my first and only," she said. "I regret that."

Another friend, who's been a widow since she was in her forties, did take the plunge, but she ditched him pretty quickly. "We wanted different things out of life," she told me. "He wanted me to do his housework, and I didn't."

This makes me ponder if I really want to walk these byways again. The answer is no.

"Is that you? Are you still in Australia?" The email arrived unexpectedly. I hadn't seen him for thirty years, and I was hesitant to send a photo. Most of us like to be remembered the way we were. When I did send a picture, he replied, "You're still gorgeous!" I wasn't sure if the exclamation mark expressed surprise or enthusiasm, but for a moment, I felt young again.

Making sense of the lifecycle: Care-giving

Our local baker's shop goes to some trouble to recruit pleasant and friendly part-timers to work after school. They're really sweet, and it's lovely to have a teenager ask after my welfare – and even listen to the answer. When I told her that my days are sometimes tedious as my husband's sole carer, she reassured me: "Well, I'm sure it doesn't feel like work when you're caring for someone you love."

I wanted to reply (but I didn't), "Well, you don't have to dislike them for it to be work."

I used to start the morning routine by positioning his walking frame so that he could get out of bed safely. Then I went outside to get his newspaper. One step by one step, he would descend the stairs: Bad leg first – going down the stairs (to hell), and good leg first – going up the stairs (to heaven) – just as the physios taught him.

Every step had been painful for him since his faulty knee replacement eight years earlier. He left one walking frame at the top of the stairs. Another awaited him at the bottom. I'd put systems in place to support him, and we seemed to be managing – but managing was as good as it got.

I became increasingly concerned one night as I watched a science program on TV about telomeres. In laypersons' terms, these are the part of the human gene structure thought to influence longevity. This has been researched by comparing people with long telomeres with people at high risk of getting sick and dying early, namely carers. So I was killing myself by looking after him. Stress is the factor contributing to poor health outcomes for carers. Whether it's because they get no time to themselves, because their sleep is disturbed every night, or because they must cope with a bewildering maze of health and welfare services, stress is pretty much a constant. I've heard that stress is not just about how much work we do. It's also about the number of different things we deal with at a time. Apparently, five is about the limit. *Five*!! That barely constitutes multitasking for carers. The devil is in the endless, repetitive detail of the work of caregiving.

Routine was boring, but unexpected events were often frustrating. He had an electric 'lift' chair, so power outages left him suspended mid-air. If the backup battery failed, he was also stuck in the 'recline' position. Fortunately, power was normally restored before he needed to go to the loo. On one occasion, when power was restored, it was time to take him to his doctor's appointment, but we had to wait an hour because there had been two accidents on the freeway. There was a connection between the accidents and the wait time because all traffic was diverted to side roads. This caused congestion, so people were late to appointments and, instead of treating people (like us) who were on time, we had to wait whilst the latecomers went in first. And so my days frittered away, as did the eight years I cared for him.

There are resources out there for carers, but I had to become an infomaniac to find them.

"Have you got a cab voucher? You get a discount on taxis if you're in a wheelchair."

Really? Trust it to be a female taxi driver who imparted this information. None of the taxi drivers in the previous two years had mentioned this. I downloaded the appropriate forms, which had to be signed by Lyall's family doctor. When I gave them to him, he seemed surprised.

"Oh, didn't I tell you about these?"

Not too long afterwards, I tried to sort out some kind of exercise program or hydrotherapy that might assist in reducing Lyall's pain levels.

"You do realise," said the health professional, "that he can get a community care plan that subsidises allied health support. Just ask your doctor."

Why hadn't the doctor told me?

It wasn't easy for me to get information because I often didn't know there was a question to ask. For example, when getting my husband ready for a stay in respite care, I noted that the aged care facility wants all electrical equipment to be checked and tagged. I get that. It's due diligence and fire prevention. It was also an important stipulation for me because reading was the one remaining pleasure in my husband's life, and I wanted to take a reading lamp for him. So I rang to ask if they have a process for checking and tagging.

"Oh, you needn't worry about that. We're happy if it's a new item and you show us the receipt."

Well, that's easy and cheaper, but why didn't they say that in the documentation? This was my story of caregiving: Half information; no information; misleading information; and misguided information.

In my early days of being a full-time carer, the outcome wasn't good because I didn't know what I didn't know. Since then, I've honed my questioning skills. Even so, hospitals present particular problems because of the chain of command. In fact, I read in one carers' newsletter that a presiding doctor didn't even like next-of-kin involved. To get information about her husband, this particular carer masqueraded as a junior doctor and joined the ward rounds. Onya! A bit of direct action goes a long way.

One problem is that a simple request for information can be perceived as a challenge by health care professionals.

"Well that's looking good," the ophthalmologist said to my husband in a follow-up consultation after a cataract operation. "I'd like to see you again in nine months' time."

"How does that happen?" I asked. "Do you do a call-back, or should I put that in my diary and ring you for an appointment?"

I was treated to a defensive explanation telling me that if he called back outside of the twelve-month referral period, it would be considered advertising. I didn't argue, but I already knew that other doctors have a call-back process and that their reception staff just remind me if a new referral is needed. What he was really saying is that his rooms can't be stuffed to provide the service.

"I'm just looking for a process," I replied. "He has multiple health issues, and he can have up to ten doctors involved in his care at any one point in time. I just need to know how to manage the situation."

His neck corkscrewed around as he turned to look at me – finally, some recognition of what I'm up against as a carer. "Oh, so you ring us."

Thanks! That's all I was asking.

Ah, the banks! I hadn't seen them coming down the track. It became necessary for us to have new debit cards, so my husband was required to answer some security questions. I wasn't allowed to stay on the phone or coach him in any way, even though I had power of attorney. He failed. Most people would if they have short-term memory loss.

"So how do we cope with this?" I asked.

We found a way around it, but it took time and was yet another complication.

Eventually, I grew in knowledge. I even became a bit of an information resource for Perth friends, Robyn, Janina, and Jean. All of them are now caregivers for husbands or parents. I just happened to be the first cab off the rank.

Janina's analysis of caregiving extends beyond the medical advocacy and physical care that I talk about. She talks about the time-consuming, emotional work that carers do. She calls it emotional s**t work. It's the work that leaves carers emotionally exhausted, especially when caring for the elderly at home, because age can carry with it a multitude of health problems, including dementia, impaired mobility, hearing and sight loss, and incontinence. Of course, it's often the case that carers are in this on their own.

Lyall had six children, and they were largely AWOL in the eight years I looked after him. It would have been lovely if they'd taken him out regularly to give me a break. For a while, one of them did. She and her husband took Lyall out to lunch once a fortnight. I paid for them all, and they referred to it as, "Lightening my wallet." Nice joke if you are the one making it.

And then there's the resentment – yours and theirs. One of the women in my aqua aerobics class, Birgit, spoke of her husband's ill-temper and jealousy when she cared for him. Her eyes filled with tears, "When my husband was dying, he kept saying I smile too much. 'Stop smiling,' he would say."

In my case, it was as if Lyall blamed me for looking after him. I faced irritability rather than gratitude, and nobody ever asked how I was. It was always, "How's Lyall?" I wanted it all to stop, but there were only two ways that was going to happen: nursing home or death (his or mine). How could I wish either on him?

If the dependent person suffers from self-inflicted wounds, then resentment grows. Wendy wrote the other day to debrief about her situation. "I'm responsible for my sister, who is a couple of years younger than me, but she's aging badly, so she's more like thirty years older, thanks to her smoking, eating copious sweets despite her diabetes, and chronic lack of exercise. She grows worse every year, and we had a three-month episode, starting in March last year, which entailed hospitalisation in a public hospital, falling, concussion, and the need to move from a walking stick to a walking frame. All of this places physical, mental and financial strain on me. I worry about having a stroke or something incapacitating."

It's important to have friends to talk to, but I found that Lyall's visitors generally caused me extra work as I ran around getting them tea and coffee. It was particularly galling when his visitors came up with good ideas about how to manage Lyall's care – as if I couldn't work it out for myself.

"Get him a whiteboard so that he can jot things down. It will help him to remember things."

But he won't remember what the whiteboard is for!

One friend came to stay and started translating Lyall to me: "What Lyall means is …"

She insisted on sitting with Lyall during the day, which I experienced as implied judgement that I should be spending more time with him. However, I had the physical s**t work of care to do, such as shopping and laundry. I also had significant household maintenance to attend to, including building a disability room for Lyall. All this had to be squeezed in between as many as three medical appointments on some days. I simply couldn't sit with him during the day, though I did in the evenings. So, what I should have said to my house guest is: "What Lyall meant was that he likes to be alone so that he can sleep and read when he wants, and he can fart if he needs to, and old men on a fistful of drugs four times a day need to let their wind go free quite a lot." Her presence all day was, in fact, inhibiting.

Whilst I was caring for Lyall, I was contacted by UK Cousin Dan. He'd been listening to the BBC 'Woman's Hour' program on his car radio. The topic was caregiving. One interviewee grabbed his attention, and he thought I might like to hear what she had to say. Her commentary explored how the physical and emotional s**t work (in some cases having to deal with actual s**t on a daily basis) diminishes a marital relationship. She had become her sick husband's nurse and could no longer be his wife. She wouldn't even get changed in front of him for fear that undressing might be seen as a 'come-on.' However, some spousal carers do want to be loving to their husbands, even if it's just providing nice food, wine and holidays, but it's difficult.

Janina called by last week. She needed to debrief. "I just want to feel like a woman again, and I want to interact with him as I always did. Instead, I find myself yelling at him because he tells me the same thing over and over again, and he puts things away in the wrong place all the time. I hate myself for the person I've become."

So not only lack of acknowledgement and respect from others, especially your spouse, but self-respect has also disappeared. I told her to get some respite, but therein lies a tale.

Getting respite is very difficult. I jumped through all the hoops. Lyall's needs, and mine, were assessed, and I was allotted a possible nine weeks of respite a year. I was also made aware of the Independent Living Centre (ILC), which helps to broker respite care places and subsidise costs. However, *there aren't many respite rooms available.* It's as if the government creates the ILC, and that keeps them happy, and the ILC unsuccessfully seeks respite care places for clients, and that keeps them happy. So everybody, except me, was happy because I still had nowhere to leave Lyall if I wanted to get away for a break.

Dealing with government bureaucracy is frustrating particularly because of the amount of paperwork involved. I had to go through this each time I wanted to get respite care for Lyall. On one occasion, I received ten documents. I worked for eight hours to complete them, but this did include a lot of time on the phone trying to find out how to complete the task and to whom I needed to send what.

"Now, this twenty-two-page document," I asked over the phone, "do I have to print that off? Is it possible to print and sign only the last page and scan that back to you?"

I was told that the last page only would be alright. Yet a Justice of the Peace once told me that I should never separate the signed page from the document to which it refers but, by this stage, I was ready to kill to simplify this process. Fortunately, I didn't have to.

"No, wait, you don't have to do anything with that form."

Then why send it?

I then rang the Independent Living Centre. These wonderful women had been helpful during previous meltdowns: "Well, I'm packing his bags and leaving him on the hospital steps," I declared during an earlier attempt to get respite. "I haven't had a break in two years, and I'm going."

I'd already tried a long list of aged care facilities, and the best offer I'd received was to contact them seven days before, and they'd know. Presumably, if a resident died, there'd be a respite room – but I couldn't plan a holiday on this basis. I lobbied the Federal Minister for Aged Care, and even he admitted that residential aged care services are not obliged to keep respite rooms.

I couldn't even feel sorry for myself because the ILC ladies told me that they have difficulty, even when searching for carers who are school children when they need to study for their exams. Somewhat angry about such situations, I contacted the Carers' Association, and they told me their youngest carer was six years old. There wasn't a thing I could say to the woman on the phone. She could cap every one of my stories. When I complained about the ten documents, including one twenty-two pages long, she said,

"Oh, I know, I know. I have a child with multiple disabilities, and it's a forty-page document just to get her out for a weekend."

Really?

I smiled because she was doing a fair imitation of Sybil in the BBC sitcom 'Fawlty Towers'. Sybil's endless phone calls with friends consisted of, "Oh, I know, I know." And, I know, I know that there are such things as compliance, quality, and due diligence that influence the number of documents I must complete. I respected these processes as attempts to improve the quality of aged care, but somewhere, sandwiched between these demands, are the carers who have to double-time just to get away.

Many of my friends are now carers. Like me, they try to organise a social life to keep everybody thriving and not just surviving. This is all part of the emotional s**t work. I booked a cruise to give my wheelchair-dependent husband a holiday. I booked carefully and emailed the cruise company to ensure assistance with embarkation.

"Just ask in the departure lounge."

I did, but on the day, I was directed from desk to desk without assistance. At the bottom of the ramp, I stonewalled: "I was told I'd get assistance. I can't push this weight up the ramp."

A passing employee pushed the wheelchair to the deck and dumped us. There were no directions and no assistance to get to our cabin. It was difficult pushing the wheelchair along the narrow corridor from the lifts to our cabin whilst negotiating the cleaning carts that lined the route. It was alright though because cheerful cabin attendants enjoyed the show as they squeezed against the wall to allow me to struggle past. They really were very keen for us to "Have a nice day." One even offered advice as I struggled through a heavy door.

"You should go through backwards."

It's so nice to know that there are still officers and gentlemen around. Staff are not allowed to help for occupational health and safety reasons and, I presume, indemnity if they caused an accident with the wheelchair.

The practice for the emergency evacuation of the ship provided clear instructions: Go to your assembly point. Do NOT use the elevators.

"How do I get there with a wheelchair without using the lift?" I asked.

"Use the elevator. It's just a practice."

Lack of briefing or assistance caused mistakes. I used the wrong set of lifts to get to the café and had to circumnavigate an overflowing swimming pool at night. Too late! I discovered that the wheelchair serves as a kite in the breeze. It took off with me in tow, skidding through the water. It was also surprisingly skiddy pushing a wheelchair over the carpet, but it was only six trips a day to and from meals. There was no other reason to emerge from our cabin. We don't gamble or go ballroom dancing, and the men's bellyflop competitions were clearly out for us, and we don't do bingo or karaoke. There was disabled access to the main pool, which was packed with kids. The adults-only pool was not accessible. We'd been told that tour buses are accessible but didn't realise that the boats that ferry passengers to shore are not. Cabin-bound, we tried TV: BBC World; CNN; and American programs in Portuguese. What about a cuppa? There are no tea or coffee facilities in cabins, and room service was a forty-minute wait.

"A holiday at home would be better," I grumbled. "You'd have your newspaper and TV channels, and it would be easier for me than wheelchair marathons."

When I got home, I complained about this to Janina, and all she could say was, "Oh, I know, I know."

"You've got to have some gallows humour," a UK friend told me, "or you'll never get through this."

We'd been emailing about the emotional s**t work involved in being a caregiver. I thought about gallows humour (or black humour as it's sometimes called), but it seemed unkind to laugh at the sick and disabled even though it was sometimes unavoidable, as with Lyall and his use of remote controls. He had to manage two black remotes – one was for his electric 'lift chair' that rose up to help him get from sitting to standing. He also had a black remote for the TV, and sometimes he got the two mixed up. I couldn't help but laugh as he bobbed up and down in his chair, trying in vain to change TV channels.

One evening, Lyall had a stroke. He started speaking gobbledygook but thought he was making sense, so he didn't want me to call an ambulance. I asked if he understood why I was sending for the ambulance.

"Yes," he replied. "It's because I'm not properly cooked."

A friend's husband landed in the same hospital at exactly the same time. He'd had a heart attack. As Lyall's stroke and his heart attack were potentially life-threatening for both men, I decided to try a bit of gallows humour and, when I rang my friend, we did have a bit of a cackle about the potential for a two-for-the-price-of-one funeral. However, she was really worried about the extent to which her husband's life was being prolonged without due regard for the quality of life if he pulled through. She really didn't mean to be funny when she discussed this with me. She told me that when he was admitted to hospital with a heart attack, he'd been paddled thirteen times. That's a lot! Then she paused for a notable period before blurting out, "So I was a bit miffed really." That has now become part of our language of friendship. Every time we're annoyed about something, we say, "So I was a bit miffed really."

For example, "Today I was smashed in the face by a thug who snatched my handbag with my life savings in it. So I was a bit miffed really."

Perhaps that's the point of humour, as Janina said, with one of her legendary one-line summaries of complex ideas: Humour is Dencorub for sad places, and caregiving is a sad and lonely place.

Making sense of the lifecycle: Medical advocacy

I've done a frightening amount of medical advocacy for my husband, Lyall. His problems started with a knee replacement. The surgery was good, but the implant was faulty. The orthopaedic surgeon knew this within six months of the operation, but he didn't tell us and so Lyall suffered muscle wastage in the years it took us to find out what happened. He never really had a hope of a good recovery, even after the re-replacement of the implant. Apparently, Australian doctors were advised not to keep patients informed to avoid panic, and unnecessary re-replacement surgery. It would have been nice to be given the choice.

"Do you think this could be Lyall's issue?"

Two emails arrived on the same day from Rosemarie, in Perth, and Aileen, in Toowoomba. They'd both heard an ABC radio health program that told of faulty knee and hip implants. I immediately contacted the Health Consumer Forum. They put us onto a class action, noting that it would be necessary to obtain the serial number of the knee implant in order to progress a complaint. I rang the orthopaedic surgeon's rooms, but I was stonewalled because I asked for a 'batch number.' Three phone calls later, I got an answer because I asked, with terminological exactitude, for the 'product code.'

This was my first insight into the lack of empathy that was to become my lot as a carer and as a medical advocate. I also asked why the risk of a faulty implant had not been mentioned during any of my husband's follow-up visits complaining of intense post-operative pain. I still have it in writing that the surgeon had not thought it relevant.

Lyall had multiple health problems starting with Temporary Ischaemic Attacks in 2001. More than a decade later, he was diagnosed with Normal Pressure Hydrocephalus, and he had a mild stroke. He had so many specialists, even his family doctor found it difficult to keep up. It wasn't unusual for me to correct his records, pointing out that Lyall couldn't possibly be on four different lots of pain relief at the same time, "… least of all that one. Don't you remember … the neurologist wrote to you saying, 'Never again'?"

Yet being a carer is a bit like being the tramp in Charlie Chaplin's film, 'The Millionaire.' The tramp was invited in to be wined and dined when the lonely millionaire wanted company in the evening, and he was booted out the following day, when his host sobered up and became aware of the company he'd kept. In a similar vein, carers are variously invited in, or excluded from, health care processes.

One orthopaedic surgeon clearly thought I was in. As he demonstrated the required exercises for my husband's post-op recovery, he looked at me and noted, "You'll have to make him do them every half hour."

I drove home from that appointment in tears. (Fortunately there are no laws against driving under the influence of unreasonable expectations.) Did this surgeon seriously think that I had nothing better to do than down-tools every thirty minutes to remind my husband about exercises? I know, I know – I worked it out for myself, and plenty of health professionals have told me: Put systems in place. I tried a timer to remind him to do his exercises, but he couldn't remember what the timer was for when the bell rang. Please don't even suggest spreadsheets or whiteboards because, as well as a faulty knee implant, he also had dementia.

During one of his hospital stays, when he was near death, I became aware that there had been no overview. The admitting orthopaedic surgeon was concerned with his knee, and the pain management specialists were concerned with pain management. The ward orderly brought the food, then took it away again, uneaten.

"Has anyone noticed that this man hasn't eaten for five days?" I asked of anyone who would stand still to listen.

"Could we bring in a physician to take an overview?"

I asked this of the surgeon, the pain management specialist, the cardiologist, every nurse on every shift, and the ward orderly, who proved to be the most interested in this case. Eventually, a young intern was sent in to 'deal with me.' He hedged, prevaricated, fenced and clearly disliked my inclination to deconstruct his arguments: "So what you are saying is that you are not prepared to bring in a physician to provide an overview."

"You're rude," he replied and walked out.

It matters who you are, I think. I discovered that my insistence on being called 'Dr' (PhD Dr) sometimes disrupts the gestalt of health professionals. Some even asked if I'm a real doctor.

"Yes," I replied. "I had to write a thesis based on original research at post-graduate level."

A sister traveller in this caregiving journey – a nurse – told me that she overheard two medicos as they exited a consultation session with her terminally ill husband. "The wife seems quite cluey, doesn't she?"

'The' wife! Well, I suppose it's better than 'the Mrs.'

Health professionals hold ambivalent expectations of carers. I've had to divert their attention to my husband in some cases, asking them to speak directly with him. In other cases, I've been excluded from the process, and sometimes we moved around each other in circles.

For example, when my husband had been in hospital for six weeks and wanted out, I asked a nurse: "Is there a ballpark date for his hospital discharge?"

"You'll have to ask the RMO (resident medical officer). She only works part-time."

"Really? I saw her every day last week."

"Oh, *that* doctor. Yes, she's full-time."

"May I see her?"

"She doesn't work weekends."

Three days later, I managed to catch the RMO.

"How long will he be in hospital? He's pushing to come home."

"You'll have to ask the consultant."

"I never see him. What's the normal process for conveying information to the primary caregiver?"

No answer.

"You see," I pressed on, "there are other factors to consider. He already has an appointment with the vascular surgeon at another hospital. Should I now cancel that?"

"I don't know."

"Can you note this conversation with the consultant and provide me with feedback?"

"I'll try, but he does have his own style."

His own style! Geez, I once had my own life.

Later that day, my husband rang from the hospital. "The consultant is coming."

"Would you like me to stay on the phone so that I can speak with him?"

"No, I'll handle it."

"Well, be sure to discuss a possible discharge date."

A short time later, my husband rang back. "The consultant said I'm definitely not to have an injection in the knee."

Qué? I hadn't even known that was on the cards, but I asked if he'd discussed a discharge date.

"No. The consultant just left."

By now, I felt like Alice in Wonderland, so I telephoned the ward. The phone rang for a long time. When I got through, I asked to speak with the consultant and was told he'd just left the ward.

"Ahh, probably whilst I was trying to get through. Can I speak with the RMO?"

"She says she spoke with you yesterday."

"Yes, but that was raising questions. Now I'm looking for answers."

"Well, that's what she said."

"What's the normal process for conveying information to primary caregivers? Clearly, I'm going about this the wrong way."

"I'll put you onto the nurse manager."

I was left hanging, and I ditched the phone call. Almost immediately, my phone rang again. This time it was the hospital radiology unit.

"May I speak with your husband?"

"He's in hospital."

"Which one?"

"Yours."

"It doesn't say in the notes that he's in hospital."

"Well he is."

"I'm supposed to give him a knee injection."

"But the consultant has just seen him and said no knee injection."

I rang my husband back to confirm that this is what had been said.

"Yes. Under no circumstances am I to have a knee injection because of the risk of infection."

So, feeling like I should be on the hospital payroll, I rang back radiology. "I'd double check that if I were you."

My husband consented to the replacement of the faulty implant in his *right* knee, but in the week prior to surgery, he'd had massive pain in his *left* leg. Suspecting deep vein thrombosis (DVT), I took him to his family doctor three times. They rolled their eyes at me for being 'Dr Google' and holding my strongest opinions in areas in which I had the least knowledge. But they did the right thing and checked him out with X-rays declaring him fit for surgery. I practically carried Lyall into the hospital because he had pain in *both* legs.

Following surgery, the pain in his *left* leg exceeded that in his *right* leg – which should have been worse because of the re-replacement. (You should be able to keep pace with this detail, he only had two knees). Endlessly, I drew attention to the problem.

"Oh, it's just a touch of tendonitis," the pain management specialist said, casually squeezing my husband's left calf muscles.

One week later, I entered his hospital room to find a nurse dressing his right leg post-op wound.

"His left foot is blue," I observed. "Oh, we'll soon get him back into bed and it will pink up," she said.

"I don't think so," I replied. That's when I bypassed doctors and nurses. Instead, I rang the customer service people: "What is this @*%$# hospital going to do to save my husband's life?"

I worked in universities for forty years, so I knew that I'd get action if I made it a risk management issue. Within four hours, Lyall was transferred to the cardiology ward.

"Oh, you must be Lynne," the cardiologist said as I entered his ward. "Congratulations, you've saved your husband's leg, if not his life."

It transpired that his left artery was completely blocked. A vascular surgeon was called in. He shook his head in disbelief.

"This should never have happened," he sighed. "Your husband has a blocked artery in his left leg. To clear it, I have to give blood thinners, and that will cause a haematoma at the site of the right knee replacement."

It did, so Lyall ended up with three operations in a week:

1) re-replacement of the faulty implant;
2) vascular surgery; and
3) an operation to manage the haematoma.

This was the first time I saved my husband's life by insistent advocacy. It didn't do my self-esteem a lot of good. I sensed they wanted to write across the top of his file: 'Watch out for *the Mrs.*'

Sometime later, Lyall was diagnosed with Normal Pressure Hydrocephalus and had an operation to insert a programmable brain shunt. A year later, he had a stroke and had to have an MRI. I overheard the receptionist tell the nurse that he had a non-programmable brain shunt. I interjected, noting that it was programmable. The import of this conversation is that the MRI knocks out the programming, which risks radically altering brain pressure, which could have fatal consequences.

"Are you sure?" the nurse asked.

Some two hours later, after finding and checking his hefty folder of notes, she exclaimed, "Yes! You're right."

So this was the second time I saved his life.

It was a small matter to get his brain shunt reprogrammed after the MRI. It's done with a magnet on the outside of his ear and takes about ten seconds. The first time I saw it happen, I commented that I wouldn't tell my friends I had a hubby whose brain could be reprogrammed in ten seconds; otherwise, they'd all want one.

When we got to the neurology department, I

heard one doctor tell another to reprogram him at 0.5.

"It's not 0.5. It's 1.5," I interjected.

"Are you sure?" they replied.

One young neurologist tried to be sympathetic but unwittingly implied that I must be mistaken: "Oh, I normally work in paediatrics, and I give 'my mums' a card so that they remember the correct pressure."

I knew the correct pressure. They pointed to the notes written by the specialist dealing with his stroke. "He's got it wrong," I said. "The last time I brought him to neurology, they changed the pressure *by* 0.5 not *to* 0.5."

I looked down at my husband in his wheelchair and wondered what it must be like to have people arguing over your head about the correct pressure for your brain. He'd given up. He was, by now, completely disempowered and he left it all to me. There was more checking back through his files: "You're right!" they said.

So that was the third time I saved my husband's life.

Eventually, Lyall entered residential aged care, and I transferred him to the care of their on-call general practice (GP) doctors. Even though I understood that the aged care organisation and family medical practices are separate entities, I felt that continuity of care might be enhanced by fitting in with established systems. In any case, his former GP couldn't be expected to attend home visits in a different suburb.

The new GP service had an innovative structure with peripatetic doctors covering many aged care facilities using nurse practitioners to coordinate services at each centre. It sounded good. In reality, things didn't play out well, but this may have more to do with how things were managed than with the innovative structure.

What went wrong?

The peripatetic service did not provide out-of-hours care as I'd hoped. This resulted in the use of locums, who, with limited patient history, played safe and referred to the hospital – often unnecessarily: "We don't know why he's here," the Emergency Department staff said when I rang to enquire. So they sent him home. That cost my private health care insurance around $500 each way and deflected ambulance services from needy cases, as well as filling emergency department beds.

There was a lack of continuity and consultation, both of which are fixable by good management. Following the initial transition to the aged care facility, we waited a mandated one month before a formal family conference. They wanted to make their own assessment of the new patient. This did not include an interview with me, his carer, for the previous seven years. There was too much room for error in this process, and the first of a series of unnecessary hospital visits occurred during this time. The chain of communication from patients to enrolled nurses (employed by the nursing home) to the nurse practitioner (employed by the GP service) and from them to the GPs meant that much was lost in translation. Whilst the peripatetic organisation had genuine potential, its processes left patients wanting. In our case, both the doctor and the nurse practitioner were on holiday at the same time, leaving a temporary nurse practitioner in charge. This resulted in inadequate monitoring of warfarin levels.

For years I'd worked collaboratively with Lyall's family doctor to monitor his warfarin levels, which should not rise above the INR measurement of three. Warfarin is, after all, rat poison. Long story short, in the absence of the doctor and the nurse practitioner, Lyall's INR rose to a dangerous fifteen. I was called at 9pm on a Friday evening by the enrolled nurse left in charge of the nursing home overnight. Whilst the residents slept, it was her job to go through all of the residents' test results. She reported an INR of nine. She was ringing to inform me. That was her duty.

"What are you going to do about it?" I asked.

She thought maybe wait till Monday.

I thought not. I knew that a Vitamin K injection could assist in such cases. I insisted on calling in a locum doctor, who ordered an ambulance. The hospital emergency department doctor rang to say that Lyall had suffered internal bleeding and that his INR level was, in fact, fifteen. I felt deflated because, on this occasion, my medical advocacy hadn't been able to save Lyall from yet more pain. I did complain to the aged care organisation. I should have complained through formal medical complaints processes but I didn't. I knew that Lyall was getting close to death, and I was worn out with medical advocacy.

Making sense of the lifecycle: Ruth's death

Dear Ruth

It's Thursday, 29 April 2021 – exactly six months since you died on 29 October 2020. That was a Thursday as well. In your last days in hospital you wouldn't let your husband, Andy, out of your sight. Even if he just popped to the bathroom you asked him not to forget you. "Who could forget you?" he replied. Who indeed! You were a beautiful, vivacious, intelligent woman – successful in your legal career in the army and in your sporting endeavours. Winning almost a dozen medals in the USA Warrior Games, and the international Invictus Games, was already a lot to make your life unforgettable, but we also did a lot to make meaning together in our family life. We travelled the world; planted trees; camped across Australia; attended political rallies for world peace; and we went to concerts and art galleries. Your father and I supported your education (five university qualifications was quite a lot) and I created many opportunities for you to feel part of your extended families in the UK and Australia. A sense of belonging is important to us all, and you still belong to me and your brother, Sam. We always talk about you.

When the cancer returned, it was clear that your days were numbered, so I posted you the memorabilia I'd kept from your childhood. I've kept memorabilia for you, Sam, your Dad and me so that we might all have opportunities to reflect on our lives in old age. You weren't going to be old, so I wanted you to have a chance to think back on the way we were. You organised these memories into scrapbooks so that you could be remembered in the way you wanted. I'm writing, now, to tell you how we remember *the last year of your life.*

You planned your own military funeral with Father Charles officiating. He made it clear, during your funeral service, that he was doing your bidding. The funeral was a grand affair and well attended. Everything went as you wanted: Bagpipes, and bugles to sound the last post and reveille. We marched slowly behind the gun carriage that carried you in your coffin. I was moved to see your husband doing a slow march at the head of the cortège. You two were soulmates, and it is so sad that you couldn't live out your lives together. Sam and I walked behind him, as your family, and I was pleased and proud to have him beside me. Many of your friends from your childhood walked behind us. Our former neighbours, your 'other sister and brother', Nicole and Russell, were there. They were in tears. I think you would have been surprised at the number of people from your past who attended, even if they hadn't seen you for many years. This was your community, and the reason why you returned to Perth to spend the last months of your life. They all remember you with love. Your school friends still meet in your honour, and Jenneke called by to give me a plant, last December, thinking that our second Christmas without you might be a sad occasion. I was very touched by her kindness.

I recently went down to the Porongurups to spend time with Father Charles, and he told me that you cried a lot during your last meeting with him. The injustice of dying so young upset you. I felt the same way because I made the beautiful body in which you lived for thirty-seven years, and I felt cheated that it had let you down so badly. I was devastated by what happened to you. A mother's instinct is to protect her children, however old they are, and I couldn't protect you from the ravages of cancer. I was helpless in the face of the pain you suffered, and I couldn't keep death at bay. You told me about your last meeting with Charles. He was staying at the Archbishop's residence. The Archbishop walked past and gave you his blessing. This provided some comfort to you, but you told me that it was very hard planning your own funeral. Of course it was, but the planning kept you busy and it may have helped to keep the awful reality of death at arm's length.

Shortly before you died, you organised a party that turned out to be your surprise wedding reception. I heard, in your husband's eulogy at your funeral, that you had become engaged several years before, and you made a speech at the party announcing that you'd married a few months earlier, in May, in the company of just two close friends as witnesses. We all stepped up to the plate to support your party plans. Sam and Jane paid for your make-up and hair, I bought the drinks and you excitedly organised a new dress and shoes. On the day, you looked beautiful but very, very frail. I don't know how you *managed to stay the distance, but your doctors had equipped you with portable pumps filled with pain killers. You did it! Well done you. Lots of photos were taken and those of you and your husband taken at sunset are so, so poignant because this was the sunset of your relationship. You died four days later. It seems you hung on for your party. After your death, we were told that you'd been given just two months to live when you arrived back in Perth some eight months earlier. Sam and I hadn't known that, but I'm pleased you lived on for an extra six months. We had a chance to spend time together after years of living in distant cities and when, on your last morning of lucidity, you turned to me and said, "Help me, Mama. I'm frightened," I felt that we still had the mother and daughter bonds of your childhood. I will always remember you in this moment.*

I was uncomfortable at your party because your half-siblings were there. Their treatment of me in the last years of your

Dad's life meant that we were no longer in touch. One of them made the speech toasting the bride and groom. It made mention of your half-siblings, and some friends, but not me or your brother, Sam. You gave me a bouquet of flowers, but there was no acknowledgement of your brother. I was surprised and worried at the depth of Sam's hurt about this exclusive behaviour because he's a laid-back kind of bloke. The next day you asked what I thought about the party. I felt trapped because, if I said anything negative, then my honesty would undermine your dream party, but I had another 'child' to consider. I said I thought you looked beautiful, that it was a lovely setting in the university boat club overlooking the Swan River, and that the catering was excellent. I also said that I was disappointed in the speech because it excluded Sam and me. My honest reply upset you. This was passed on to those who perpetrated the exclusive behaviour, which occasioned subsequent hostile interaction with Sam that bewildered us all. Those involved didn't like being called-out. The repercussions even played out on your Facebook memorial page. I had to ask for offensive material to be removed. This was not your fault, Ruth, but it was an awful experience. This isn't how I want to remember you, and I'm working hard to get past it to find my daughter again in my memories of our family life together.

You were upset by my honesty and spoke with Sam. He rose above his own hurt and used the occasion to let you know how much he'd always looked up to you, as his big sister, and he told you that he loved you. I don't know if you ever fully understood that. I was also at pains to let you know how much I cared, telling you that you'd been front and centre of my life since you were born. That night, Sam came to my place to sort out some photos of our family. He popped them in a small album and took them to the hospital to look through them with you. He wanted to assert the *significance of 'us' – our family: Lynne; Lyall; Ruth; and Sam. He showed the photos to your husband, telling him that family dynamics hadn't always been as they now appeared. He said that he was beginning to see that.*

Your army managers suggested that you write a letter to your pre-cancer self. You did. You wrote a well-crafted 'Dear Me' letter on which this 'Dear Ruth' letter is based. Your letter was released on social media and it was trending number one in Australia as you died. You have been remembered by millions of people, but it's how you were remembered by your family that counts, and half of your family is British. So, I wrote 'Ruth's Story' for inclusion on the family's 'Hartland Britton' website. It contained your 'Dear Me' letter, so it's there forever.

Your aunts and cousins were proud to claim you as one of their own. Did you know that your UK cousins all switched the picture on their Facebook profiles to one of them with you? You have been remembered internationally – and lovingly – by your British family.

You died in your husband's arms. He'd been at your side for days and weeks and months. He was exhausted. He called your brother when you died. Sam and Jane picked me up, and we drove to the hospital, arriving at about midnight. Sam and I kissed you on the forehead to say goodbye. Lying on your back, you looked so much like a photo I have of you as a sleeping toddler. Together we decided on an undertaker and Sam, Jane and I waited with you until they came. We thought it was important to keep you company.

Your funeral was filmed and watched worldwide. The pomp and circumstance and the music was a spectacle that nobody will forget. The eulogies were perfect. I didn't cry very much until I got home and I watched your funeral online. Only then could I be alone with 'my girl'. When you were a baby, I used to dance around with you singing the pop song, "Nothing you can say can take me away from my girl." It was 'our song'. But cancer did take you away. So did your father's family dynamics of exclusion that had been perpetrated for many years. So much so that I felt I was an intruder at your funeral. Fortunately, your army boss stepped up to the plate and offered to be my 'chaperone'. I said yes immediately and he supported me in a manner befitting a mother at her daughter's funeral and also his role as a Major in the Australian Army.

I was in Croatia when your first diagnosis came through. We skyped, and all I could see on the screen was a lost little girl. I offered to return immediately, but you didn't want it. When I got back to Australia, I was still looking after your Dad, so it was difficult for me to get away. In any case, you rebuffed my overtures to come to see you. I put money into your bank account, and Sam's, so that one way or another you two might be able to fly to see each other. That didn't happen, but it's important to me that you know that we tried. In the end, Sam and Jane offered you one of the most generous gifts of all. They named their new baby after you. Elsie Ruth will keep your memory alive.

I don't know why your dying and death brought challenges over and above the sadness and loss that I naturally felt. I can only guess at the reasons for the tone of the interaction with your half siblings, but absolutely nothing can justify the things that were said. It's incomprehensible that anyone could treat another person that way at a time of grief. This is not how I want to remember your death or your funeral.

As you requested, the wake was held at the surf club. Your sister-in-law, Jane, organised the catering, and I invited a soprano friend, Harriet Marshall, to sing two arias, one honouring your love for your

Dad and one to highlight the love that you and your husband had for each other. Jane's brother, Mark, organised the montage of photographs that played on a loop during the wake. Everyone congratulated Sam on the speech in which he honoured you as his big sister.

Sam and I were both deeply hurt at a time when all we wanted to do is grieve for you. The hurt and bewilderment is still there, but the details of what happened have now faded and I am now remembering my Ruth: Her liveliness, humour, determination, and full-on engagement with life. When I came to visit you in Canberra, in early 2020, we even talked about the fact that you had done far more in your thirty-seven years than most do in their allotted three score years and ten. You did a lot, Ruth. Well done. Sam spoke with you about our plans to share our lives together at Blackbutt Road — your childhood home —and you told him that you were pleased that we'd all be looking after each other. All's quiet on the western front now, and we intend to have evening drinks as we overlook Jackadder Lake and, at the going down of the sun, we will remember our Major Ruth.

With my love, as always, Mum x

Values: Making sense of politics

I'm a 1968er. It was the year of student revolutions around the world. I was an undergraduate in Liverpool at that time, and I learned, from what was happening around me, that social change for the better might be possible through political action. As a post-war baby-boomer, I was also influenced by one of the most famous post-Nazi statements about the importance of remaining engaged and having your say:

> *First they came for the socialists, and I did not speak out — because I was not a socialist.*
>
> *Then they came for the trade unionists, and I did not speak out— because I was not a trade unionist.*
>
> *Then they came for the Jews, and I did not speak out— because I was not a Jew.*
>
> *Then they came for me—and there was no one left to speak for me.*

But I didn't know how to speak out. Politicians and political processes were remote from my world as I grew up in the UK. So, I loved Australia from the moment I arrived because exercising my political will seemed so much easier here. Access to power was better than anything I'd experienced before because Western Australia had such a small population – just over a million in 1973 when I arrived. So, if I didn't know a handful of state or federal politicians myself, then I knew someone who did. I felt empowered to be a small fish in a small pond. In any case, there were also a lot of politicians to know. Australia seemed over-governed to me. The Federal Government has two houses of parliament, and each State, apart from Queensland, also has an upper and lower house. The two Australian territories have their parliaments, and sitting beneath all of this are the layers of local governments. That was an awful lot of government for an Australian population of 13.38 million in 1973.

I joined the Women's Electoral Lobby in the 1980s, where I met female politicians. I remember finding it auspicious that Senator Pat Giles helped me carry my baby daughter, Ruth, in her bassinette. I made a wish that Pat's qualities might rub off on Ruth. Years later, when Pat died, Penny Wong, a leading federal politician, described Pat's qualities in a speech of condolence to the Senate: "she was one of a generation of Labor women who brought progressive policies affecting women and families to the very heart of this Senate and the government." Which mother would not wish her daughter to be so empowered?

The contrast between British and Australian politics was drawn in sharp profile when I applied for a British passport for Ruth. I needed help, and I didn't have the access to power in the UK to which I'd grown accustomed in Australia. Ruth was born in November 1982, but sexist British citizenship laws changed in January 1983, just two months later. The old law said that a British man could pass on his British citizenship to his children, but a British woman had to pay $80 to register the child as British. Not only was this sexist, it was also weird, because, when it comes to parentage, the one thing of which a baby can be certain is its mother. The problem was that the old law continued to prevail for those *born* before January 1983. This perpetuated sexism for years to come. I thought it should be all children *registered* after January 1983. So I decided to lobby as many UK politicians as I could, including my mum's local MP, in Gloucestershire, and British Equal Opportunity officials. I eventually got a reply from the latter, which sent me into orbit. It was gobbledegook replete with administrative jargon worthy of a Sir Humphrey speech in the British TV comedy 'Yes Minister.' I could have sent it to the scriptwriters for immediate inclusion in the program with very little editing. I was, however, interested to read that British equal opportunity legislation did not necessarily affect other laws, so it was perfectly OK to have discriminatory citizenship laws.

In Australia, equal opportunity legislation prevailed over other laws. Anyway, after that, I got busy raising my family, working, and writing my PhD thesis. It wasn't until 1994 that Lyall started to insist, "Lynne, we really do have to get Ruth her British passport." Sam was no problem because he was born after the law change. By this time, Lyall was retired, so I asked him to get on with it. He did. By then, it cost $280, so I should have shut up and paid $80 in 1983.

I'd been in Perth only a few weeks when there was a State election and I became aware that, not only could I vote, but I should. I was pretty scornful when I discovered that voting is compulsory in Australia, but I've done an about-face on that one. When you look at how few votes it can take to become an American president, it's positively scary. Compulsory voting favours participative democracy.

Australia also has a preferential voting system, which I thought contrasted favourably with the UK's first-past-the-post processes. But it didn't necessarily secure fairness in the lower house because there remained significant differences in the number of people in electorates. Those electorates with smaller numbers were larger in geographic area. These were the vast rural areas of WA. This system was seen to ensure a rural voice in politics. This remains the subject a debate: Should the vote of rural Western Australians count for two or three times as much as that of urban WA voters?

I slowly made sense of Australian politics and, eventually, I joined the Australian Labor Party (ALP). When my son was born, one of my leftie mates bought him membership so that he became the youngest member of the ALP in Australia. I was delighted. I remember, particularly, going to an ALP fund-raising dinner at which the after-dinner speaker was a witty and rabble-rousing unionist. His speech was interrupted suddenly when the door opened, and there stood a bridal couple. They must have mistaken the ALP dinner for their own wedding reception. Quick as a flash, Jack turned this to his advantage, and, looking straight at the bride in her white wedding dress, he said, "Come on in, love. If you're in labour, this is the right room."

Australia has offered me new perspectives on the world of politics, particularly about post-colonial countries. These new insights don't help much when I'm back in the UK, where I've found myself under fire because British friends and relatives think that colonialism was a pretty good thing because "Well, we did the Aborigines a favour, didn't we? They were nomadic. They had to be brought into the modern era, didn't they?"

Since living in Perth, I've also learnt more about Asia, especially Malaysia, where my lifelong friend, Mazlan, argues cogently about the consequences of colonialism for his country. When they gained independence, they were forced to accept about a million migrants overnight when the British left. Fledgling Malaysia had to incorporate the cheap labour originally imported by the British to work in the rubber plantations.

By Australian standards, the drive between Perth and Geraldton isn't far, just four hundred and twenty kilometres. Even so, when I drove there with Lyall and our friends, Val and Brian, I facilitated a line of conversation to keep the driver awake, and to engage fellow travellers.

"What was your first political memory?" I asked.

For Lyall, it was the sinking of the British battleships, the Prince of Wales and the Repulse, off Singapore in 1941. He recalled picking up on his mother's fear as she leaned over the balustrade of the veranda, speaking to her neighbours in hushed tones. As a nine-year-old, Lyall couldn't imagine why she spoke so quietly. The Japs weren't here yet. There was no real need to whisper. But, from his Mother's point of view, the sinking of the battleships meant that was it now: Australia was exposed to invasion, and Mother

England could no longer protect her colonial child.

Lyall's mother, born on the goldfields of Western Australia, had never travelled outside of Western Australia, yet she always spoke of England as 'home' because that's what Australian kids were taught at school. Lyall had an Australian school history textbook from 1912. It was a slim volume, given that it purported to be a history of the world. It started with Adam and Eve and then romped through major milestones to the Boer War, detouring via the story of Cain and Able to make the point that a rebellious child had been welcomed back by his parents. And, thus it was with Mother England, apparently. She welcomed her colonies back into the Commonwealth when they had the temerity to become independent. This implication was specifically emphasised in the 1912 school book.

Well, Mother England didn't need to worry too much about her Australian children: they voted to keep the Queen. Even Prince Phillip thought we were mad. The core issue at the time was the particular vision of a republic that was proffered for consideration – not the fact of republicanism.

Lyall was philosophical about the outcome of the referendum. If Australia didn't like what was on offer (and I think he voted against that model) then we might as well stick with a democratically elected government and a ceremonial head of state, which might just as well be the Queen.

"Why would you want to pay for a head of state if some other bugger is willing to fund the position for you?" he joked.

Lyall was less flippant in 1975 when the Governor-General, the Queen's representative in Australia, sacked the elected government. There were dramatic demonstrations around the country which echoed the sacked Prime Minister's rhetoric: "Ladies and gentlemen, well may we say 'God Save the Queen', because nothing will save the Governor-General."

Back on the road to Geraldton, Val and her husband, Brian, both thought their first political memory was the announcement of World War II. This had a profound impact on children, especially if their fathers went to war.

Some fifteen years younger than the others in the car, I noted that my first political memory was the 1956 Suez crisis. I was eight years old and living on an isolated farm just outside Broadway (UK). It had no electricity, so there was no radio or TV, so no news. I knew nothing that was going on in the outside world. I had to catch a bus to school, but, often as not, Mum and I were given a lift by one of the trucks passing by. One day, I asked Mum what the trucks were doing.

"They're building an airstrip. The country might be going to war, and we don't want to get caught on the hop, do we?"

What does that statement convey to an eight-year-old? How could a country hop? I had a mental image of the map of Britain hopping around the globe.

Iconic political moments are the scaffold around which we build our memories. Each generation identifies in terms of its own noteworthy events. Everyone in my generation remembers what they were doing the night President Kennedy was assassinated. I was a fifth former at high school, and I was at a party with the boyfriend of the moment. For my kids, their defining moment was probably 9/11 and the destruction of the Twin Towers in New York. They would probably also mention the Bali

Bombings, which killed eighty-eight Australians. For my grandsons, it will be COVID-19 and maybe the Russian invasion of Ukraine.

Israel was born the same year as me, and the associated wars and resistance that accompanied its birth peppered the news as I grew up. I came to take a close look at the Middle East when I lived on Kibbutz Ma'anit in Israel for six months in the early 1970s. Those were the days when living on a collective farm was the trendy, left-wing thing to do. These days I daren't mention my kibbutz days because many now associate Israel with right-wing, nationalistic, anti-Palestinian politics. I sit on the fence with these issues because Palestinians have a right to live comfortably in their own country – just as Australian Aborigines seek to do on their own land – and it's hardly the fault of Palestinians that European colonial powers carved up the Middle East in such an expedient manner.

On the other hand, the Holocaust was a turning point in modern history for its calculated mass murder of Jews. They have a right to live safely somewhere in the world, though I guess Palestinians might have preferred it if Jews had taken up the Kimberley option in Western

Australia (though the Kimberley Aborigines might have had something to say about that).

I travelled to Israel with an old school friend, Gwyneth. The import of this statement is that we shared history classes at school. One afternoon, we visited the Crusader castle at Acre, where our Palestinian tour guide spoke of a "band of marauding Barbarians who came over and raped and pillaged the countryside." I nudged Gwyn to ask who he was talking about.

"The Crusaders," she replied. "Not the way we heard it at school, huh? Doesn't he know they wanted to rescue the Holy Land from the Infidels?"

It turns out the Palestinian Guide had a point. In 2000, Lyall and I travelled to Syria, where we learned much more about the behaviour of the Crusaders, which incited an anger among Muslims that may well persist to this day.

One day, I said to my students, "That was after the war," and they replied, "Which war?"

I'd been outed as a true baby-boomer. There were many conflicts after World War II and I learned of many of them as I travelled the world. I've been to Hiroshima, where the Americans dropped the Atomic Bomb; Yad Vashem - the World Holocaust Remembrance Centre in Israel; the Cambodian Killing fields; Dachau, the Nazi concentration camp; the site of the Sandakan Death Marches – a series of forced marches in Borneo; and the Vietnamese tunnels of Củ Chi. It's awful to realise that so much of what I've seen is about war, and it's disheartening to think that the political optimism born in 1968 seems to have achieved so little in the grand scheme of things.

But I want my grandchildren to know about and learn from this history. I also want them to know that the standard they walk past is the standard they accept. They come from a family of activists who did try to make the world a better place, at least at the local level. Their grandmother (me) helped develop women's health and sexual assault crisis centres. Their great grandfather (Jack Hunt) was a member of parliament, and he played his part in attempting to protect workers' rights in the Wittenoom Asbestos mines. Their Grandpa Lyall was active in the trade union movement. Equity and justice underpinned family values, so much so that I smiled to myself in 2016 when I received our postal votes for the plebiscite on same-sex marriage. I was going to vote yes, but I knew that Lyall was homophobic so, momentarily, I considered not giving him his voting papers because I didn't want us to cancel out each other's votes. I reasoned that he might be too demented to vote. This was, in fact, a very real issue, so I rang the Electoral Office to ask what I should do.

It was decided he should vote, and, in any case, I couldn't bring myself to deny him his rights. As it transpired, I underestimated his 'fair-go' Australian principles of equity and justice. I gave him the papers and re-explained the process of postal voting. Then I left him to it. As I left the room, I heard him say, "Ah well, I suppose I'd better give the poor bastards a fair go."

Values: Making sense of feminism

I was slow off the mark in regard to feminism because I didn't know I was supposed to be a second-class human. I had a strong mother, three older sisters, and an absent father. Even all our dogs were female. Women were my world. I went to an all-girls high school and then studied sociology in a department comprising a majority of female students. Only when I encountered the world of work did I cotton on to structural sexism. I was one of two undergraduate students at my university to secure graduate employment at the well-known UK department store, Marks & Spencers. It was considered a prestigious graduate appointment. The other graduate was a male student. He was put on a management track, and I was offered a position in the personnel department, which looked after the welfare of employees – a nice caring job for a girl. His starting salary in 1970 was £1,400, and mine was £1,200. I didn't take the job.

Of course, I was aware of sexism, even though

I didn't have a name for it. I could see male power over women at play in my Dad's domestic violence, but I saw it as an individual matter. I knew, quite simply, that I would never allow a man to treat me like that. The day Dad went through my handbag displaying the contents along the mantelpiece was the day I learned to discard men from my life if they weren't worth keeping. Oddly, the intent to humiliate, the smallness, and the calculated meanness of this act sticks in my mind more than his verbal and physical assaults on my mother. Why would a father do that to his daughter? I can't imagine treating my kids that way. The only possible reason is control, and I resisted it. Inadvertently, Dad fostered my feminist politics.

Mum's contribution to my feminism was complicated and convoluted. She demonstrated an indomitable spirit and strength in finding employment and in raising a family without the help of men, but she wasn't a feminist. Her life was riddled with contradictions. She grew up in a rural, patriarchal community in which sons inherited farms, but not daughters.

When Mum tried to discuss the disparity in

inheritance between siblings, one of her brothers opined, in his Devonshire accent, "It be up to your husband to look after thee."

She was disempowered because she was a woman, but she endorsed the traditional role of women even when it came to discussing university entrance with me. I was the 'first-in-family' to go to university, and I was ambivalent about enrolling. I would variously say, "Mum, I don't think I'll go to university."

To this, she replied, "Well it is a bit of a waste of time for a girl."

Then, when I changed my mind and decided I would go, she said, "Well you might find yourself a doctor to marry."

With this kind of encouragement, it's a wonder that I eventually earned the title of doctor for myself. Marriage and family were her primary goals for her daughters, but she knew the importance of women's economic independence from bitter experience. She wanted all of her daughters to have a skill that they could 'fall back on'.

My feminist ideology crystallised in the world of work. Perth friend and colleague Janina and I both started work at a college in Australia in the mid-1970s. We were both young British female sociologists, and we quickly became aware that our starting salary was below that of newly appointed Australian males. It was a new college, so the union busied itself with negotiating the conditions of service, including study leave. The draft document announced that 'a lecturer may take his wife and children on study leave with him' – meaning that their fares would be paid. The blokes on the union executive thought I was a real hoot when I objected to the exclusive language. "Well, you know what we mean," they said. I did.

I taught a lot of mature-aged students in the 1970s. These were two-year trained teachers who had to convert to a three-year qualification. Most of them were women. They'd lived through the years when female teachers were required to resign from permanent staff when they married. Thereafter, they were re-employed on annual contract appointments. The lack of tenure meant they were subsequently disadvantaged in terms of leave provisions and superannuation. Having suffered these structural impediments to their careers, they were now required to upgrade their qualifications.

It's unbelievable that, in Western Australia, resignation on marriage was a requirement for female teachers until 1969. The tale of Dorothy Hewitt shows how farcical the situation was. Technically, Dorothy could be fired because she'd been married and divorced but there was no rule against a single mother with three kids.

Dorothy was a well-known West Australian author. Her autobiography 'Wild Card' describes a turbulent life in which she ran away from her first marriage in WA to live in Sydney with a man who turned out to be mentally ill. She returned to Western Australia with their children and enrolled at Claremont Teacher Training College. She wanted to be a teacher so that her working hours would coincide with her kids' schooling. Also, in those days, teacher trainees were paid to study on the condition they went where they were put when they graduated. This ensured that isolated and remote schools had teachers. It also gave Dorothy an income while she studied.

I was drawn into Dorothy's orbit in the late 1980s because I interviewed her for an oral history of women teachers who graduated from

Claremont Teachers' College – except Dorothy didn't graduate. She was expelled because she was divorced.

She told her story for the 'Claremont Cameos' book that I edited with Janina. She said she'd been carpeted by a senior man at the college.

> "It had come to his notice that I was a married woman (because they didn't have married women, of course). Not only had I been a married woman, but I was a divorced woman and this was absolutely verboten. I knew they had widows at the College, so I said, 'Well, what's the difference between a widow and a divorced woman?' He said, 'There's no need to tell a woman like you the difference between a widow and a divorcée. Who was the guilty party?' I laughed, and this infuriated him. He got very unpleasant and told me that I would have to pay back all the money, which they'd invested in me for that year. I was summarily dismissed as a person not suitable for teaching young people, because my moral standing in the community was

so low. I went away and got in touch with a lawyer, who told me that I had every right to call myself legally single, a 'femme seule'. The lawyer also said that the College would not be able to get the money back from me, so I wrote them a letter informing them that I was absolutely within my rights to have gone to the College under my own description of myself. I was very angry at the time and the fact that I couldn't do much about it made me even angrier."

The 'Claremont Cameos' book was born of an event that excluded women's stories. Claremont Teachers College was the first tertiary educational institution in Western Australia. It was founded in 1902 as a primary teachers' college. As such, it had high numbers of female students. It closed its doors to teacher training in 1987. This was commemorated with a garden party at which men celebrated the achievements of men, and women didn't get much of a look-in. A female graduate of the college picked up on this and wrote a letter of complaint to the local newspaper, which I read. At this stage, I was working in health, not education. So I rang Janina to ask, "What are you women in the Faculty of Education going to do about this?"

We came to the conclusion that we should interview female graduates of the college to tell their stories. We got a women's research grant and adopted a community-based approach by advertising for women prepared to undergo one day's training about interviewing techniques. We also advertised for female Claremont graduates who might like to be interviewed. We then paired one trained interviewer with one graduate. I've forgotten exactly how many interviews we did, but I think it was close to sixty. Some of the tapes were edited into radio programs that were put to air across Western Australia. These are now digitised and housed in the Battye Library (WA's social history collection) as well as in Edith Cowan University's (ECU) archives. The women's stories have been told and preserved.

So, that was it until 2002, when ECU celebrated its centenary based on the opening of Claremont College in 1902. Janina and I secured funding to publish a book about female graduates of the university's antecedent college – Claremont. It was based on a selection of the original interviews – one chapter per woman. We practically had to turn people away from the launch because Western Australia had such a small population that almost everybody had been taught by a female teacher from Claremont, or they had grandmothers, mothers, aunts, sisters and female cousins who'd trained there. Several hundred people wanted to be at the launch. The print run sold out.

Janina and I marvelled at the stories in the book. Many of these female graduates had been sent out bush for their early teaching appointments, and many fell in love with local farmers, married and stayed there. They had to resign because they were married, but they were well educated, so they became leaders contributing enormously to their rural communities. One story is about Western Australia's first female Aboriginal teacher, and another tells of the first woman to be a mayor in WA. Many of the women were the product of post-World War II migration, so they became leading lights in multicultural education. One conducted original research and published on the subject of WA's vast array of orchids, and another became a novelist.

My favourite story was of a woman who was asked to start special education. Until that point, kids with special needs just languished at the back of mainstream classrooms. Can you imagine living in the very small society that was WA in the mid-twentieth century? You had no journals about special education and no experience – nor did anybody else. Where would you start? What would you do? It's a compassionate story of a woman who saw the world from the point of view of her pupils. She designed the curriculum in terms of their needs, and she learned from parents. The story that sticks in my mind concerns teaching a child to brush his hair. She demonstrated by brushing her own hair, and then handed him the brush. The problem was that he then brushed her hair. She'd hit a knot that she couldn't untangle. Then she saw another child brushing his own hair, so she asked his mum how she'd taught him. It transpires it was an accident. They'd both been looking in the mirror at the same time, and her child had copied her. Soon afterwards, the new special education school was the proud owner of a mirror.

So, this was my contribution to feminism. I made sure women's stories were told. I sent my husband back to the drawing board with his list of names for inclusion in his 1979 biography, 'Westralian Portraits'. Thanks to me, there are at least some women in there. When he was asked to edit a history of the Yilgarn shire, I made sure I wrote a chapter about women in the Yilgarn. This chapter was really the first significant piece of writing I'd done. It started me on the writing and publication road I'm still on.

On 40C days in Perth, when I can dive into my backyard pool in Perth to cool off, I always think of those pioneer women in the Yilgarn. How did they survive? My chapter tells some of their stories, and it also tells of the contribution of the Country Women's Association, known as the CWA. My father-in-law used to deride it by calling it the **C**hin-**W**aggers **A**ssociation. I don't think many would see the CWA as feminist, but they provided the woman-to-woman support needed in the Australian outback.

Every time I drive through country towns and see the CWA Rest Rooms, dating back decades, I wonder what female farmers would have done without them when they came into town. Where would they feed their babies or change their nappies? I'm sometimes asked to make a contribution to International Women's Day events, and I often read out a short extract from my 'Women' chapter in the Yilgarn book. It's a letter of resignation written to the CWA in 1934. It's full of compassion and so certain of women's capacity to change the world for the better. I come close to choking up when I read it aloud — and if this isn't feminist, I don't know what is.

> *It is a grand thing for the womenfolk of our land to club together, with an objective such as that of our Association. Might I leave this message to members of your association? The longer I live, the more am I convinced that any social reform on a large scale, will be brought about through the agency of women, and not by men. The hand that rocks the cradle rules the world, and when we, as women, realize the tremendous responsibility resting upon us, and are prepared to shoulder those responsibilities, then will be seen in this fair land a social reformation that will sweep the powers of evil before it. That power is ours, and if only we will use it for*

good, then will a generation arise who shall call us blessed. May your Association prosper is the earnest wish of, yours sincerely, Eva Hanton

I like to think of myself as being part of that generation that Eva hoped would arise. I'm very aware that my feminist activism is built on the work of suffragettes and women across the centuries before them. In fact, I got a bit excited just recently because I thought my great-grandmother had been an activist in boycotting the 1911 British census. She wasn't, but I was intrigued (and disappointed) that I'd never heard of the boycott. It was a very clever political strategy. The Suffragettes' motto was, 'If we don't count, then we'll not be counted'. In other words, if women didn't have the vote then don't count them in the census. They avoided being part of any household on the night of the census. None of my friends, feminist or otherwise, knew of the boycott. This says something about the lack of teaching about women's issues in our schools and universities.

Among other approaches, I used humour in my teaching to raise awareness of women's issues. For example, I taught the value of punctuation by referring to the English professor who wrote the words, 'Woman without her man is nothing', on the blackboard and asked her students to punctuate it correctly. The male students wrote: 'Woman, without her man, is nothing'. The female students wrote: 'Woman! Without her, man is nothing'. Teaching women's health meant discussing breast cancer prevention. For those not in the know, the mammograms that detect breast cancer flatten a woman's breast between two glass plates – and I do mean flatten. To show what this means to women, I used a simple cartoon of a man attending a clinic for a penis X-ray using the same kind of equipment. Say no more!

I was active in second-wave feminism in the 1970s and 1980s. I participated in consultations about new equal opportunity legislation, and I enjoyed the fact that in a small population like Perth, I felt that my activism, and that of other women, actually did have real outcomes. My main area of activism was in women's health. I researched and published a lot about the women's health movement and about domestic violence. I started women's health courses. I organised community-based women's health conferences where women told their own stories, and I supervised Master's and PhD theses on women's health. I also sat on the committee of Perth's Sexual Assault Referral Centre, where I watched as the feminist fervour that informed its inception slowly collapsed into the black hole of the corporate management processes required for government funding. But if we wanted the Sexual Assault Referral Centre to survive — and we did — then we had to take the money and comply.

At work, I sat on the equal opportunity committee, which was a bit of an eye-opener. At that stage, the vice-chancellor had the right to sit on any university committee. He didn't normally exercise that right to the full, but he was clearly cautious about letting a bunch of feminists loose in the decision-making structures of the university, so he attended our committee meetings — and he dominated. We realised that we were letting him take charge, so we caucused and made a plan. First of all, we would all speak through the chair of the committee. We would also orientate our body language to the committee chair so that the vice-chancellor was cooled-out. We would make sure we used the agenda papers and put motions forward so that we set the course of the committee. Actually, all of this is normal committee procedure.

Feminist sociologist, Dale Spender, advised more direct action. "When a bloke does something stupid in committee meetings, women rush in to rescue him," she announced. "Don't do that! Ask him to repeat it – twice if necessary! Take notes!"

She turned resistance into an art form. Her research demonstrated how men jostle for position at committee meetings. It's all talk and no listening. Women ought to be able to do better than that, but do they?

Outside of the university, many feminists disliked the committee procedures we used to effect on the equal opportunity committee. For my part, I disliked the fluid structure of the feminist meetings I attended in the 1980s. I witnessed established members of feminist organisations ruling the roost whilst newer chums sat around contributing little. I tried to speak out about giving voice to newer members, and I was invited to put up a paper for discussion. Much of my paper focused on the need for some structure to the meetings. This was scornfully dismissed as too masculinist, and one woman really went on the attack. Nobody offered me support, so I left the group.

Feminists opposed committee procedures because they can be used to block communication, and they can be disempowering for those who don't know how to use them. I get that, but it's equally disempowering to have no limits on a vocal and established gang of mates. I couldn't see that the girls' club was much improvement on the boys' club. I wasn't the first to spot this problem.

Jo Freeman's seminal 1970 article, 'The tyranny of structurelessness', told us that, really, structurelessness is impossible. She argued the need for due process. My point exactly. Jo Freeman's article is still all over the internet, so it must have relevance today. Her article survived my cull of office papers when I retired. I can't throw it away. It's an iconic tract in my life.

Making meaning through feminism has been difficult. I was active in the women's health movement for almost a quarter of a century, and the thing that made my blood boil the most was female genital mutilation (FGM). Yet, when I attended a pre-meeting for the 1995 Beijing Conference on Women, I witnessed a female African delegate call the women in the room 'Western imperialist feminists' because we opposed FGM. Senior women from the World Health Organisation, and female Australian politicians, countered by defining FGM as a health issue – not a cultural matter. The aim of the pre-consultation sessions was to achieve consensus on a document about women's health. To avoid being held up, the process bracketed out any statement to which anybody objected at any of the pre-meetings worldwide. By the time the document reached Perth, it was all brackets. Consultations in other countries had resulted in objections even to the term 'women's health'. Where can you go with that?

So, precipitated by the Suffragettes, and furthered by the second-wave, feminism continued into the 1990s when it became an 'F' word. My own daughter refused to identify as feminist, despite the fact that she became a lawyer and a major in the Australian Army. I became disheartened as I watched younger women exploiting conditions of service, such as maternity leave, for which my generation of feminists had fought. I still watch as girls and boys are crafted into gendered roles, but I draw strength from my grandsons who question all this chat about girls and boys. At school, they're taught that all kids can do anything – and they are taught about domestic violence. I've been interested that my grandson, Thomas, has questioned me about why my dad wasn't such a great father. I can't tell him the full truth now, but he'll read it in this book when he's grown up.

I was both inspired and disheartened by Sam Mostyn's address to the Australian National Press Club in 2021. She's President of 'Chief Executive Women'. Her comparative statistical analysis showed that, internationally, Australia has slipped to sixtieth place on some measures of gender equity. In addition, there are very few women in the current federal cabinet; women remain under-represented in board-rooms around the country; and the gender pay gap is a disgrace in a country which now boasts high rates of women's participation in university education.

Women's equality in Australia has gone backwards since my days of second-wave feminism. She said that "The best time to plant a tree was decades ago. The second best time is now."

Her tree analogy summed it up: we have to try and try again.

I felt deflated because I did plant as many feminist trees as I could – but for what? She contrasted the slow progress of gender equality with the fast political action when COVID struck in 2019. Just imagine, Sam mused, if politicians moved equally quickly to keep young mothers engaged with the workforce.

Then suddenly it happened. At the 2022 Australian federal election, the ruling Liberal party was ousted and the opposition Labor party was elected, albeit with a decreased vote. The real winners of the day were the independents – all of them described as professional, well-educated women. They got sick of waiting. They just went for it with a grassroots, community-based approach largely based on environmental principles. Political analysts assessed that women's votes had effected the change. But then a feminist journalist asked why these successful candidates were described as well-educated women. She couldn't remember any male candidates being described that way. 'Plus ça change.'

Values: Making sense of courtesy

Grace Tame was Australian of the Year in 2021. She was recognised for her leadership in a law-reform campaign known as #LetHerSpeak, in which she had successfully petitioned against Tasmania's Evidence Act. This legislation prevented the publication of any information that identified survivors of sexual assault, which meant that survivors couldn't speak about their abuse or abusers.

In her year of office, Grace became a powerful voice for women. She was incisive in her analysis and quick to deconstruct paternalistic attitudes. So, when the Prime Minister responded to serious incidents of sexual abuse within Parliament House by announcing that he'd had a chat with his wife about it, Grace pulled no punches.

It seems the Prime Minister's wife had advised, "You have to think about this as a father. What would you want to happen if it were our girls?"

In her subsequent National Press Club speech,

Grace retorted, "It shouldn't take having children to have a conscience [and] having children doesn't guarantee a conscience."

Her abuser was a father. So there was no love lost between Grace and the Prime Minister, which was evident at the Australia Day events in 2022 to which Grace was invited as the outgoing Australian of the Year. Her body language in the presence of the PM was variously described by some politicians and journalists as icy, childish and rude.

Writing for the Australian edition of the Guardian, Katharine Murphy took a different tack. She recognised that young women, like Grace Tame, were not raised to shut up in the face of authority. To which I would add that Grace became Australian of the Year precisely because she spoke out, and because she maintained the rage against powerful men.

I wonder if Grace had heard of the 'Smile Boycotts' held in New York during the second wave of feminism in the 1970s. Secretaries, receptionists, and women working in similar capacities stopped smiling for the day, driving their male bosses to distraction. It was a deliberate strategy to point out that women are expected to be emotionally available to men. Grace's strategy was deliberate as well. She was seizing the moment to tell the world that this prime minister never had, and never would, understand the rights of women.

In her Guardian article, Katharine Murphy went on to say that the attack on Grace Tame's so-called poor manners "begs a lot of questions: who decides who can be rude and the circumstances in which rudeness is permissible? Who appointed the rude police? Can we appeal their rulings?"

This is what I'd like to know as well because, as a parent, I decided what was rude, and my decisions were often contested. I was teaching women's health when my daughter, Ruth, was about seven. As I prepared my teaching, I came across a clever Canadian film about the prevention of child sexual abuse, so I brought it home for Ruth and her brother, Sam, to watch. It contained a catchy little song for children to sing, 'My body's nobody's body but mine, you run your own body let me run mine.' They were both quite taken with this song, so I felt like a good mother because I'd done my bit to protect them from child sexual abuse. However, the next morning, when I was rushing to get the kids off to school, and me off to work, I found myself in conflict with Ruth. I wanted to do her hair in bunches because it was a quick hairstyle. She wanted plaits.

"Mum," she declared in a knock-out point, "It's *my* body."

Well, there was no arguing with that. I was sulky about being hoisted on the petard of my own rhetoric, but Ruth was being assertive, not rude.

Janina reckons it's important to distinguish between intentional and unintentional rude: "I'm gobsmacked by people who are intentionally rude and want to broadcast their cultural superiority. Do you remember Ellen, who used to work with us? She'd leave me speechless as she corrected people's pronunciation over the coffee table. Where does such toxicity come from?"

My heart sank when I heard this because Rosemarie and I make a collection of people's funny mistakes in communication. We don't do it with malice aforethought, and we laugh at words, not people. My point is some are screamingly funny, even in the direst of circumstances. My daughter's husband gave the eulogy at her funeral and I was enchanted when a friend told me that she'd enjoyed his urology. I'm also fond of UK Jane's story about her Scottish grandmother who sang "Gladly, the cross-eyed bear" until she read the hymn book: "Gladly the cross I'd bear."

I first met Lyall when he was thirty-nine and already completely grey. When I introduced him to a friend, she told me that he was "very extinguished."

Rosemarie's a stickler for grammar and language and almost forensic in spotting funny mistakes and malapropisms. At one stage, she collated them for my annual Christmas letter. The best of these include: 'You would have to be a mime-reader'; 'She's a vivacious reader'; 'the abolution blocks'; Crème de Meth (my all-time favourite); 'She's self-depreciating'; and, 'He was arrested for cardinal knowledge.' Given the subsequent arrest and trial of a certain Australian Cardinal for alleged sexual impropriety, maybe that wasn't a malapropism. I hope we're not being rude because we're having fun with words.

On balance, Janina wants to leave a patch for rudeness in our lives so that we can defend ourselves against attack. Her opinion is informed by a childhood experience when she was at school in Tanzania, where she had a formidable eight-year-old enemy. In Janina's unbiased opinion:

> *"this girl showed great potential for turning into an overweight and over-opinionated woman like her mother. She always wanted to be the fairy in the Xmas play and I was always the one chosen, so we were set for a stand-off. One day, she told me that my father was having an affair, and had been seen at a bar with another woman. How does an eight-year-old get to hear that kind of information? Anyway, I didn't know the niceties of the situation, so I went home and told Mum. All hell broke loose and my whole family drove off to her house to check the facts. She was all innocence and her mama cooed that her daughter would never say anything like that. Dad was so scared that he was very pleased to accept the denial. Both my parents turned on me and called me a liar and a trouble maker. I remember thinking that no one would believe me. Why insist I was telling the truth when*

they're all smugly in the safe version of the story?"

Eighteen months after the Tanzanian incident, Janina was living back in Wales, where she joined other kids playing in the street. One kid, Steven, called her 'a big fat farting horse,' so she told him that if anyone was fat it was his mother. He told his mum, and she barrelled down the road, her face an incandescent hue.

"I remember thinking that if I didn't speak up for myself it would be Tanzania-Gate all over again, but I had a problem. How could I tell them what Steven had called me? After all, 'farting' was a rude word and definitely not in the vocabulary book at my convent school. I decided to tell the assembled crowd what Steven said. Result? There was a pause, then much laughter. I learned that being rude is necessary at times. In any case, a rude woman to some is assertive to others" – a bit like Grace Tame, really.

I was once asked to write a piece about rude behaviour for an online magazine. The editor had just experienced an incident and she was furious. "I stood up for a much older woman as soon as I saw her getting on the bus, but a teenage guy sat down in the seat! The older woman had to stand (and so did I). I was livid. The poor woman was almost falling over and no one cared." She followed up with a picture of a wired-up young woman occupying two seats on a full bus. Headphones on, and engrossed in social media, she had no awareness of the needs of others.

Yet, generally, we are so hard-wired to be courteous that it's impossible to be rude. I used to invite my first-year students to reflect on the extent to which they are a product of their own society by asking them to contravene expected social behaviour. Often, the simplest ideas were the best – but just pushing into a queue proved too much for many of them. They couldn't do it. In general, though, I don't like too much conventional tut-tutting about rude behaviour. It seems so very narrow and suburban to me. So it's unsurprising that I love Ricky Gervais' stand-up comedy, in which he is so rude and yet so very humane. In fact, I would say, if you're going to be rude, do it well, like Australia's former Prime Minister, Paul Keating. People practically lined up to be insulted by Paul. Some of his top insults include:

- He's all tip and no iceberg,
- It was the limpest performance I've ever seen ... it was like being flogged with a warm lettuce.
- He's simply a shiver looking for a spine to run up.

Definitions of courtesy and rudeness are gendered. I remember staff room conversations about important issues, such as the need for child care, and equal pay for women, but we were certain to be interrupted by a male colleague saying, "But I like opening the doors for women."

Our rehearsed retort was, "It's not the doors you open for us that we're bothered about. It's the ones that you close."

When Liverpool Phil visited Australia one Christmas, he gave me a book entitled, 'Get in touch with your inner bitch.' In a light-hearted way, it explored how to deal with other people's rudeness. It advocated standing your ground, like Grace Tame, by saying, "I don't think so."

For example, I know one woman whose husband decided he wanted more variety in the breakfasts she cooked for him, so he wrote a list of possible breakfasts for her consideration.

"I don't think so," she said.

At one stage of my career, I gave a lot of talks to women's groups in the community called, 'The power of gossip,' to revaluate the much-demeaned term 'gossip'. They were about the power of women telling their stories *and* getting a hearing. The first of these talks was for an International Women's Day Breakfast in Kalgoorlie. When the organisers met me at the airport, they were thrilled to bits. They'd never had such a good turnout. Over two hundred women came to find out about the power of gossip.

I'd planned the breakfast talk so that I practised what I preached. I gave them some background on the useful exchange of women's information inherent in gossip, and then I mentioned the need for each to get in touch with her inner bitch. After that, I gave them their space to gossip about the last time they should have said, "I don't think so" – but didn't. It was a bit of a mistake, really, because I couldn't get them back. I had to curtail the rest of the talk. They had a riotous time as they shared stories about when they should have said no, and how they might have said it – courteously, of course.

Values: Making sense of religion

Descartes declared "I think, therefore I am."

My own self-evident statement is, "I'm English therefore I'm Anglican," which suggests that I wasn't doing much thinking as I grew up Anglican. Rather, I entered into a ready-made set of established religious values and ways of being. I was baptised at St Anne's Church, Nuneaton. For the two years I spent in the Girl Guides, I turned out for church parades, and I went to Sunday school, where I sang a song at their concert which taught me that I should love God and speak his will:

> Two little eyes that look to God
> Two little ears to hear his word
> One little mouth to speak his will

I said my prayers at night:
God bless Mummy
God bless Daddy

God bless all the world, Amen.

Even as a toddler, I didn't rate my 'Daddy' as being worth many of God's blessings, so I turned to another prayer:
If I should die before I wake
I pray the Lord my soul to take.
This wasn't optimistic as children's prayers go. Basically, I didn't find much joy in religion, even though my family culture was insistently Anglican.
My year was shaped by the Christian celebrations (and holidays) of Easter, Whitsun and Christmas, and the days of the week in my village were marked by church bells calling us to morning and evening service on Sundays. There was bell practice on Monday evenings and wedding bells on Saturdays.
Anglicanism was the State religion in England, so attendance at State schools included morning assemblies comprising Anglican hymns and prayers. Lyall was fond of watching 'Songs of Praise' on television. It's a program that features hymn singing in different churches around the UK. He loved the English countryside scenes, but he was always amazed that I could sing ahead of

the congregation because I'd learned the hymns off-by-heart at school assemblies.

He was fond of saying, "I wouldn't have been able to sing the next line if you offered me a million quid."

I wasn't aware of other religions until I went to high school, where I discovered that non-Anglican girls weren't required to participate in the religious aspect of morning assemblies. It was a question of Catholics and Jews drop-out – and there was only a handful of these. They returned for school notices.

Anglicanism meant being 'proper'. Mum liked to buy me a new hat to wear to church at Easter, and she grumbled at me for slouching as I walked to church with her. She taught me to bob up and down at appropriate junctures of church services, but I really wasn't engaged. Even the attempts of Sunday-school teachers to entice me hadn't worked. They gave me stamps to stick into my Sunday-school attendance book. In retrospect, I see that the inventors of supermarket customer loyalty programs, like Green Shield Stamps, tapped into a rich cultural heritage that offered market advantage in a nation primed to understand the rewarding nature of stamps.

I'd opted out of religion completely by the time I was thirteen, so I was never confirmed into the Anglican Church, yet it remained the wallpaper of my life until I lived on a kibbutz in Israel for six months in my early twenties. I discovered that 25 December was just an ordinary day of the working week for Israelis. New Year was in September, and the first day of the working week was Sunday. I worked in the kibbutz social club, so I had cleaning duties on Sunday mornings. I usually switched the radio to the BBC World Service to listen to 'Family Favourites.' This connected me to my 'roast beef and Yorkshire pudding' meaning of Sundays. My Israeli co-worker insisted on changing the station to Kol Israel. It became a weekly cross-cultural tussle.

My kibbutz hosted some sixty volunteers each summer, and they returned the favour of our free labour with weekend trips around Israel. One trip involved climbing three mountains in one day: Masada at 2am to avoid the heat of the day; then Ein Gedi before cooling off in the Dead Sea. This was followed by a climb to the monastery at the site where Jesus fasted for forty days and forty nights. By this time, I was tired. I staggered up the hill next to a Brooklyn Jewish guy to whom I ventured the opinion that it was small wonder that Jesus had hallucinations after climbing this mountain.

He looked askance, "You don't honestly think that he sat here for forty days and nights without food, do you?"

I was dumbfounded. "I suppose I don't. I've just never thought about it."

My experiences in Israel continued to tear down the Anglican wallpaper of my life. I travelled there with a school friend, and we visited the site of the 'loaves and fishes' miracle, which caused her to write to her Anglican mum asking how she could possibly believe that so little food could be shared among five thousand people.

"But that's the point!" her mum replied, offering her own contemporary explanation. "These people weren't educated. They spoke in concrete terms. They didn't have abstract concepts such as socialism, collectivism or communism. So what Jesus meant was this: if everyone shares what they have there should be enough to go round."

I was hooked. I loved this re-narration of the taken-for-granted Anglican meanings in my life, especially if they suited my left-wing political views.

I didn't baptise my children. I couldn't stand the hypocrisy of ritual admission to a community of faith that failed to engage me. It would have been difficult, anyway, because my background was Anglican, and Lyall's was Catholic.

When I was pregnant with our first child, I raised the subject of its future education. As a feminist, I favoured single-sex education, should our firstborn be a girl. At that stage, the evidence showed that girls achieve better in single-sex schools. Unfortunately, in Perth, the only single-sex high schools were private schools. Even worse, private schools were religious schools – and that's when the fight started. No way would I let a child of mine, especially a girl, go to Catholic school. (I'm opposed to the implications of Catholicism for women's reproductive health). No way would Lyall let a child of his go to a Protestant school. (He thought they were too elitist). We were well into the debate before I started laughing because neither of us was a practicing Christian. This was like two agnostics arguing about which religion not to raise our child in.

Yet, when Ruth and Sam began studying English literature in high school, I realised that I'd done them a disservice because they lacked the metaphor of their Judeo-Christian heritage. So I decided to tackle sixteen-year-old Sam.

"What do you know about the New Testament?" I asked him.

"Hasn't it got something to do with Jesu of Naru," he replied.

"Sit down and listen, son. We have a long way to go here."

The books I bought to offer them some knowledge of religious traditions lay unread, but the global travel we gave them in childhood did something to make up for the shortfall in their religious education. My aim was to give them strong humanitarian values with or without religion.

It doesn't really matter much which lens you use to study sociology. Essentially the same understanding of social processes will emerge. It just depends on what interests you, and the sociology of religion intrigued me when I was in the third year of my degree at Liverpool University. I'd had some exposure to the study of religion in the previous two years when I read Max Weber's 'Protestant Ethic and the Spirit of Capitalism.' He gave me my first insight into how religion might influence culture, behaviour and social change. Protestantism, he thought, was more conducive to industrialisation than Catholicism.

I was pleased to discover that it's all about our own constructions of meaning – and that we can invest anything with our own meanings of the sacred. We all have sacred and profane places, and Liverpool University was my sacred place in which I came into my own understanding of the world around me. It was such a liberation from the confines of my rural upbringing. Being there in the 'Swinging 60s' might also have had something to do with it. If ever I were to be asked which place in my life is most sacred, it would be my undergraduate Liverpool world. I was a born-again sociologist. I'd found something that helped me to develop my own meanings in my own life.

Despite my intellectual engagement with the

sociology of religion, the essential spirituality of religion has always escaped me and, it would seem, my Perth friend, Val.

"I would call Charles a true believer," Val observed during a recent telephone conversation. It's just as well because Charles had been the priest in her Catholic parish. She'd never felt herself to be a true believer but contented herself with the sense of belonging she felt with a church that had been her lifelong companion. She'd never left her church. Charles had, temporarily, but he returned. He was a migrant to Perth at the same time as me, and we were both sociologists. Even better, we'd both studied the sociology of religion, so we could swap notes to help in each other's university teaching. He'd done a fascinating study on the sociology of death and dying in which he'd shown social patterns in the time of death – meaning that people of each religion hang on to life until after a major religious festival. So, for example, there can be a surge in Christian deaths after Christmas and Jewish deaths after Passover.

Charles eventually became my PhD supervisor. I'd just submitted my thesis for examination when I received a phone call from Bev, who was finalising her own PhD under Charles' supervision.

"Have you heard from Charles?" she asked. When I told her I hadn't, she said, "Well, I'm not going to tell you anything. You're lifelong friends, so he should tell you himself."

I hate it when people ring with some hot goss and then don't tell you what it is.

I arrived home from work one day to find Lyall with his hand atop a pile of post. "I bet you a million dollars that you'll never guess what invitation arrived today," he declared.

I didn't fancy the odds, so I searched through and found an invitation to Charles' ordination. In his late fifties, he'd decided to become a Catholic priest, and we were invited to his ordination. This put Lyall into a rare-old Catholic spin. He forbade our daughter, Ruth, from wearing a strappy tee shirt, and marched ahead of us into St Mary's Cathedral like a regular patriarch. You can take the man out of the Catholic Church, but you can't take the church out of the man. Ruth was a bit grumpy when she saw other girls wearing revealing tee shirts, but, apart from that, the ordination was a joyous occasion.

Charles was ecstatic to be enfolded, once again, in the arms of Catholicism. I've just been reading his book 'Jesus Matters.' It reveals the intimate and intellectual nature of his relationship with faith and spirituality.

Charles really is a true believer, and so is another friend, Diana. In the early 1970s, she prayed for safety before setting off on a long car journey. Within hours, an oncoming truck caused her to take evasive action. The car rolled and she came to a halt upside down. She heard a voice saying, "You'll be alright." She also had a very real sense that she'd been saved for a purpose – "Something big," as she puts it.

She was alright. Only two cars came along this lonely stretch of road, one of which contained a doctor, and the other some strong lads who helped to right the car. The sense of purpose came later when she worked as Translation Director for an International Bible Organisation through which, in her words, "God used her to help people throughout the world grow in their faith."

Religious experience, spirituality, and a sense of community have created meaning in the lives of friends, and faith has been ever-present, as Janina describes it, "like a warm comforting bath with no need to keep topping up the water," but it can also be hard work. Even my Buddhist friend, William, reckons that "Faith is a decision at times," and Charles often thinks that his faith is held by sheer grit rather than any holy feelings, guessing that, "Perhaps that is how we all make meaning – through determination and sheer grit."

Values: Making sense of secrets

There was little administration to do when Lyall died in 2018. He'd visited his lawyer a short time after I retired in 2010, so his estate planning had been in order for years. His main income source was his defined benefit superannuation, and this type of pension can be inherited only by a spouse, so there was a small amount of paperwork to do for this, including submitting the exact birthdates of all his kids. I went to his Death Certificate to make sure I noted the details correctly. This was the first time I'd looked carefully at the list of kids. To my surprise, there was one more than I'd known about. I thought it must be a typo, so I rang the funeral parlour, and they insisted that the document was accurate as confirmed by the Registrar of Births, Deaths and Marriages.

I started to ask around. Lyall's children from his first marriage declined to share information other than to say that the extra child's name is on all of their birth certificates. It's not on my children's birth certificates. I then received an anonymous, poorly written letter with incorrect spelling. Lyall would have referred to it as a letter written by 'a thumbnail dipped in tar,' in a reference to Banjo Patterson's poem, 'Clancy of the Overflow.' It directed me to Lyall's sister for information, but she hadn't spoken to Lyall since about 1980, so there was little point barking up that tree. It all felt very grubby. It certainly lacked the dignity owed to Lyall in death. I also became alarmed. I was living alone in a large house. Who was the person who wrote the letter? How does s/he know my address?

I rang Pam in Queensland. She's a friend and a lawyer.

"Hang on," she said. "Let me go and find my birth certificate. I'll see what the exact wording is."

The wording runs along these lines, 'Is there any other issue from *this relationship.*' This explains why the extra baby's name was not on my children's birth certificate (nor were those of their half-siblings) because my relationship with Lyall was new and different from his first marriage. I was in shock, and I was also angry because nobody would give me any information. Seemingly it was none of my business.

Depriving people of information falls into the definition of bullying, and I knew how to deal with that: Blow the story wide open. Don't protect the bullies with your silence. Of course, I've been condemned for this as well.

"That's the trouble with you, Lynne. You always want to talk about things."

So I wrote an email to all of Lyall's kids, for whom I had an address, and I included his cousins. I thought that, being closer in age to Lyall, they might have heard something about the baby girl that I now call the 'The seventh child.' In fact, she was the first of Lyall's documented seven children. I also asked a local friend who'd known Lyall since they were young. No, nobody knew anything. One of Lyall's daughters did reply to say that, in the eighties, the 'seventh child' had returned to Kalgoorlie to find her parents. This particular daughter had acted as a go-between in regard to consent forms and had been sworn to secrecy.

As it turned out, none of Lyall's other children knew about the attempt by their eldest sister (the seventh child) to contact her birth family. This was secrets within secrets. By the time I discovered the story on Lyall's death certificate, the truth could be sought only from Lyall's first wife. So one of Lyall's daughters went to ask her mum. The story that fell out is not mine to tell.

What I can tell is my story.

The implication of the secret of the seventh child is that my husband had deceived me for our entire marriage. As one of his cousins said, "That's the kind of stuff you clear up before you get married."

I was chatting with my son, Sam, about this just recently, "I married late and dated a lot in my twenties, so I didn't think it necessary to give your dad a full roll call of previous boyfriends, but I did tell him anything that might wrong-foot him if he were to find out, and I think I'd have let him know if I had a child floating around somewhere."

The implication for other family members, including my son, is that they might have a sister, half-sister, or cousin who they've never met. Some would like to.

I went to London from 1978 to 1979 to do my Master's degree. Lyall and I had already been an item for two years, so we wrote many letters to each other, which we kept. I'm just re-reading them now before throwing them out. In one letter, we discussed honesty in marriage, and there it was in black and white: "I have no secrets from you, at least none that are current or relevant."

All I could think was, "You bastard! You kept the secret knowingly and deliberately."

This wasn't the only secret Lyall had kept from me. Just three years before he died, he told me that his father and mother had abandoned him when he was twelve.

"You were abandoned at age twelve! Why haven't you told me about this before?" It was quite a secret!

"I was ashamed," he replied.

Things started to click into place. I'd always felt blocked by Lyall because he would never discuss issues of importance to me. I can still see him tapping his hand on the arm of his chair in time with his statement to emphasise: "I will not worry about things over which I can have no control."

The secrets, that are now revealed, indicate that there was much in his life over which he'd had no control, and these had intergenerational consequences that rocked down through the years, damaging my marriage with him and my relationship with his kids. The man I married because of his principled approach to life turns out not to have lived by the fundamental principle of honesty with his wife.

I took a particular interest in secrets when we developed the Hartland Britton Family Website - that's my mother's family in Devon. We had to make decisions about the stories worth telling and those that should be kept private. The questions I asked myself were: "Who needs to know this stuff, and how does this story add value to history?"

I chatted with Janina about this. She thinks that "There's ambivalence about secrets – about when they're good, and when they're harmful. Clearly, what was kept from you were bombshells – enough to make you revise what you felt about your husband and your marriage. But are there some circumstances when whatever's hidden or not spoken about is done with benevolent intent? It also depends on when and how the information is revealed. For example, I think that I should have been told secrets about some of my family matters at the time they became known. To have them dumped on me thirty years later was hurtful and puzzling. Similarly, I haven't told a friend about her husband's invitations to have lunch with me. I didn't then because I thought it was a hiccup in their marriage. They didn't need me making it worse, and I won't now because – well, what's the point?"

We wouldn't have laws around privacy if we didn't value our right to keep our own secrets, but secrets do control the flow of information, and this can be weaponised. My UK cousin Dan, who worked on the family website with me, thinks that "secrets are like a cancer slowly eating away at people. Although, I appreciate that the truth can be hard to hear and share."

He has a point. I know that, among my family and friends, there are plenty of stories showing intergenerational trauma arising from secrets.

"I'm thinking of writing a piece about secrets," I said when I was back in Cheltenham having coffee with a group of school friends.

"Well, you can have mine," they chorused. I'd been intending to tell them my story about Lyall's secrets, but the conversational basketball bounced away and didn't return.

Niki told her story first. She left school before

the rest of us. At the time, we'd understood that it was because her dad was being transferred elsewhere to work. In fact, she was pregnant, so he'd asked for a transfer so that she could have her baby away from our hometown. She had a daughter, who was raised as her sister. I'd heard this story a few years earlier when Niki came to stay with me in Perth. She'd sworn me to secrecy, and I'd kept my word, but on this day, in the Cheltenham coffee shop, it became apparent that everyone else knew.

"Bloody hell, Niki, I've been keeping that a secret!"

It's only now, in her seventies, that Niki is finally addressing issues arising from this secret, up to and including communicating with her grandson as a grandson, and not as her nephew.

Back in the UK, Catherine told me that she was born around the time of her dad's death. Her mum had remarried, and she'd been raised by her mother and her step-father. Eventually, her mum died, and Catherine sorted through her old family photos. She had a moment of insight and called her step-dad to say, "You're my dad aren't you?" Her mum had jumped the gun on her dying husband and passed off the child as his so that the baby's birth date looked respectable.

In a classic upstairs-downstairs story, another friend, Rick, was the product of a wealthy homeowner and the maid. The pregnant maid was married off, and Rick grew up thinking of this couple as his parents. Uncle Alan did call by from time to time, bringing money and gifts, but Rick was unaware that Uncle Alan was his father.

Does this matter? Why air any secrets? Should I even be writing about them? Does it really matter if she discovered that her husband visited sex workers during their marriage? Does the world need to know that one of her kids was the product of a one-night stand and that she went missing to protect herself from family opprobrium? Does it add value to my understanding of her to find out that she tried to commit suicide after years in pain?

All these secrets have been kept by people who've been part of my life, and their specific stories will remain untold. They have a right to their secrets, although, collectively, their stories sadden me, and I regret that the course of their lives was changed and kept secret, all for the sake of what others might think.

I went to a talk by British author Martin Amis a few years ago, and he declared that we reveal only about five per cent of ourselves. I don't think he'd be able to back that statement with evidence, but I think it's a point well made. We do keep a lot to ourselves. We do want privacy in our lives, and we do craft an image of ourselves based on what we allow others to know. This means guarding the information we share. Yet, some secrets should be told.

"There are good secrets and bad secrets."

The note outside my grandson's classroom alerted parents to the subject of child sexual abuse – currently part of the kids' curriculum. I could see why they adopted this approach because it's difficult for five-year-olds to make sense of a world in which they are asked to keep secrets about surprise birthday parties or presents. Yet, the school tells them not to keep secrets when an abuser asks them to keep quiet about their special friendship.

From a kid's point of view, when is a secret not a secret?

Similarly, the women's health movement in which I worked challenged secrecy about domestic violence – scream quietly so the neighbours don't hear. Certainly, my mum didn't want people, especially her Devonshire family, to know what happened to her. When I did break the news about the intergenerational consequences of my dad's violence, my great-niece, Becky, now working in feminist public health issues, wrote to say how proud she was of me and my sisters for surviving and thriving.

"I've often felt there was a lot that I didn't know about those days, and whilst I wish they could have been happier stories, it certainly helps piece together how we've all come to be where we are, so thank you."

Lifestyle and culture:
The meaning of travel

Hometown friend, Brian, reckons that when he first met me when we were eighteen, he saw me as the snobby girl from Pates who could speak French. That's not the way I saw myself, but I'd lived with a family in France during summer holidays as part of my French studies at school, and they'd broadened my horizons. My 'French Dad' was a rural doctor. My 'French Mum' was a pharmacist. In the mid-1960s that was quite an achievement for a woman in rural France. They lived in the Pyrenees, and had two children. My job was to teach English to their eleven-year-old daughter, but I generally mucked in with the family, and I was congratulated on my helpfulness, so I guess I did the right thing.

They were sophisticated and, I suspect, they felt a little superior to the British. Which French person doesn't? My 'French Mum' went through my wardrobe and pronounced my taste in clothes satisfactory. So they should have been because this was the mid-1960s when London's Carnaby Street ruled, and Britain's Mary Quant led the world of fashion designers. Even so, I became her project, for which I remain grateful. She was like my personal finishing school. She took me to have my hair cut in a stylish bob; she bought me a new dress, and she introduced me to French music, in particular Edith Piaf, Francoise Hardy and Charles Aznavour.

They had a *Citroën* DS car, which rose up on its suspension on ignition. I was dazzled. My 'French Mother' drove me around in it, and used my time as a captive audience in the passenger seat to educate me about philosophy – something taught in French schools but not in my English school. I was gobsmacked to discover that Hitler wrote 'Mein Kampf.' Until then, I thought the only thing he did was chuck bombs at English cities. They used the car to drive us across to the Riviera, staying at Juan Les Pins, and visiting the casino at Cannes.

These were the days of the old French Franc, which was in serious need of revaluation. My

'French Father' was most amused when he ordered a bottle of champagne at the casino because the zeros started on the left-hand page of the menu and extended across to the far side of the right page. A young cousin of the family travelled with us as my companion. She and I shared a hotel room, and we escaped after 'lights out' to visit teen nightclubs on the beach. It was pretty exciting stuff. The family also rented a villa on the beach in Spain and had a boat that they used for water-skiing – which I learned to do. If this was how the other half lived, I wanted more of it. The meaning I made of my life and my ambitions changed under the influence of my French family.

I went to stay with them for a second summer after their daughter had come to visit me in England. On our return to France, my 'French Father' drove to meet us in Paris. He took us to the top of the Eiffel Tower for our first meal. Experiences like this didn't happen to many seventeen-year-olds in the mid-1960s. As we drove out of Paris, he apologised that he hadn't been able to take us to the Moulin Rouge. The age of majority was twenty-one, and we had to wait.

He promised to take us there when we were of age. That day never came. He died soon after, aged thirty-eight.

He was a foodie before that word existed. Bearing in mind that I didn't even know what a steak was – or yoghurt – before I lived with this family, I was a willing learner. He knew the exact restaurant to visit almost anywhere in France. On the Riviera trip, we stopped in Le Vieux Port, in Marseilles, to have lunch at the restaurant reputed to have created bouillabaisse. Driving south from Paris, we dined in Orleans at a restaurant that specialises in truffle omelettes. Much of this was lost on me. I thought it was mushrooms.

In Barcelona, we went to Los Caracoles, which I recently recommended to a friend travelling to Spain. He reported back that he'd passed it by. It seemed yuppie and trendy. It probably was when I was there, but I was getting used to this lifestyle. This family was hugely influential in expanding my horizons.

Immediately after graduating from Liverpool University in 1970, I toured the USA by Greyhound Bus. It was the thing to do, and many students of my generation availed themselves of the services of the British Universities North America Club (BUNAC). This student organisation provided a guidebook, a cheap return airfare to the USA, and a Greyhound Bus ticket, that lasted for ninety-nine days. I went just after the cost had risen slightly. Before that, the whole deal was advertised as '$99 for 99 days.'

I went with Sue, one of my Liverpool flatmates. We flew first to New York, and I have a photograph of us there in the days before the Twin Towers were built. The route we took around the USA was partly determined by who we knew and where they lived. We'd met an American exchange student in Liverpool, so we went first to Boston to visit her. We circled around the USA, taking in major cities and sights, including Niagara Falls, Chicago, Mt Rushmore, Yellowstone Park, San Francisco, Berkley, Disneyland, Santa Fé, Grand Canyon and Washington.

Bus-hopping worked well for most destinations, but in Yellowstone Park, we had to team up with a group of French students doing a similar tour around the USA. We hired a car together and drove around visiting the 'Old Faithful' geyser en route. That night, around the campfire, I discovered, for the first time, that British and French students really are taught different perspectives on history. Goodness knows why he was talking with me about Napoleon, but he rehearsed a number of battles Napoleon had won. I hadn't heard of them.

"But what about Moscow and Waterloo?" I asked.

He seemed hazy on these, and so, indirectly, the BUNAC trip gave me insight into the Britishness of my outlook. I didn't know, for example, that African Americans generally sat at the back of the bus. Unwittingly, I invaded their territory. Nobody seemed to mind, though I did wonder why my hands got so greasy. It was from holding on to the backs of seats as I disembarked. It was the era when excessive amounts of hair oil were used to straighten Afro hair.

I went to Israel by chance. I was at a loose end for the summer of 1971. So, when my school friend, Gwyneth, phoned to see if I'd like to go with her to work on a kibbutz, I said yes. As I found out later, working on the collective farms, known as kibbutzim, was the trendy left-wing thing to do. I became fascinated by the determination of Jewish Israelis, who had carved a living for themselves out of Zionist ideology, and the bare land. Kibbutz Ma'anit grew apples, oranges, grapefruit, avocados and other fruit and vegetables. I grew weary of picking apples and eventually got to work in the avocado fields. This was more fun. There was a certain challenge in manipulating a small net on the end of a long pole around the avocado before manoeuvring the snippers around the stem to cut the fruit off the tree. The fields were at some distance from the kibbutz, so we took breakfast with us and picnicked in the fields. It was all very bucolic.

The working day for volunteers, like me, began at 5.30 am with just a quick drink and snack to start the day. After working in the apple orchards for a few hours, we'd return for a Middle Eastern breakfast of fruit, salad, daisa, and eggs. This was followed by a few more hours of picking fruit until lunch. The rest of the day was our own.

The Kibbutz had a pool, and we spent many afternoons lounging and talking. The conversation was intelligent. This is where I learned about Judaism, and absorbed alternative interpretations of the Bible. In many ways, it was a time of deconstructing old meanings in my life. The mystery of Christianity faded through Israeli experiences such as entering the Church of the Holy Sepulchre in Jerusalem, where we were greeted by street hawkers trying to make a quick buck by selling crowns of thorns – brambles gathered from hedgerows. In Bethlehem, local men tried to gain advantage by tempting young women to go with them to see the fields where the shepherds were. My departure from organised religion was now complete.

On the kibbutz, I met a volunteer who wanted to travel. He could speak five languages and had considerable travel experience, so we teamed up and embarked on a backpacking trip to Australia. At that time, backpackers mostly did the hippy trail between Britain and Australia, travelling through India and Afghanistan. We wanted to be different, so we planned to travel via Eastern Europe, across the Soviet Union on the Trans-Siberian Railway, and then by boat to Japan. After that, we had no plans except to reach English-speaking Australia, work for a couple of years, and earn some money to travel back to Europe via South and North America.

We had a shared interest in all things Israeli and Jewish. I'd already read a lot of Leon Uris: 'Exodus'; 'Mila 18'; and 'Armageddon: A Novel of Berlin.' This background reading influenced our plans for the first part of the trip. First, we caught a train from Brussels to East Germany. Crossing the Berlin Wall at dawn, I looked down and saw the dog pounds that guarded the border. It was an eerie, threatening experience, but visiting East Germany seemed quite normal, and the Stasi wasn't interested in us. After East Germany, we caught a train to Warsaw and sought out the location of the Warsaw Ghetto, where a handful of Jews kept cultural memories alive in a small museum. I realised that Leon Uris had done his homework here. I saw the milk churns he'd mentioned in 'Mila 18,' in which the inhabitants of the Ghetto buried their stories and their possessions. They wanted the world to know what had happened to them. The power of storytelling was beginning to dawn on me.

The train journey between Warsaw and Moscow was like travelling through the film set of 'Fiddler on the Roof': Wooden cottages, villages, dirt roads. It was picturesque when viewed from the train, but not easy to live there, I'm sure. Our journey was punctuated by the sound of hammer and sickle when we stopped in the night because the wheel-base needed to be adjusted to the Soviet railway gauge – deliberately created by the Russians to inhibit the advance of invading armies. Our journey was facilitated by Intourist, understood to be part of the Soviet KGB, and a surveillance unit for foreign visitors, among others. However, they were also a help, and we needed them in Siberia when we took a break from the long trans-Siberian train trip choosing to fly between Irkutsk and Khabarovsk. We sat separately on the plane so that we could both have a window seat.

Unbeknown to me, my travel companion took a photo at Irkutsk airport. This wasn't allowed, and he was spotted by a flight attendant who wouldn't have looked out of place in the Gestapo. She reported him. He anticipated what might happen. He took the film from his camera because it had our Moscow photos on it, and he handed it over the back of his seat to me. I didn't know what was happening. I just put the film in my handbag, as requested. He replaced it in the camera with a new, blank film. When we got to Khabarovsk, all passengers remained seated, and great-coated soldiers boarded the plane to escort us into the airport. The Intourist woman, who awaited us, explained that it was an innocent mistake, so they settled for ripping the film out of his camera. We still had our Moscow photos. This turn of events means that I'd innocently carried the hot goods through the inspection. We boarded the train to the coast, where we caught our boat to Japan.

We spent a month in Japan – a country that bamboozled me. It's so different culturally that I read an anthropology book to make sense of it all. Ruth Benedict's 'Chrysanthemum and the Sword' was written in 1946 to help the conquering American troops understand the vanquished Japanese people and their culture. The title illustrates her assessment that Japan is a country of extremes – of beauty and violence. I don't think that makes the Japanese particularly different from any other culture, except that their beauty is more delicate and exquisite than most.

After a month in Japan, I was glad to get to Taiwan. After living in Liverpool for five years, with its significant Chinese population, I felt entirely comfortable to be back in Chinese society. We caught a bus along their east-west highway, so-called I joked, only because of its altitude. For the most part, it was a scary ride along narrow roads which dropped away sharply. Next the Philippines. Despite the beauty of the rice terraces and the intrigue of head-hunting tribes, I think my predominant memory is of the worst toilet block I've ever seen in my days of cheap backpacking. This contrasted with the opulence of staying with relatives who were senior in the World Bank. They lived in a gated community next door to the brother of President Marcos. We dined and swam at the Polo Club, and generally lived the elite life of the ex-pat community for a couple of weeks.

We moved on through Hong Kong, Thailand, Malaysia, Singapore and Perth. I learned a lot on this trip about the western definitions implicit in my geography lessons at school. I realised that the Far East isn't very far from anything for the people who live there. In fact, it's quite close. I no longer speak in terms of Asia because the range of countries and cultures is too diverse to be captured in a single concept.

My British views of the world were particularly

challenged in the Philippines, where I visited American war cemeteries that stretched as far as the eye could see. I knew there had been battles in the Pacific, but my British education had focussed on Europe in World War II. In my mind, the Pacific was a bit of a sideshow.

So, by the time I was twenty-five, travel had given rise to many new meanings in my life. By the time I was seventy, I'd visited almost eighty countries. Travel is now part of my identity, and this is the way others see me. A few years ago, I bumped into some backpackers at an isolated bus stop on Magnetic Island in Queensland. We talked about backpacking, and I mentioned my trip from London to Perth in 1973. Within seconds, I had five young men sitting at my feet listening to tales of REAL backpacking.

"My goodness," one of them said, "You didn't even have backpackers' hostels in those days!"

I'd never thought of myself as the Grand Dame of backpacking, but I enjoyed their reaction and claimed the title.

Lifestyle and Culture:
The meaning of music

Music is the metronome that ticks off the milestones in my life. I graduated from children's songs through pop music to folk, classical music, and opera. It's not a linear journey because I revisit different genres all the time. Even children's songs have re-entered my life now that I'm a grandmother. Essentially, I'm a 1960s pop tragic. The music of the 1970s and 1980s passed me by as I busied myself with travel, family and career, but I circled back to these lost years in my retirement, encouraged by Ben Elton's musical 'We Will Rock You' and the film, 'Bohemian Rhapsody.' Freddie Mercury and Brian May proved an unmissable, if late, entry to my life.

I'm a baby-boomer, and I was a teenager in the UK when 'England swung like a pendulum do,' and Carnaby Street fashion ruled the world. Elvis was still significant but a bit passé for me. He belonged to my older sister's era. When I was twelve, in 1960, Cliff Richard and Adam Faith divided my class at school. I favoured Adam Faith. He seemed a little more edgy to me. In reality, both sang banal teeny-bopper songs. Much the same happened with the division between fans of the Beatles and the Rolling Stones. This all reflected issues of identity, which were writ large in the fights on the beaches between British teenagers who saw themselves as Mods and Rockers, in accordance with fashion and musical preference.

My childhood tastes in music were shaped by the BBC. We were one of the first families in the street to get a television, which happened when I was about four years old, in 1952. So my earliest musical memories are associated with the theme tunes of children's programs such as 'We love Muffin, Muffin the mule,' and 'Andy is waving goodbye.' If you're singing those tunes in your head as you read, you were also in front of the TV as a child in the early 1950s.

I was about fifty when I saw the saddest thing I've seen on TV. It was a BBC comedy skit. A producer of my vintage had taken it into his head to gather, in a bar, the star puppets of my early 1950s children programs (Andy Pandy, Looby Loo, Muffin the Mule, and Sooty). They were drowning their sorrows as a group of has-beens. It wasn't at all funny. In fact, it was a break of sacred trust with the childhood memories the BBC itself had created.

Following an early start with television, I had a few years without TV or radio, mostly because I lived in a house without electricity. So my theme-tune musical memories cut back in with 'The Avengers,' 'Dr Who' and 'Coronation Street.' A dog I know particularly objects to 'Coronation Street' and howls his way through until the music stops. I can't say I blame him.

Before I went to school, the BBC dominated interpretations of popular music: 'Billy Cotton's Band Show' (with the catch-cry, 'Wakey wakey'); 'Workers' Playtime'; 'Family Favourites'; and 'Children's Favourites.' These became the memorable programs of the first five years of my life.

Where would I be now, as a grandmother, if I hadn't been a fan of 'Children's Favourites'? I can still sing, 'I'm a Pink Toothbrush, You're a Blue

Toothbrush.' Danny Kaye was big when I was little. He sang – and I particularly liked – 'The Ugly Duckling.' But there were other favourites such as 'Nellie the Elephant' and 'Tubby the Tuba.' In the 1980s, I evolved into loving the children's music of my kids' generation when Australian Peter Coombes was top of the tiny tots' hit parade. 'Spaghetti Bolognaise' and 'Wash Your Face in Orange Juice' were firm favourites. Coombes has a generation of fans who are now in their thirties, so he was persuaded to do a pub gig in Melbourne to play his children's songs. He was apprehensive. He thought it wouldn't work. To everyone's delight, his thirty-year-old fans spilled out onto the streets, all wearing their triangular pirate newspaper hats and singing 'Newspaper Mama' along with him. He was a smash hit – and deservedly so.

My 1960s UK baby-boomer generation grabbed opportunities to forge their tastes in music and resist the BBC's music monopoly. This establishment organisation was reluctant to give in to the challenges of the emerging pop scene. Elvis' gyrating pelvis may have had something to do with it, though that hardly mattered on the radio. So, if you can't beat them, move around them. Pop music broadcasting moved off-shore. My sister and I used to listen to Radio Luxembourg with our hands pressed to the side of the radio to improve reception. This radio station made Jimmy Savile famous. His infamy as a paedophile came later, whilst working for the BBC.

Radio Caroline started in 1964. It was a pirate radio station that broadcasted from a boat in the English Channel. They were fought with everything the establishment could throw at them. The story of that struggle is told in the 2009 Film 'The Boat that Rocked'. In the end, the BBC had to relent, creating extra channels to accommodate diverse and emerging tastes in music.

I started going to gigs when I was about twelve. My long-suffering mother took me to see Cliff Richard when he appeared at the Odeon in my hometown – Cheltenham. She also took me to see Billy Fury. I didn't see the Rolling Stones when they played the Odeon. Instead, I caught up with them at the local Wimpy Bar (think MacDonald's). I went, after school, with a group of friends. We were still in uniform, and we may have felt that gave us an entrée because Brian Jones, the founder and original leader of the Stones, came from Cheltenham. His sister had been a few years ahead of us at our girls' school. We chatted and got autographs. It puts the Stones into their 1963 context to understand that the only performance venues in Cheltenham were small cinemas. They were the warm-up group for the headline act – The Everly Brothers.

What amazes me now is that small-town, rural Cheltenham had so much to offer in terms of pop music. I saw the Beatles at the Odeon. My mother queued for much of the day to get tickets for three school friends and me. We had seats close to the front. I remember two things. John Lennon had announced that they liked Jelly Babies, so I was pelted from behind by jelly babies that fans threw toward the stage. I also remember that I was annoyed by the screaming. I wanted to hear the music. Paul McCartney later reflected on these years, noting that the screaming covered up many a musical mistake on their part. My nephew, Martyn, recently found a photo of the Beatles for sale online. It was taken at the Cheltenham gig on 1 November 1963. He circulated the advertisement to me, and I passed it on to school friends. It elicited quite a response. I'd hazard a guess that about a quarter of my school saw the Beatles that night, and many of us had mums who queued all day for our tickets. Bless them. Quite a few of us grew up to become teachers, and we all acknowledge that actually seeing the Beatles when we were fifteen gave us considerable street cred with our students through the years.

Small-town Cheltenham had a surprisingly strong pop music scene. The Town Hall held weekly dances. I danced to the 'Troggs,' 'Hollies' and 'Searchers' – all big names at the time. The Yardbirds visited the Athletic Ground. I was part of a judo display from my youth club, and I shook hands with them. The Promenade, the elegant main street of Cheltenham, was closed off for a short time in the summer months so that we could dance in the street to local bands, and enjoy the eye candy of the male French exchange students from Cheltenham's twin town, Annecy. My friend, Jacky, tells stories of the Blue Moon nightclub where she saw Jimi Hendrix in 1967. That's unbelievable. JIMI HENDRIX in little ole Cheltenham!! Why wasn't I there?

I had my musical fads and fashions as a

teenager. I couldn't wait for the New Musical Express to arrive each week, and my mother also bought me the monthly Beatles magazines. I rarely missed the new pop programs: 'Juke Box Jury'; 'Ready Steady Go'; and 'Top of the Pops.' I aped the female presenter, Cathy McGowan, with my heavy-fringe hairstyle.

On weekends, I went with school friends to a music shop in Cheltenham, where the trendy thing to do was squeeze into a sound-proofed box to listen to the latest singles through headphones. These were the days of vinyl. One memorable coffee shop had phones on the table so that we could call the DJ to play our choice of music. We thought we were the ants' pants. Dad bought my sister and me a Dansette record player in the early 1960s. The first record I ever bought was 'Concrete and Clay' by 'Unit Four Plus Two.' In retrospect, I'm pleased with my choice. It had quite complex syncopation and avoided a banal teenybopper style.

I started at Liverpool University in 1967. The city's connection with the Beatles was a bonus for me, but they were long gone by then. The vacuum they left was filled, in part, by the Mersey Beat poets, some of whom combined to form The Scaffold, still famous for their songs 'Lily the Pink' and 'Thank U Very Much' – the latter resurrected in 2020 as 'Thank U Very Much for the NHS' during the COVID Pandemic. I saw them at the Everyman Theatre in Liverpool, but mostly I saw bands at university dances. Recently I found some old student newsletters listing the bands that played in those days. I was disappointed that I couldn't remember seeing them.

The bands that played for dances at my hall of residence included: 'Mindbenders'; 'Unit Four Plus Two'; 'Easybeats'; and the Liverpool band,' Colonel Bagshot.' At the University's Student Guild, we saw, among others, 'The Kinks' and Francoise Hardy, the French songstress.

Folk music attracted my attention when I went to Liverpool University, but I'd been a fan long before. Pete Seeger's 1963 'Little Boxes' railed against life in suburbia. The yearning for something different from the 'ticky-tacky' lives of their parents led my generation to the flower power movement, represented in song by Scott McKenzie's 'If You're Going to San Francisco.' I did go in 1970 as part of a Greyhound bus trip around the USA. It was all very 'of the moment.'

Folk music is storytelling, and it's a cross-over to poetry. I can't multitask when listening to folk songs. I'm compelled to sit and just listen to the power and cleverness of the words. Leonard Cohen's famous 'Hallelujah' sounds meditative – almost hymn-like, but it's about the bitterness of a failing relationship. Ralph McTell is a top-shelf guitarist, wordsmith and advocate for social justice – 'Streets of London' is about homelessness and loneliness. My singer-songwriter cousin, Dan Britton, arranged for a gift to me from Ralph McTell. It was a four-CD box set 'Affairs of the Heart.' It was signed out to my name 'With love from Ralph.' So I have it in writing that he loves me, and it's framed in my study. It is still possible for seventy-three year-olds to be fangirls.

I learned to love opera and classical music when I studied for my Master's degree at the London School of Economics (LSE) 1978-79. LSE is just a short walk from Covent Garden Opera House. I still don't know a lot about classical music, but my home and car radios are permanently tuned to 'Classic FM,' and I find the commentary of the presenters informative.

Seeking to improve my understanding, I joined a classical music cruise of the Danube in 2018 with a Queensland friend, Pam. Sightseeing was incidental to the musical events. There were two musicologists on board who gave lectures associated with the composers of each country we visited. Given that we fell asleep in one country and woke up in the next, this meant quite a few lectures. I was intrigued when they explained the influence of folk music on classical music composers Liszt and Dvořák among them. They discovered and catalogued hundreds of ethnic folk tunes. It was a pleasing continuity between my love of folk and classical music. On our way down the Danube, we listened to orchestral rehearsals, visited the homes of Mozart and Dvořák, dined in palaces to the tune of local ensembles, and attended workshops to watch Europe's up-and-coming opera singers put through their paces. The highlight was attending the Vienna Opera House for Saint-Saëns' 'Sampson and Delilah.' The staging was stunning, and the Opera House is grand in the extreme.

"Oh, so, if you know Gill and she knows Paul, that means I'm within two degrees of difference from Paul McCartney."

It was in the late 1990s, and we were waiting for a university senior executive meeting to start. My colleague was thrilled to bits by our conversation. By this stage in life, we might have been seen by students at our university as crusty old academics, but we thought our conversation was pretty cool. I'd never thought of being at one degree of difference from Paul. The Gill in this story was at school with me, and we both completed post-secondary education in Liverpool – a city to which we both return as often as possible. On one of her visits, she'd met Paul and Linda McCartney and became something of a family friend. Gill's connection with pop music continued through her adult life in San Francisco and, at one stage, she was in Chris Isaak's road crew. He was popular in Australia, so Gill and I were able to catch up when he did tours Down Under. So, through Gill, I was able to meet Chris. By now, I was approaching fifty years of age. I still loved pop music, and I enjoyed his gigs.

I don't know exactly, what makes a musical memory iconic, but an outstanding event for me was a comparatively small concert in Mirepoix,

France in 1965, where I saw 'Les Compagnons de la Chanson' – Edith Piaf's backing group. I went with my French family at a time when France hadn't yet fully recovered from Edith Piaf's death in 1963. She was the soul of France, so a concert by Les Compagnons de la Chanson was part of the grieving process for locals. 'Les Trois Cloche' wasn't quite the same without the soaring voice of Edith. However, the sonorous tones of her backing group still conveyed the profound meaning of the three church bells of life: birth, marriage and death.

I've been three times to Handa's Opera on the Harbour in Sydney, seeing: 'Carmen'; 'Aida'; and 'West Side Story.' They were all lively and innovative productions involving, variously, camels and American vintage cars. For this opera series, the stage is over the water, and the audience is tiered up the hillside of Mrs Macquarie's Chair overlooking Sydney Harbour – one of the most beautiful in the world. So the Sydney Opera House and the Harbour Bridge provide the backdrop to the performance. It's a magical setting reminiscent of another iconic musical moment in Israel in 1973, where I attended a performance by Mikis Theodorakis after his 1968 release from jail during the Greek dictatorship. His concert was in the Roman Amphitheatre at Caesarea. I sat on the stone seat of the amphitheatre overlooking the Mediterranean, lit by the moon, listening to 'Mauthausen,' a piece he wrote in jail using the Jewish concentration camp as a metaphor for his own experience of imprisonment. Can you imagine an audience full of Israeli Jews, many of them concentration camp survivors, listening to such a song? You could have heard a pin drop. Very little comes near this iconic musical moment because it was politics, scenery, and passionate music rolled into one fabulous evening.

In 2017, I had another Mediterranean musical moment. I'd returned to Greece for the first time in decades to visit one of my Liverpool University lecturers, Professor Nikos Kokosalakis, and his wife Ada. They booked tickets for a performance of Puccini's Madam Butterfly at the Odeon of Herodes Atticus on the slope of the Acropolis. I would never have thought that I'd have the opportunity for such a musical experience. Sadly, it started to rain, and I was disappointed for Nikos and Ada that their plans were cut short. I did suggest to them that it's possibly more original to dine out on the story of seeing two-thirds of Madam Butterfly in Athens rather than the full thing, but I don't think they were convinced. Record times were established as they raced to get their instruments out of the rain. I was astonished by the athleticism of the orchestra. I've never seen musicians move that quickly.

It was close to New Year's Eve 1978. My soon-to-be Australian husband, Lyall, was visiting the UK for the first time and had managed to get last-minute tickets to 'Die Fledermaus' at the Royal Opera House, Covent Garden. We were both enchanted by the production, particularly when the Opera Company extended the party scene to offer a surprise New Year's gift to the audience – a performance by the famous pianist Daniel Barenboim and also ballet excerpts by principal ballerinas of the Royal Ballet Company. As we left, the chauffeur-driven Rolls Royce cars lined up to collect their black-tie passengers, and it had started to snow. It was a Christmas card scene. Lyall's eyes were out on stalks.

"It isn't always like this," I informed him, as he

soon found out when we realised that the extension of the opera to include piano and dance performances risked missing the last tube home to the start of our new life together.

Lifestyle and culture:
The meaning of customer service

On our first morning in New York in 1996, we breakfasted at a diner. As we sat down, four orange juices hit the table. The waitperson was swift to act.

"I'm allergic to oranges," Lyall said. "Do you have anything else?"

On our second morning, three orange juices and one pineapple juice hit the table as soon as we arrived.

"Good grief! How did you remember that?" I asked, in awe of a woman who must serve hundreds of customers a day.

Of course, the quality of service in America is partly dictated by the expectation of tips. Lyall always disapproved of this because he saw it as subsidising the employers' profits. He thought that wait staff should be paid a proper wage. I agreed with him about tipping, but for different reasons. I always thought of a tip as a thank-you for special service and not an expectation.

It isn't customary to give tips in Australia. Workers are guaranteed a minimum wage – at least they were until it was discovered that one fast-food chain was underpaying school kids doing part-time work. Lyall not only opposed tipping because it subsidises employers but also because it establishes servile relationships. As a family, we'd never been big on intrusive, servile, or even haughty service, preferring friendly local ethnic restaurants where we could take our own wine. In fact, we had an in-joke in our house about 'Dad's white table cloth look'. Lyall hated the fuss and nonsense of silver service, but these occasions were sometimes visited upon us, and Lyall sat with a fixed grin on his face, willing the evening to come to an end.

Waiters in the USA have a big job to do negotiating menus with far too many options. We wised up quickly and curtailed the time it took to place an order.

"We'll have four of the specials with the eggs sunny-side-up, sourdough bread, and black coffee."

The trick is to be specific, but we came to expect anything in a society that provides so much choice. At one restaurant, we ordered ribs. The waitperson flourished his way through the order. We were so mesmerised by his sleight of hand that we lost concentration.

"And sides?" he asked.

Lyall's chin hit the floor. An unexpected choice had blindsided him.

"He means salads," I whispered quickly, realising that Lyall thought he had a choice of sides – left or right ribs.

Lyall and I generally favoured the multicultural, laconic and relaxed Australian version of service and hospitality. Or, at least, I did until Rosemarie and I took a driving trip around the southwest of Western Australia in 2021. These were difficult times for the tourist trade. COVID lockdowns had demolished the tourist industry, and zero international and interstate travel meant that backpackers weren't around to work in regional hospitality services. Staff shortages meant that many restaurants were closed from Sunday to Wednesday. I rang the tourist bureau in the relatively large town of Albany to suggest that local restaurants self-organise to provide a roster of opening days rather than have all closed for four days and all open for three. This idea was a step too far.

The restaurants – mostly pubs – that were open all week didn't take bookings, so it became a bit of a bun fight to get a table. Even then, the evening was far from relaxing: We had to queue separately for food and drink in a system streamlined to save staff time. Rosemarie asked for the dessert menu at a pub in a small rural town. She was met with blank stares and puzzled expressions, so we started to play the 'You would have thought' game: You would have thought they would at least be able to serve some ice cream.

Everyone was friendly and extremely welcoming throughout the southwest trip because we were doing what the government had asked, namely getting out and spending money to boost the post-COVID regional tourist economy. It was just a bit difficult to find things to buy, especially food.

Down-to-earth Australian outback helpfulness and friendliness can be endearing, or it can be bumbling. I cringed to think how Americans might react to the boat cruise operator who waved a life jacket at us, noting that we all know what they are and that we didn't need to know how it worked because there was only one on board and it was his. It was laconic Australian humour at its worst, yet I still prefer it to overly slick, 'Have-a-nice-day' formulaic service.

A few years earlier, I'd driven Lyall and our friends, Val and Brian, on the Monseigneur Hawes Trail in Western Australia. He was an outback priest who'd built a number of churches, which now have heritage status. The Perenjori church was first on the list. It was locked, but the notice on the door said the key was at the tourist office. When we found the tourist office, it was closed. So I asked at the nearby garage.

"Well, it would be closed, wouldn't it," the garage bloke said. Apparently, all the locals knew this. "Why don't you try the Telecentre?"

The young woman there didn't know and didn't want to know anything about the church key.

"Does anybody know where the key might be?" I asked, wondering what it would be like for international or interstate tourists trying to negotiate the Monseigneur Hawes Trail. A couple of women who were in the Telecentre collecting their mail took pity and rang someone they thought might know. Yes! Mrs Williams did have the key, but she had a doctor's appointment at 4pm, so we had to get to her house quickly.

"Where will I find it?"

Nobody actually knew the address. "It's on a corner with lots of oleander plants around it."

When I eventually found the house, I knocked on the door and was given the key, together with the instruction to leave it under the wheat bag when I returned it because Mrs Williams would be at the doctor's. Well, I knew that already. I was practically a local by this stage.

"You can't say that! That's rude." I exclaimed.
"Well, I did."

I was chatting with my hometown friend, Brian, who had re-visioned his life from city stockbroker and agricultural economist to rural chef running his own restaurant and hotel. One of his clients had complained about his crème brûlée and he'd told her to "get a life." I later checked him out on tourist websites and found that clients described him as a 'character', calling him Bas after his alter-ego Basil Fawlty in the British TV series 'Fawlty Towers'.

I didn't quite know what to make of this. Did I think he was rude, or was I squeezing the 'characters' out of my life with bland definitions of good service? Maybe the characters are actually the attraction.

Ray chortled as he recounted his favourite Bas stories. "I lived near a pub in Cambridge whose landlord was a complete nutter – a Wagnerian aficionado. The food was glorious, but the clientele had to endure him playing thunderous Wagnerian music over the sound system. If unsuspecting newcomers had the temerity to request that the volume be lowered, they were ejected from the premises.

"We regulars hovered in delicious anticipation of the confrontations."

Years later, when he lived in London, Ray encountered an Asian Basil Fawlty. Outside his restaurant, he had a sign saying 'Spices from the subcontinent: salmonella from the water supply.'

The other day, I started to unpack my groceries at the check-out, assuming I was next in line, when a customer pushed past me, pointing to the two items she'd left to reserve her place whilst she completed armfuls of shopping. I had assumed these items belonged to the woman just completing her purchase. This was an unimportant issue in the general flow of life's events, so I let her move ahead of me. When my turn finally arrived, I told the young girl serving me that I hate it when people push in like that.

"Oh, I didn't mind. I could manage it," she said.

"But I'm not talking about you. I'm talking about me – the customer," I replied, remembering that this wasn't the first time I'd been treated this way.

I followed up on a deal at a restaurant for a Mexican meal with a free margarita cocktail in the same shopping centre. The food was poor, and the cocktail was even worse. When I mentioned this to the waiter, she tried the cocktail and concluded that she thought it was alright.

"I suppose that makes it OK then," I replied.

She was inclined to agree.

The chef of the crème brûlée story is often faced with difficulties arising from online bookings at his hotel. Clients think they've paid when the system requires payment on arrival. One altercation led to a client walking out without paying, so Brian told him to f***off. The client reported him on social media, and Brian apologised.

I wouldn't have: The customer isn't always right.

So, where's the balance? Where does customer service sit on a continuum that meanders past Baz, to obsequious silver service, and to the formulaic extreme of 'have a nice day' responses in fast food outlets? I think I'll order crème brûlée and listen to Wagner.

Lifestyle and culture: The meaning of one-liners

"Lynne, I feel uncomfortable with this."

There are few things worse than a boss who has read as far as page three of an assertiveness training manual.

"Then, please, let's go and sit somewhere more comfortable, but I will still want to speak with you about the lack of consultation in this department," I replied.

'I feel uncomfortable with' is a one-liner that makes my skin crawl with frustration. It originated in assertiveness training manuals in the early 1980s, if not before. I don't like it. It's inauthentic – a slick American solution to handling conflict that doesn't tally with my straight-talking Anglo/Australian culture. Even worse, it was co-opted by my boss to evade every meaningful concern in the department. He'd learned the words but didn't understand the meaning of the song. Even so, I appreciated his efforts to manage his aggression that had occasionally manifested itself – like when he told me that I shouldn't be at work because I had small children.

'At the end of the day' is one of my least favourite one-liners. It transmits as a self-evident statement without actually providing evidence. It also implies that the speaker is reasonable and others aren't.

Some years ago, I was on a committee overseeing research into consumer health. The committee's purpose was to involve health consumers in the research design, and they comprised the majority of the committee. But the research was funded by the Australian Federal Government, so the committee had to include a Canberra public servant. He was out of tune with consumer health issues and had a predilection for persuading the consumer health representatives that, 'at the end of the day,' he knew what he was talking about, and they didn't.

The majority of his interjections were prefaced by 'At the end of the day.' As the invited research consultant, I let this pass for a while until I couldn't help myself.

"But, Michael, what about at the beginning of

the day? Does the time of day affect the research design?"

This deconstructed the meaning of his one-liner and disrupted his gestalt enough for others to have their say. So, at the end of the day, the consumer reps were quite happy with progress.

One-liners come in different guises, and I've never quite worked out the difference between proverbs, aphorisms, corporate-speak, clichés, platitudes, and quotable quotes – but I do know that I'm prone to using one-liners. They're like a Greek chorus in the script of my life, and they can be an effective form of communication – good summary concepts.

At my retirement do in Queensland, my colleague, Michael, made the farewell speech. In preparation, he'd canvassed our department to collate a list of my one-liners. One concerned change-leadership with limited resources. I always sought to 'get best bang for buck.' Sure, it's an Americanism. My British mother would have said that we have to 'make the best of it.'

All this came back to me recently when I was chatting with a friend about her workplace concerns.

"You need to get best bang for buck,' I said – almost automatically.

"Oooh, Lynne. I couldn't possibly use that kind of language where I work."

I've known this dear friend for nearly fifty years, so I understood immediately where she was coming from. I quickly reassured her, "I think the bang refers to fireworks or bombs, and not workplace sex."

One-liners work well in management to focus attention on important issues such as the need for sustainable systems of working: "What if we were all on the same bus that went over the cliff. Who would know what to do?"

The 'bus-off-a-cliff' metaphor is not new, but it does crystallise meaning. It was difficult for us to promote university teaching and learning in a cash-strapped environment and in a regional university set in its ways, so I always proffered the notion that there must be 'a quid in it for everybody.'

People need to see that change will help them in their work. I've even invented some one-liners. 'That's a pyjama decision' was one of them. When my kids were little, I believed in developing their ability to make decisions – but only decisions I determined for them. They could choose blue or yellow pyjamas, but they couldn't choose bedtime.

This came to mind at a university meeting that occupied the time of many senior staff for over three hours. Do a cost-benefit analysis on that! I suddenly realised that the significant decisions had already been made. We were just choosing the colour of our pyjamas, not bedtime. It was a conversation stopper when I announced that this was 'a pyjama decision,' but when I clarified my meaning, they saw the light.

One-liners can illuminate meaning in a flash, especially if you're good at them, like my friend, Janina. She's so expert that I sometimes wondered if she rehearsed them in the morning in order to drop them into conversations during the day. Not so, as I found out in 1994 when Janina and I attended the launch of the latest, jazzy, high-tech advertising video for the university. It was years after gender equity legislation was introduced and long after universities had adopted equal opportunity principles, but this video didn't have a woman in it. Unbelievable!

Janina and I were sisters in friendship and

feminism, so she sensed my rising tension as I watched this apology for an advertising video unfold. She leaned towards me to proffer her opinion, "It's rather like a technological codpiece for the intellectually under-endowed, isn't it, Lynne?"

That's exactly what it was, and she couldn't possibly have rehearsed that in the morning.

Shared meanings sit behind the one-liners that emerge in the shorthand language of friendships. Just last week, I spoke with Rosemarie about a relative who wouldn't even ask her own grandchildren for help. She feared rejection, so she made excuses, "I can't ask him on a weekend; he might be baking." So now, whenever Rosemarie and I realise that it may not be worth asking for help, we just say, 'They might be baking.'

'Being dealt with' arose from our conversations about friends who squeeze us into their oh-so-busy schedules.

"She popped by for five minutes between appointments yesterday," I said.

"I think you've been dealt with," Rosemarie replied.

I don't know anybody who doesn't bemoan that they think of suitable retorts ten minutes after conversations have finished. On these occasions, an arsenal of ready-made one-liners can come in handy. My Queensland colleague, Ren Yi, still quotes back at me a one-liner that I taught him: 'That may be a reason, but it's not an excuse.'

A one-liner that helps me when I'm being stone-walled is: 'I'm not playing skittles.'

In the interests of cross-cultural understanding, I sometimes change this one to 'I'm not playing ten-pin bowling.' It refers to conversations in which the other person has a problem, but if I offer helpful suggestions, they knock them down one by one. I now stop when the first pin is knocked down because it means they don't want helpful advice. They just want to moan. That's fair enough, as long as I understand the name of the game.

My mother raised me on one-liners, and she proved to be right in much of the wisdom she imparted: 'Clean as you go. Muddle makes muddle,' always comes to mind when I don't feel like tidying the kitchen before going to bed, but there's 'no time like the present', so I get on with it. Mum probably reasoned that 'cleanliness is next to Godliness,' and I really shouldn't 'put off to tomorrow what I can do today.' In any case, it's best to 'strike whilst the iron's hot.'

Ask anybody you know, and they will be able to trot out their parents' one-liners.

I've always defended proverbs on feminist grounds because many reflect the home-grown wisdom of women, oft derided as old wives' tales. Mum had one to cover most of life's events, including farting, on which subject she quoted lines supposedly on a headstone somewhere in the south-west of England: 'Wherever you be, let your wind go free, for holding it back was the death of me.'

That's one I wish I could forget. One-liners, however defined, were the backbone of Mum's parenting. She always reckoned that it's the hours before midnight that make for a good sleep. That may have been her own neat way of getting her kids off the bed early, but her justification was that 'Early to bed and early to rise makes a man health and wealthy and wise.'

Maybe it's a family thing because my Canadian cousin, Diane, reported a similar one-liner in her family: 'Nothing good happens after midnight.'

Well, actually it does, but there's now some evidence that the traditional wisdom in these one-liners is true: it is, indeed, the hours before midnight that count. That's probably because the 'early bird catches the worm.'

It's when one-liners swamp everyday conversation that I grow weary of them. I used to buy fruit and veggies at a rural Queensland shop. It was here that I realised that there's a limit to my support of home-spun wisdom. It was never-ending:

- Better safe than sorry
- You can't judge a book by its cover
- The grass is always greener on the other side of the fence
- You've got to laugh or you'd cry
- Every cloud has a silver lining
- A bird in the hand is worth two in the bush

Make it stop! I survived the banality of the conversation by counting how many platitudes I heard in one shopping spree. The maximum was nineteen, and I was living alone, so I didn't buy much. The reason I don't like platitudes is that they contribute nothing to the conversation.

They're a waste of breath, and I'd rather just be silent. Clichés and platitudes are overused one-liners, and they lack original thought. They are uncritical and can be used to dismiss intelligent and meaningful observations.

Rosemarie popped by the other day with her hands over her ears, "If I hear anyone else say 'it is what it is,' I'll scream."

As one-liners go, this one had grown in popularity during the 2020-2021 COVID lockdowns in Australia. Fatalistic acceptance was our only choice. However, another friend, Anne, quite likes it as a simple, clear one-liner that has the power to neutralise: "over-analysis; over-emphasis; over-stressing; and over-reaction." She finds a gentle sense of acceptance in it. Ah well, 'one woman's meat is another woman's poison.'

One-liners make meaning for us through the language we speak without us even realising. I've seen a few Shakespearean plays, but never Hamlet. So, when the old Laurence Olivier film Hamlet was on TV one night, I decided it was about time I filled the gap. I was gobsmacked. I thought I must have been mistaken. I must have seen it in a theatre somewhere. I felt I knew almost every line, and I probably did, because English is my first language and Shakespeare embedded one-liners right through it.

The extent to which Shakespeare created one-liners or simply used the idiomatic expressions of his time is a moot point, but who, in the English-speaking world, has not used one or other of the following in their modern versions?

- Though this be madness, yet there is method in't.
- To thine own self be true.
- The lady doth protest too much.
- I must be cruel only to be kind.
- There is nothing either good or bad, but thinking makes it so.

I take great exception to the latter because plenty of awful stuff has happened in my Australian family that no amount of thinking will make good. Then there's the Shakespearean one-liner that Americans had to learn off by heart during the period of the Trump presidency, 'Madness in great ones must not unwatched go.' They were a bit slow about it but, as Winston Churchill said, 'We can always count on the Americans to do the right thing after they have exhausted all the other possibilities.'

One of Churchill's one-liners that I used endlessly with my students was, 'Ending a sentence with a preposition is something up with which I will not put.'

This was probably a step too far for young university students with whom my first priority was to tackle the influence of Australian English on written expression, "It's would *have*, not would *of*." But then, as Mark Twain said, "Anyone who can only think of one way to spell a word obviously lacks imagination."

Conclusion:
Making sense of me

Mum had a dressing table set comprising a decorative mother-of-pearl hairbrush and hand mirror. They were 1940s in style – possibly earlier, maybe art deco. When I was ten, I loved to sneak into her bedroom to play with this paraphernalia, but if I spent long enough looking into her mirror, I started asking myself, "Who am I?"

Then another voice would come back asking, "Who is it asking who am I?" It was a mildly disorientating feeling – a bit like being on a train when the train next to you moves, but you think it's you.

Clearly, I was making meaning, and making sense, of my world in a way that is typical of kids of this age. I saw it in my son, Sam, when he was ten. His rather quaint expression was, "It's funny when you come to think about it …"

My grandsons, Oli and Thomas, are now aged ten and eight, and their lines of questioning about the world are part of this same reflective process, as is this book, 'Making Meaning: Making Sense.'

As my colleague, Rachel, said in her book, 'Reaching One Thousand,' "We narrate ourselves into existence. In everyday life, we understand ourselves through a kind of ongoing story." As Rachel sees it, "If we cannot tell stories about ourselves and our world, it seems we cannot really develop a sense of self."

But stories don't remember themselves. We select and craft our sense of self. Some stories stick because they fit the narrative, and others slip away because they don't. Some become well-guarded secrets that, when uncovered, cause us to re-narrate our ongoing story, as with my discovery of a seventh child on my husband's death certificate.

There is a fluidity to Rachel's notion of an ongoing story that my mother echoed when I rang her for her seventieth birthday, "But I'm still me, I'm still Alma." Yet this book shows that my own stories jostle against each other. There is ongoing fluidity, but there are also discontinuities and unexpected peaks and troughs. When I was eleven, in my first year at high school, I remember a group of us sitting around planning how we wanted our lives to be. We drew pictures in the air as we contrasted a flat-line, comfortable life with one in which we zigzagged up and down the peaks and troughs of a more exciting and challenging lifestyle. As if we had the choice! It's just as well that we chose the zigzag life because it happened anyway.

At some stage in my sixties, I was back in Cheltenham, and I met my classmates for a pub lunch. I took a moment to look around the table, and I could certainly see the troughs that we'd anticipated when we were eleven years old. One classmate had experienced the death of her baby through sudden infant death. I also saw the classmate who nursed three husbands through serious illness to death.

In memory of our English Literature classes, I wanted to paraphrase Oscar Wilde and say, "To lose one husband, Diana, may be regarded as a misfortune; to lose two looks like carelessness," but I couldn't because the Oscar Wilde script didn't extend to three tragedies.

Next to her was Niki, whose daughter was raised as her sister, and she sat by Jacky, who'd recently been told that her husband, John, had six weeks to live because his brain was riddled with cancer. In fact, he didn't have cancer at all, and he's still alive. That was quite a roller-coaster ride.

Next to Jacky, I saw Carolyn, whose first husband left her for his secretary when their baby was eighteen months old. Years later, after they'd had three children together, her second husband left her for his secretary. It crossed my mind that maybe Carolyn should have done a secretarial course to evade these troughs, but that quick quip would not hold her two husbands to account for their behaviour. I didn't know what to say to her when we met.

"Bloody hell!" I said.

"Bloody hell!" she replied.

So that dealt with that through the shorthand conversation of long-term friendship.

I've also had my share of troughs, including an alcoholic and violent father, blended family trauma, and a husband with multiple health problems, who I looked after for eight very long years. This is not to mention that I was badly bullied at work to the point that it came close to destroying my career. Instead, through my agency, and success in teaching awards, I was promoted.

Troughs can become peaks, as Carolyn observed, "To be honest, Lynne, it was no bad thing that my two husbands left. If they hadn't, I wouldn't have had the life I've had. It's enabled me to travel more, make new friends, start new hobbies and interests, and become completely independent."

Carolyn took charge of her life, and I did the same. I became 'me' because I made decisions and took a few risks. I gave up my first steady job and backpacked around the world, ending up in Australia. I'm thrilled to bits that my cousin, Dan, has just written a folk song that refers to me at that time. His lyrics book-end our 'Britton' family migration, alluding to the first and last (me) to migrate. He's called it 'The Pioneers Call,' He does own up to some romantic and artistic licence in the lyrics that tell my story:

> *"She knew there was a better life.*
>
> *She was young, brave and strong.*
>
> *She pulled that rucksack on her back,*

and sang the pioneer's song.
She swapped the green of England,
for the outback's dusty red.
Waved goodbye to her family,
with big dreams in her head."

It's a nice romantic spin on my younger risk-taking years.

Most of all, I took charge of my own education. My intellectual development through school and university and my subsequent career as a university academic are absolutely fundamental to my sense of self. The things I'm proud of in my life are my qualifications, especially my PhD. I'm also pleased that I've co-edited four academic books and written nearly sixty journal articles and book chapters. I also made almost forty educational videotapes for my students. The almost one hundred conference papers I presented mean that I became moderately well known in my niche areas of women's health and academic development, especially after I won the 2002 national prize for social science teaching and the top prize: Prime Minister's Award for

Australian University Teacher of the Year.

Later, in 2009, I was chosen for an Australian Executive Endeavour Award, and in 2010, I was awarded Emeritus Professor at the University of Southern Queensland. I'm now 'Professor' for life. In my mind, these things are 'me,'

I recently caught up with Bev, with whom I worked and studied for many years. We hadn't seen each other for ages, so we had a lot of hot goss to share. This ventured in the direction of how much we both value our intellectual engagement with life. She touched her head and her heart saying, "This is me."

It's me as well, Bev.

Many of my stories, particularly those about music, travel, politics and feminism, tell the story of my baby-boomer generation. We were born into our parents' grey and beige world of post-war frugality. In Nuneaton, where I was born, our house had an outside toilet and no bathroom. My sister and I had a Saturday night clean-up in a tin bath in front of the living room fire. I can still feel the absolute pleasure of everything being clean at once: Bath, hair wash, clean nightie, and clean sheets. It was a much-needed bath night because our playground was the slag heaps from the coal mines and the dusty streets where I played with my older sister and the neighbourhood kids.

Food was still rationed when I was born. I can just about remember buying sweets (lollies/candy) with ration books. Mine was a life of limited expectations. Travel was unheard of in the British working classes. Neighbourhood was the limited horizon. I don't know how it started, but I knew, from a very young age, that I didn't want this small, narrow life of my childhood when I grew up. I didn't want to be conventional, full stop. I moved towards a more bohemian life. In fact, my favourite photo of my young self was taken on New Year's Eve, 1971, in a London pub, with a gang of Liverpool University friends. I had long black hair and a black polo neck jumper. I looked like a hippy. This was the 'me' that felt comfortable.

The British National Health Service was born in the same year as me. The advent of the Welfare State in the UK meant that the families of baby-boomers had greater security than ever before, if not greater wealth. Kids of my generation were a national project. We were the future of national rebuilding after World War II. We had free milk at school, and cheap school lunches of the meat and two veg variety. We were vaccinated, at school, against polio and TB, and we had more opportunities than our parents, including a free university education, with grants to pay our living costs. This meant that many, like me, were the first in family to go to university.

My baby-boomer generation is now defined by its mini-skirted fashion, pop music, and radical politics, in particular, the 1968 year of student revolutions. We created new meanings from the advantages we were given. This is the era in which I developed my sense of self.

I think I became me not only through the opportunities provided to my baby-boomer generation but also in opposition to social expectations. In this context, second-wave feminism did much to shape how I wanted to be in this world, even if others didn't quite go along with the person I became.

Hometown friend, Brian, was perplexed. "I don't understand this feminist stuff. You've always loved men."

I have. I enjoy male company, even if I do have

to moderate my behaviour so as not to intimidate them. I learned this from a rather strange conversation that my husband started one day.

"What if you were to drop off the perch first, Lynne. How do you think women would react to me?" Lyall asked, preening perceptibly.

"They'd be knocking the door down," I replied.

"Really, why's that?"

So I pointed to the demographics, noting that there are fewer men available in older age groups. Women have to make do with what's left over. "If things happened the other way round, how do you think blokes would react to me?" It was my turn to ask.

Lyall gave this some serious thought and offered a considered response. "They'd be intimidated by you."

Not long after this conversation, I returned to the UK and went to Liverpool to stay with life-long friend, 'Liverpool Phil.' I repeated the conversation I'd had with Lyall and then said, "So, when I asked what blokes might think of me, what do you think Lyall said?"

He dignified the hypotheticals with a thoughtful response. "Well, not that I think this personally, but I think they'd be intimidated."

So, both my husband and close male friend think I'm intimidating. I returned to Perth and repeated this whole story to one of my stepdaughters, who said, "My father-in-law is intimidated by you."

At this point, I lost interest in the topic because I knew that I couldn't disappear into the wallpaper much more than I did with her father-in-law.

"Do you remember your birthday? Your dad and I were parked at a table with your in-laws. Well, the whole night I asked after their health, their kids, their parents, their jobs. I did nothing but facilitate their conversation and take an interest in them. They didn't ask me anything. It was all about them. So if that's me being intimidating, stuff it!"

There's no escaping that my mother had an extraordinary influence on me. I know that this is true for most people, but I suspect that my chaotic childhood meant that I clung to her to an unusual degree. When I was about eleven, my two eldest sisters owned and ran a small hotel in Devon. Mum used to send me down there for my summer holidays. I don't know if she'd simply had enough coping with my dad, or if she was trying to get me away from him, or if she thought I might help my older sisters – or maybe all three reasons. Now that I look back, though, it was quite a big ask of Audrey and Joyce to take on board their two younger sisters when they had their own little children to care for and a hotel to run. It was, however, an opportunity for the four sisters to be together.

Given that Audrey got married when I was three, and Joyce when I was four, we hadn't actually lived together very much. One day, all four sisters were together in the hotel kitchen when Joyce stopped in her tracks, "Oh! I felt just like Mum then," she exclaimed.

The other two demurred, "How can you know how Mum feels?"

I was only eleven, but I looked up and said, "I know what Joyce means." I've often felt like Mum. It's just a feeling that sweeps over me. This level of bonding with my mother has helped to shape the meaning I make of my life, particularly through her one-liners.

I was encouraged to reflect on what it means to be me by Mum's one-liners. If ever I complained to her about the behaviour of other kids at school, she would quote me two lines from a Rabbie Burns poem, "O, wad some Power the giftie gie us, to see oursels as others see us!" In other words, look to your own behaviour first, and assess yourself in terms of how others see you. Well, I don't mind looking at my own behaviour, but as for seeing myself reflected in their eyes – I don't think so! I prefer to go along with the mantra, which suggests that I can manage my own behaviour, but I can't control how others see me. In fact, I'd go so far as to say that the way others see me often has more to do with their issues than my behaviour.

A case in point is when I rang a UK relative to wish her a happy birthday. It took me a week to get through. When I did, I was treated to a sad but distressing account of my many sins including, surprisingly, that Mum had helped me with my homework. I was forty-five at this stage, so I was a little taken aback by this schoolgirl grievance, but I quickly realised that I'd been in Australia for a quarter of a century, and I hadn't been around in the UK to address any emergent narratives about me. I also hadn't been around to cause an argument like this.

This story of my life needed a fact-check: "But Mum left school when she was thirteen. How was she going to help me with French, Latin and Algebra?"

Things got worse over the years and towards the end of the 1990s, I was manoeuvred out of visiting Mum in her own home. The new arrangements were made without my knowledge or consent. I received a phone call telling me that I would be seeing Mum elsewhere. I felt quite powerless. This had all been decided for me, and it meant that I didn't get back to my hometown, Cheltenham, for quite some time. No matter, I still had the 'giftie' to see myself as others saw me, and I saw no truth reflected in this telephone conversation nor in my banishment.

My sisters are, respectively, nineteen, seventeen and five years older than me. Clearly, I was an accident, the fourth of four girls, and the youngest by a long chalk. My cot was the bottom drawer of the chest of drawers. No special arrangements were made for my arrival, and probably none could be afforded. My early childhood memories are that I trailed around after my older sister and that nobody much considered my point of view. This was no bad thing. There are freedoms in being ignored, and, to this day, I hate to be controlled or micro-managed because I wasn't accustomed to having people 'on my case.' I still respond poorly to petty authority and nit-picking.

However, freedom can also mean neglect. I look back now and see an unsupervised young me doing things I wouldn't have allowed my kids to do. As a teenager, I was a vulnerable young girl roaming alone across the Cotswold Hills on my school holiday walks. It's noteworthy that my house was in the village where the serial killer, Frederick West, rented a caravan, and his wife, apparently, was at Bishops Cleeve Primary School with me. This does give me a 'there but for the grace of God' feeling, especially because a girl from my school was one of his victims, and she lived in a nearby village. Yet, as I see it, this freedom did encourage me to travel off the beaten track. I've had a lifetime of travel visiting seventy-nine countries by the time I was seventy. The sense I made of my world has been heavily influenced by these travels, but no matter where I roamed, I always had a sense of belonging with a place I called home.

Mum made sure that I felt embedded in her large extended family in Devon, which endorsed the importance of bloodlines. You belonged if you belonged. I remember feeling quite embarrassed when I returned to Devon in my late twenties to find my Auntie introducing me to an in-law of the same name as me. She put her arm around me and announced, "This 'yer be our Lynne."

Although I'm sure it wasn't intended to be exclusive, it did seem so, given that the other Lynn had contributed much more to family life in Devon than I ever did. I'm not going to pretend that this extended family was there for me because they weren't. In fact, I barely met some of my older cousins. The point is, Mum made her daughters think they belonged, and, to those we saw more often, we did.

These days, some cousins of similar age are also my friends, and they're an important part of the meaning I make of my life. It does seem to matter that we're descendants of the Britton family and that we share grandparents, great-grandparents, and memories. My sense of self is anchored in our shared extended family. I was the first in this family to go to university, but there is now generational change, and many nieces and nephews (and greats-) routinely enjoy university life. Now, with similar educational backgrounds, I've sometimes wondered if someone of my ilk might pop up in the generations that follow me, so I keep a special eye on my great-niece, Becky, whose social justice principles keep her as happily engaged in feminist public health work as I was.

Perth friend, Robyn, rang a while ago to make a point. "Lynne, when will you tell the story of what you did to build a blended family. Plenty of people try, but you did it for thirty years. I know it went pear-shaped in the end, but you did do it."

I did, and being family-minded is part of my sense of self – most recently manifested in building a granny house in my backyard and sharing my property with my son, Sam, and his family. I'm glad to have him, his wife, Jane, and my grandkids Oli, Thomas and Elsie around me in my older years, but if they wish to start a new adventure, they're not tied to hearth and home. I took risks, and so should they. Each generation must make meaning of their own lives.

Recently, my eldest grandson, Oli, exclaimed,

"Oh NaiNai, I want to write, and I want to travel." Go Oli!

I've lived, moved and had my being in four places: The Cotswolds, Devon, Liverpool and Western Australia. I have a sense of place with all of them, which is closely tied to familiar patterns of friendship. It's the people I know in each location that shape my sense of place. Phil has been meeting me at Liverpool Lime Street train station for fifty years but, on one occasion, I landed at Manchester Airport, and he went to meet me there. It was all wrong! Somewhat out of sorts with the changed arrangements, we got to chatting on the way back into Liverpool about something as boring as reticulated gardens in Australia. We missed the turn to Runcorn Bridge and had to carry on to the Mersey Tunnel. That was OK because the Tunnel holds special memories of Liverpool for me, but when all is said and done, my sense of place determines that I arrive at Liverpool Lime Street, just as I did in 1967 when I first went up to university.

I claim being an accidental migrant as an important part of my identity. Living in and learning about Australia has been an adventure that I'm glad I fell into. I've been a migrant for almost fifty years, and my sense of self has been remade in antipodean form. A Darwin colleague of British background captured the shift that migrants must make when he chatted with me about his imminent return trip to the UK.

"You know how it is, Lynne. When you get back to the UK, you're exotic for all of five minutes because you live in Australia, and then they start with, 'Did you know they're changing the bus route at the end of the road?'"

At these points, we slip back into our British selves.

So, how do I make sense of the peaks and troughs of life that I voted for when I was eleven? Being a baby-boomer, with all the advantages that brought, offered many highlights. I've enjoyed the education, music and travel opportunities afforded to my generation. I'm glad that I was part of second-wave feminism and satisfied with the contribution I made to women's health. I'm still enjoying work to enhance university teaching, hopefully resulting in better learning experiences for students.

Friends who made a difference have enriched

my life. There were about twenty-five of us at our Liverpool University reunion in 2010. Among them, there were about five professors, a couple of medical specialists, some CEOs, a pilot, and people who've made significant advances in the world of research – like Steve. The patents for the Clear Blue technology in pregnancy tests were developed by a colleague of his. Subsequently, Steve headed the research group that developed it for Unilever. The rapid flow test technology, also patented by his group, is now being used in almost every home in the developed world to test for COVID. There are many things for which we might thank Steve because he later worked with the Birds Eye Company to develop tastier and sweeter peas. That's also something that affects almost every home in the developed world.

Cheshire friend, William, researched the use of clays and clay minerals as protective layers against the effects of flames and heat. One of the applications was in space – for use in satellites, shuttles, and space stations. Space is a hostile environment for plastics that corrode quickly, so William sought to coat plastic material so that it could survive. This research attracted the attention of the USA 'Star Wars' program. This led William to a posh London Hotel, where he walked through layers of military security to present his work to the Americans. After that, he moved on to something more practical. He developed packaging for coffee using layers of clay – like vermiculite. This replaced aluminium, which was thought to be linked to dementia or Alzheimer's disease. So, but for friends in my generation of university students, the world could be full of demented coffee drinkers and parents unable to tempt their children with sweet-tasting peas. It's been intriguing to witness the success of people in my life.

Do I have any regrets about the way in which my stories have jostled me into my sense of self?

Of course I do.

I regret very much that I was subject to the intergenerational trauma of my family of origin and my blended family. I regret, even more, that my daughter died a young death. I wish that universities were nicer places to work. I still see younger academics trying to do more with less in unsupportive management contexts. I regret that women's status has gone backwards since the days when I participated in second-wave feminist activism. I still worry about the way in which Mum suffered from domestic violence. I'm just plain sad that walking my toddler kids in their strollers on peace marches has come to nought as this book draws to a close just when President Putin is invading Ukraine and threatening to push the nuclear button. I also get jealous when I see dads playing in the park with their toddler daughters.

I can't help but wonder what it must feel like to be loved by your dad, but I don't have to look far to see this. My son is a terrific father to his kids. So, if I've been able to turn around my past to produce this good man, then it's a major achievement. As Perth friend, Jodie, said, "Your job is done, Lynne."

There's a story about an old-timer in the Australian outback. When asked if he'd lived all his life in remote areas, he replied, "Not yet."

Nor have I lived all my stories – not yet.

References

Benedict, R. (1946) Chrysanthemum and the sword. Houghton Mifflin Company: Boston

Bryson, B. (2015) Notes from a small island. Journey through Britain. Transworld Publishers Ltd: London

Freeman, J. (1972-73) The tyranny of structurelessness. Berkeley Journal of Sociology. Vol 17. Pp 151-164

(https://millcreekurbanfarm.org/sites/default/files/tyranny%20of%20Structurelessness.pdf)

Few, J. (2020) Sins as red as scarlet: a Devon town in turmoil. Blue Poppy Publishing https://bluepoppypublishing.co.uk/2020/07/26/sins-as-red-as-scarlet-by-janet-few/

Hartland Britton Family website https://thebrittonfamilysite.wixsite.com/thebrittons

Hilts, E. (2006) Getting in touch with your inner bitch. Sourcebook inc: USA

Hunt, Lyall (1979) Westralian portraits. University of Western Australia Press: Perth

Hunt, Lyall (2001) Towards federation: Why Western Australia joined the Australian Federation in 1901. Royal Western Australian History Society: Nedlands

Hunt, Lynne & Chalmers, D. (2021) University teaching in focus: A learner-centred approach. Routledge: Abingdon Oxon

Hunt, Lynne & Hunt, Lyall (2017) The Importance of a whole-of-department framework in learning partnerships. International Journal for Students as Partners. Vol 1. No 2. Pp 1-8

Hunt, Lynne & Trotman, J. (2002) Claremont cameos. Edith Cowan University: Perth

Hunt, Lynne (1988) 'Women'. In Lyall Hunt Yilgarn: Good country for hardy people. Yilgarn Shire: Southern Cross

Hunt, Lynne (2009) 'In search of a title' in Naidoo, K. & Patel, F. Working women. Stories of strife, struggle and survival. SAGE: New Delhi

Lee, L. (1959) Cider with Rosie. Hogarth Press: London

Robertson, R. (2012) Reaching one thousand. Black Inc: Collingwood

Russell, W. (1993) Shirley Valentine. Longmans Publishing Group: Harlow

Uris, L. (1963) Armageddon: A novel of Berlin. Dell Books: New York

Uris, L. (1958) Exodus. Doubleday & Company: New York

Uris, L. Mila 18. Doubleday & Company: New York

Waddell, C. (2014) Jesus matters. St Pauls Publications: Strathfield, NSW

Lightning Source UK Ltd.
Milton Keynes UK
UKHW011337280622
405074UK00001B/43